YogAha

Quest of the Conscious Field

Dr.Shelley Evans PhD DNM

authorHOUSE®

AuthorHouse™
1663 Liberty Drive
Bloomington, IN 47403
www.authorhouse.com
Phone: 1 (800) 839-8640

Published by AuthorHouse 04/27/2018

ISBN: 978-1-5462-3863-8 (sc)
ISBN: 978-1-5462-3862-1 (e)

Library of Congress Control Number: 2018904229

Abstract

Quests such as this, are personal journeys with every step commanding that it be taken alone. Inevitably, adventurous pursuits seeking to overcome obstacles, both symbolic and supernatural, unveil life's essence to fulfill prophetic transformation of the void. Despite potential perils or bewildering consequences, a spiritual and psychological sense of purpose or reason drives us forward. Alchemy is such a quest, in the form of yoga teaching the physics of human interaction. The Aha moments obtained throughout this yoga culminate in meaningful variants of transforming legendary lead into gold.

"The two most important days in your life are the day you are born and the day you find out why."-Mark Twain

Dedication and Acknowledgements

The author wishes to acknowledge Bill Donahue of Hidden Meanings and Dan Winter of Fractal U, for their many meaningful and scholarly contributions made freely available to the world via respective websites, videos and interviews.

This book is dedicated to my Mom and all my precious children, the Earth mother and all of her precious children. -Dawn Mother

Contents

Preface

YogAha was written as a simple gift to nurture and nourish, teach and inspire lives, physically, emotionally and spiritually. It is my hope that the availability of a simple yet fulfilling taste of a Bliss induced 'Aha' moment, will assist our deserving population on the path toward believing in themselves and imagining new possibilities into being.

Put your spoon where the soup is.

Introduction

This book is a representation of the modus operandi for both obtaining information from, and manifesting within, the field of Consciousness experienced personally as Oneness.

In honour of the "Fruit of the Light of Loving-kindness" and "Healing through Togetherness".

Yogaha's are the aha moments produced by yogic awareness tuning in to sacred space. The 'aha' moment defined by that transcendent radiance, proverbially defined as the 'light coming on', gives us certainty which translates as 'experiential coherence'. Sacred space is created through the union or yoking of the Observer's awareness with Consciousness conveying pure principle. Sort of like a zygote, or a translator interface which yields the answer only when the two different operating systems talk with each other, that light which turns on is a result of an event horizon, aka you, both transmitting and receiving simultaneously- because you were open to both sides of the equation! The resulting expansion triggers the bliss moment and is suspended as stillness, to attain liberation. If only for the moment, liberation provides the cosmic area code (which is a specific frequency) for conscious union with the blissful Spirit.

"Sacred in "Sacred Geometry" does not mean Holy, but rather pertains to that which is Permanent or Timeless Truths" ~ Jain 108

This is the sanctuary called freedom. Through the Yogaha's we come to know our oneness with the Infinite Intelligence, Pure Source Energy and Joy which gives life to all and is the essence of our own Self. I hope these concepts inspire you as a travel guide would, to explore exotic destinations. I hope these concepts nourish and pamper you as the finest of celebrated Chefs would, organically, naturally.

Read with Intention to make a lifetime change for your mind and body, for intention initiates your solution to long-term health and vitality.

Read.

(All implied calculations in this book are original discoveries of Dan Winter)

Chapter One

Awareness

*A*wareness is the secret of transforming yoga into an aha moment. And the secret of sustaining any 'aha' moment is yoga. Mind yoga that is.

Every Aha moment has its bliss portal…where do we wish to explore?

In a playful and yet empowering way, the term 'YogAha' represents tracking your awareness as it flows through the field of consciousness to trigger an Aha moment of unexpected insight. As a beginner, we sometimes don't know where to start. Just how do we make our awareness become the yogi of mind, body, soul & heart much less use it to track the flow of breath from one point to the next. I mean the field of consciousness must have designated points identifying the 'you are here' sort of signposts along the way, right? Vinyasa is the yogic term used to describe a specific sequence of poses and therefore serves metaphorically as a signpost to designate beginning or completion points. It can also can be translated as "arranging something in a distinct way," like yoga poses for example. The field of consciousness also has signposts, which can designate reference points of familiarity, so we can build upon and coordinate the sacred movement of our practice. Can you imagine every form or pose your vinyasa incorporates, not only contains an important message from the universe for you, but also your experience of that form or pose likewise provides meaningful feedback acted upon by the field of consciousness? Not unlike the concept of being simultaneously both the drop of water and the whole ocean. When your awareness contracts you experience the life force of the droplet and when your awareness expands you experience the myriad life forms which collectively are expressed as the ocean. Just as breath leads our vinyasa as it flows through our yoga practise, so too, the inhale and exhale of contraction and expansion permit our awareness to grasp Aha moments as we flow along in the journey of life. These aha moments open a portal of communication, like an exchange of information through a sacred interface. In this way, we develop a relationship with the All-That-Is. We learn to surf the inhale like it is the deep face of a moving wave, only to find ourselves host to the unridden realm. But a moment or forever later, the natural response forms the exhale, and gently we have returned home to the next beginning. As an event horizon, Consciousness is both receiver and cultivator of feeling and experience. It is the anthropomorphized yoga, aware of itself as both the sequence of forms, while also aware of your experience expressing the forms. But now, let's address this one important concept straight out of the gate, here and now. We do not have consciousness, rather, Consciousness has us! Consciousness is the field of Oneness. Alive and well, Consciousness provides for our every impulse. We do however choose those impulses by the frequencies we elect to engage with. This really brings home the reason we need to be fully accountable for every thought, behaviour and environmental influence projected upon us. Habit will certainly define our path of least resistance; however, the good news is, we can change our minds and change our perceptions which consequently, changes our life experiences. Mindfulness is the master's tool of highest value for a reason. Simply being mindful of the myriad thoughtforms floating unrequested through our subtle bodies energy field will immediately refine what our receptors are a match for. Just for fun, do a random sampling of thoughts periodically throughout the next few days. Mindfully examine the ones you catch and notice if that thought is a match to your highest good. Continue weeding out the dark, fear infested thoughts from those of utility until you can permanently evict the undesirables. We are surrounded by thoughtforms not of our own making or choosing 24/7, all our life, until we become accountable for becoming a match to those of our own choosing. Don't take my word for it, let's do a quick demonstration to highlight our innate capacity to create the life we prefer.

Think of being in the presence of someone who has been angry.

Now pay attention to the physical reaction taking place having only imagined a nano-second of this illusion. We all know how quickly we become entangled in the emotional response which locks us deeper into further review and embellishment of our imagined scenario. Allow the flashback to continue. At what point did we become defensive or prescribe 'meaning' as a barrier against such negativity? Were you able to notice if the thoughtform you responded to was originating from

- a) WHO you want to be' in the most appealing light and highest good,

or,

- b) from that seasoned conditioning automatically reacting to this type of anger?

Or have you ever felt constricted by a judgemental thought you really aren't aligned with as 'your truth'? How often do we accept random thoughtforms as an extension of our own minds rather than apprehend the actual soup concocted by aeons of human brains endlessly churning out electromagnetic vibrations? Let's challenge ourselves to be mindful enough for even just ten minutes a day, to decide if we,

- a) like the thought and want to 'be that'
- b) recognize the pattern and cause
- c) reject immediately for the direction it will take us or additional undesirable energy it will attract

It is not enough to simply reject the vibrational nuisance, although it is a good start. Now that we know what has been lurking, unsuspecting, not just in the shadows but blatantly all around us, we must fill the vacuum with a neutralizing agent. Inject an equal and opposite thoughtform to halt the discordant speculations. However, additionally, we must diligently choose to become a match for the alternative frequencies of our desired experience. What thoughtforms would 'who I want to be' engage in? What thoughtforms are a match to the experience we wish to attract? Busting free from the briny deep of mindlessly mutating thoughtforms requires initial diligence but is surprisingly easy to navigate. Yes, it requires a formidable force dedicated to shattering previous beliefs and paradigms, but you have in your DNA (deoxyribonucleic acid) these exact potent triggers for your return to full consciousness. Tasting just one breath of freedom from negative thoughtforms will have us all suiting up into the armor of a most daunting defender. Setting up this practice of mindfulness is no different than settling onto our yoga mat. The space around us does not resist the option of beginning in seated position, or simply lying on the mat, eyes closed to briefly quiet the mind. The space simply accepts us as we settle in preparation for yoga. In fact, it always adds an intriguing dimension to consider feeling into the space before we begin. Photons and frequencies are the unseen observers we routinely ignore. Despite containing unimaginable treasure, we seldom hone our awareness to take in the gifts this universe lavishly imparts. Staying connected to your breath may just be the nudge to help you notice this loving abundance. Take time for Savasana often, our mental Child's Pose, and really rest. Sometimes, just allow your body to totally relax and let the mind be free to roam and frolic in the endless thoughtforms. They too, host plenty of opportunity to align themselves with awareness and thus transform our mental yoga into an aha moment. Setting the tone for your Savasana, to stay mindful, present, and aware, will turn your yoga practice into a cosmic journey of wondrous discovery.

Gratitude as Pure Principle

Because nobody ever said, "I wish I'd skipped yoga", remember to seal each new expansion with gratitude. Gratitude for each newly forming impression of that expansion that is rushing toward your open heart. Look for signs that prove your corrected frequency is already securing your desired lifestyle. The signs have been there in superposition, waiting to be noticed. Just as the Observer Effect elegantly sets aside the notion that a predetermined reality is "out there", it likewise demonstrates with double-blind accuracy that the expectation of the 'observer', causes perceptions which define the experience. Therefore, I say to unto you, get thee behind your expectations, and to do that, lets really hunt for any sign or symbol that foretells the effect you have set in motion.

Gratitude creates the frequency fractal to match receptors permitting the cross-exchange of information. These receptors specialise in communication. They detect changes in the environment and turn them into electrical impulses conveying very specific directions. A receptor must fit with the lock 'n key precision of Indiana Jones entering the Tomb of the Gods. And just like that key which opened the vault for Indiana Jones, the frequency fractal of gratitude is also a map. This map was used by our most ancient of ancestors and remains our most venerated treasure for times to come, for this map charts our way home.

Likewise, bliss and compassion are also examples of the frequency fractal passage which lead us home to Pure Source Energy. Life in the human body is designed to be a blissful experience and our ancestors let this knowledge guide them. Yoga is one example of a core technique which was relied upon in the development and sustaining of bliss-inducing life-affirming intuitive guidance. To this day, modern science acknowledges the potential of yoga in a new light reframing socio-political reforms, arts and sciences. Bliss begets compassion and helping others, from a place of compassion, produces bliss. You can begin to see how this divine intervention feedback loop, safeguards our natural return to light. So really, what is this 'light' we hear so often referred to like it is the celebrated destination and goal of all positive spiritual quests? Science and religion both explain the same phenomenon, which is the paradox of the photon. Novelty, in the form of personal differences and unique perceptions are not only the proverbial salt of the earth, but also the quintessential factor of immortalizing our infinite and eternal nature, aka 'Light'. Any textbook will explain that a photon is a particle of light, which is equally capable of behaving like a wave, simultaneously. Giving honourable mention to the dual nature of light, acknowledges that both fields co-exist. Co-existence is deeply invested in the mutual endorsements essential for peace. Yoga complements and corroborates with these subtle fields of light to emphasise a methodology to expand our consciousness to it full realization.

Now if we convert the wavelength of light into a time factor, we can then easily intuit the optimum frequency or duration to hold a yoga pose, or even a hug for that matter. Frequency means oscillations (cycles) per second and is most commonly recorded in hertz (Hz) which is to say vibrations per second. The frequency of a wave can be calculated by dividing the speed of the wave by the wavelength. But don't let the old linear model limit the real significance behind the wave and frequency. The universe has one wave shape, the sine wave. But it is not the two-dimensional image you see on the paper of your text books. The vibratory nature of our magnificent universe uses the spiral shape to package information. Form is the only thing the universe conserves by maintaining the ratio of length, area and volume of the golden mean (Phi). As a fractal of Phi in yoga-speak, we could imply that every one of the thousands of forms or pose positions, hold a signature of meaning which is shareable, hence understood, by all DNA. Observing a master yogi flowing in distinct defined form is beautifully uplifting just to watch. And when we can align our own bodies into the perfect form of this symmetrical efficiency, our bliss quotient skyrockets and we are grateful for our practise.

Most objects in nature are symmetrical. Dan Winter explains the principle of frequency signatures called "Fourier", means that even the most complex shape is a simple sum of sine waves of different lengths. http://www.fractalfield.com/ Symmetry represents order, and don't we all just crave order and the emotional pleasure we derive from symmetry intuitively sensed as security. This is the form of security embedded in 'sacred space'. When the charge resonance of a space is symmetrically fractal, the god-spark within your own DNA is able to propagate efficiently causing harmonic inclusiveness. Harmonic inclusiveness - defines the viability of every living thing (HRV fractality) - see goldenmean.info/ holarchy. Mindfulness gives instant access to the domain of God, Goddess, All-That-Is. The ancient salutation, Dominus vobiscum (Latin: "The Lord be with you") was an acknowledgment of that which is the 'perfectly branched' fractal of our own innate 'divine' potential. Once again Divine Order guides us back to "Ananda" meaning Bliss in Sanskrit. Great strides have been made through the work of Dan Winter, in understanding the electrical and harmonic nature of sacred resonance (think phase conjugate dielectric) In fact, phase conjugation in optics is the only place physics has reliably measured apparent self organization.

Boundary Conditions

On and off the mat, we can agree in the importance of boundary conditions. Boundaries, among other constants, illuminate and convey information concerning our values. Well, in science also, the boundary condition likewise specifies values. A boundary condition is a known value that must be true for the problem that you are working on. Even though our values are subject to constant flux that require revaluations, they non-the-less are generally used to evaluate what we posit to be constants. Those constants are synonymous with belief systems. Imagine old belief systems we had relied on for the safety they represented, breaking down because new or additional information has appeared which make the old belief obsolete. It was fine to engage for awhile but would only cause harm and entropy should we insist on clinging to it. Contradictory beliefs can result in cognitive dissonance, fear and even anxiety attacks. While the Band-Aid called 'justification beliefs' may help to reduce cognitive dissonance, the true value remains buried. The simple solution is found in answer to one question. "Is it shareable with all DNA"? If the answer is yes, then you can rest at ease knowing your fractal is (very Phi able) verifiable. If the answer is found in the land of 'not so much', then expect pressure to build forcing a change. Universal wisdom may be all for indulging the diversions and detours of free will but has your back and will always offer a way back to the light.

The universe can thus be described as a geometry of pressure. Accountability and assuming responsibility for deliberate and conscious choice elicits the pressure that emotion creates. This pressure informs the surrounding environment of vital requirements. Our evolving knowledge of the subconscious domains of the psyche along with the inter-connected nature of quantum physics instructs our yoga practise insofar as it looks to the biophoton light stored in our DNA molecules. Yoga, as meditation, is the art and science of systematically being the observer. Accepting, understanding, and training occurs at each of our subtle layers. The selectively permeable sacred interface permits recognition and extraction of knowledge stored within our own biophoton center of consciousness. Under appropriate conditions, the holographic projection of ancestral domain is released as a dynamic web of light. Appropriate conditions trigger a specific frequency and may spontaneously occur during a yoga practise or be born out of a sudden aha moment. The specific frequency, once learned, will serve as a cosmic area code enabling you to return at will to these self-inducing blissful peak experiences. Our DNA plays host to a communication network we all have carried with us since our inception. It behooves us to catalyze the correct conditions that guarantee our return to full consciousness, aka, the light.

All living cells of plants, animals and human beings emit biophotons. The holographic biophoton field of the brain and the nervous system has provided the basis of memory and other phenomena of consciousness. The consciousness-like coherence properties of the biophoton field are closely related to its base in the properties of the physical vacuum and indicate its possible role as an interface to the non-physical realms of mind, psyche and consciousness.

The "ch'i" energy flowing in our bodies' energy channels (meridians) which, according to Traditional Chinese Medicine, regulates our body functions may be related to node lines of the organism's biophoton field. The "prana" of Indian Yoga physiology represents a similar regulating energy force that has a basis in weak, coherent electromagnetic biofields.

Temple was a name which indicated a magnetic field which can become implosive enough to fire self-awareness. Self-awareness is a self study obviously. Translated from the Sanskrit svadhyaya, "self-study" describes the first part of the word—sva—meaning "self." The second part—dhyaya—is derived from the verb root dhyai, which means "to contemplate, to think on, to recollect, or to call to mind." Thus, it works to translate dhyaya as "study"—to study one's own self. The aim of svadhyaya is to bring the experience of that immense All-That-Is Consciousness, in the context of you individually aware. When the mind can grasp its own underlying nature (sva) through yogic means we have re-established a fractal boundary condition. This boundary condition expresses universal consciousness that focuses the waves into the zero point and keeps it spinning. This single symmetry principle describes centripetal forces within all self organizing systems and is the actual definition of peacemaking. Illumination implies light. The means to letting light guide your footsteps would be to follow the fractal path where living plasma/charge compression and spin density is made possible by the symmetry which allows efficient charge distribution. From another angle, consider what is said about God being the truth and the light. The living (plasma/charge/ether/spirit) fountain of ancestral memory and the collective conscious exist in the fractal places and times where the lightening heart of spin enabled perfect wave connectivity. This accurately describes the bliss sensation as a flame around your pineal and your heart as well. The conditions to invite bliss and light are saturated in science lessons which teach how to join a perfectly shareable wave. Spirituality and Yoga agree with Science because this implosive compression is precipitation. In alchemy, not unlike meteorology, precipitation is a process that involves the conversion of matter from a gaseous form into a liquid form. Light is the alchemical key. Saint Germain is said to have instructed the Nine Steps of Precipitation, the first of which was to affirm and repeat "Let there be light! Let there be light where I AM THAT I AM!" The law of precipitation speaks of spiritual energies which are drawn forth out of the Universal and coalesced in Matter. We must acknowledge that we ourselves are the alchemists who will determine the design of our creation and that we must know ourselves as the Real Self and our creation as coming forth from that Self. Restoring the freedom to create is essential to our well-being individually and as species amongst the myriad star nations of our cosmos. The interaction of the cosmic forces to which we belong is symbolized by energy vibrating over the lemniscate figure eight, which is the symbol of infinity. It is also the symbol of the transfer of energy from Spirit to Matter and from Matter to Spirit. The interchange of energy over that figure eight, as observed in the practise of Yoga and T'ai Chi, is the interchange of the yang and yin of cosmic forces, of breath and of the masculine and feminine principles of Oneness.

When we were taught about the possibility of human oneness - or about infinite collapse by Einstein - or implosive fusion by the alchemists - or black holes caused by Golden Ratio, we in fact were learning about the same thing: the wave self organization in the plasma 'flame' of mindfulness itself. Whether it is the shape of hydrogen's core, the fusion in the sun, the 'soul connecting' central bond in DNA's zipper or the wave fusion (successful compressing) at the center of plasma in the brain when you have peak experience/peak perception (bliss)...this central (Golden Ratio) compression solution and fusion psychology of oneness and physics of self organization in fact, all resolve to one simple symmetry solution.

Geometry produces symmetry (from Greek συμμετρία symmetria "agreement in dimensions, due proportion, arrangement"), which allows waves proceeding from opposite directions to meet each other and stand (to phase and phase-lock.) Standing waves give the illusion of stability, segregation of momentum, and make possible the birth of matter. Pressure occurs where waves meet. Have you ever felt that your personal waves must be meeting as 'relationships' or over at the bank perhaps, or, maybe the office lunch room? Let's come back to the topic of pressure after we fill in a few of the blanks…

Ratio is sacred; scale is profane. Size is unimportant where information is concerned. Ratio is informed formation- aka, information. Every form has a different message. It is the form which we need to understand. It is the form of each posture in yoga that speaks to your consciousness. Honing and perfecting form is not just an active meditation but also a science we have yet to honour.

The universe is a hologram, which means that even the tiniest part contains information about the whole. In a universe made of waves, focus on pure principle through prayer creates a harmonic pathway, aka gravity, for the waves to nest thus forming answered prayer. Every Aha moment has its bliss portal. The 'aha moment' in prayerful (focused) ecstasy and bliss achieved as a harmonic cascade called holography, establishes a connecting field of resonation with all frequencies. Frequency specific feeling derived from emersion in gratitude, compassion or bliss will catapult our awareness straight into a portal of its own design. The designer of the YogAha, is thus a two-way artisan of joyous bliss, fulfilling union with the sacred Pure Source energy embedded within all life. Simply the feedback of your physical heart muscles responding to gratitude, bliss or compassion literally induce shape-shifting epigenetic transformations in the environmental match for your thoughts. With this negentropy comes increased order to further amplify our metamorphosis from fear and suffering into bliss and enlightenment. Fractal spacetime is the solution to self-organization and self-organization is the requirement to become like incorruptible gold, never again framed by fear. Thus, our quest becomes fulfillment understood within the bounds of fractal spacetime. (Photo below is courtesy of Dan Winter)

Quest

Quests such as this, are personal journeys and every step commanding that it be taken alone. Inevitably they become adventurous pursuits, seeking to overcome many obstacles both symbolic and supernatural thus fulfilling some prophetic void or lack. Despite perils and bewildering consequences, a spiritual and psychological sense of purpose or reason drives us forward. Alchemy is such a quest, as is the yoga which teaches the physics of human interaction. Human interaction is about charge, so here we have come back to the topic of pressure and fulfillment when understood within the bounds of fractal spacetime providing the Aha of YogAha. All implied calculations which prove this fact are by one of the finest visionaries of our time, Dan Winter. Fractality is infinite non-destructive compressibility of charge. A fractal field is phase conjugation. Gravity is a centripetal force. Fractality is therefore the cause of gravity. Phase conjugate generation of superluminal longitudinal EMF after the charge accelerates by golden ratio conjugation- thru center Planck sphere as the phase conjugate 'mirror', will propagate primarily at integer golden ratio multiples, times the speed of light exactly where the imploded charge (gravity) goes at center, thru the (phase conjugate foci)- Planck sphere. So? It's pretty fun to see formulas describing naturally intuitive clairvoyant super-sensory observations, such as accessing ancestral memory, exploring in the field of consciousness and steering implosive plasma, like TheraPhi, by intent! On a much simpler level, if we imagine ourselves inhaling the delights of coconut and jasmine somewhere wonderfully tropical, suddenly, our outlook is lighter and brighter. If we are really good at matching frequency or merging in resonance, probably we are already hearing the thundering surf and smelling the salty surf of seawater. Waves are of course fractal space-time structures whereby the internal churning of the ocean is no less an electrical charge distributer than its upper surface. We all understand the immediate and sensational increase of our attention span. As electro-magnetic beings, our natural entrainment to the five basic types of ocean waves (sound, capillary, gravity, inertial and planetary) need no scientific corroboration to convince us of the peace and tranquility that comes with seaside visits.

Creating peak attention is amplified further by natural sunshine, largely because Hydrogen, the heart of the Sun, is phase conjugate. Bliss likewise is created by conjugate, or golden ratio, EEG brainwave frequencies. And achieving bliss is what this book is all about so slug through the physics with me and I promise to keep it light, pun intended. If you are just wishing instead for a technological-guru-devise to teach you how to produce these phase conjugate, or golden ratio, EEG brainwave frequencies, welcome to the modern technological era. In the spirit of offering a shareable wave let me show you where it has been accomplished and is available through Dan Winter at www.flameinmind.com. (Winter & Botte, 2017, p. 1) We are infinite eternal Beings and can open to All-That-Is where we are one with All.

We don't really need devises to communicate for us, however, our return to full consciousness is greatly accelerated by the Observer Effect. Societies in general have already progressed way beyond the quantum double slit experiment. Think of experiencing a skill or ability through the act of observing. One example might have come as toddlers watching our parent challenged to manipulate the first wave of computers and cell phones. Thirty some years later those toddlers are now producing their own offspring who seem to wield the natural innate ability to navigate the superposition of possibilities collapsing wave functions simply by what IT parlance deem 'intuitive'. Perhaps insulting to Grandma over there but it demonstrates how observing interactions within the conscious field via a devise such as TheraPhi, will hasten our neurological development to inform our memory, aka the functioning plasticity of our hippocampus. In the very near future, bliss could be our natural prerogative, should we elect to focus attention here, thereby increasing self-organizational order or negentropy, of this bioactive field.

The All exists in us

The All exists in us and we exist in the All. Think of drinking a bottle of water while floating in a lake or pool or seaside lagoon...you are in water and water is in you. Now imagine if your consciousness merges with the water; you could be conscious of not only everything positioned in the water but also the water within everything. This is all life...you can do same exercise with fire, air, plasma, colours, etc. Expanding our awareness in this way, to experience Oneness intellectually, teaches the next step toward navigating the subtler worlds. When you consider the limitations of three dimensional senses but know we have senses unexplainable by 3-D such as intuition, gnosis, clairsentience, clairaudience, claircognizance, telekinesis, telepathy, synesthesia, premonitions and many more examples, we can accept or knowing that indeed, there is far more to life. In so doing we can begin to become free of dark limitations and trust our questions as Great Creator's gift to find our way 'home'.

There are at least nine senses and most researchers think there are more like twenty-one or so. Psionics is a broad term used to describe supernatural powers that stem purely from the force of mind and will, rather than from the harnessing of divine or arcane energies... Split up into three parts.

- Telekinesis (moving things with your mind)
- Telepathy (reading minds and speaking with your mind)
- Psychic viewing (sensing with something other than the normal 5 senses)

The "Fruit of the Light of Loving-kindness" and "Healing through Togetherness" has been already set in motion. We have emergent skills currently developing in our return to full consciousness. Emergent skills such as psychic abilities which inform the noosphere to create new context for a conscious evolution. It is like the magnetic field itself is awakening in our return to knowing or remembering, Oneness. And to help us understand centripetal life force and biologic rejuvenation of fractal fields, the sacred yet very physical demonstration referred to as TheraPhi is now lovingly engaging the planet. (Winter, 2014, p. 02) (Winter & Harris, n.d., p. 1)

Bliss naturally is the fastest way to enter this charge access and is accompanied by DNA activation of ancestral memory. Within every bliss portal is an Aha moment and within every Aha moment is a bliss portal. Both bliss and the yogAha activate what amounts to a portal in DNA through which our ancestors speak in vivid holographic encoding of the light field. So, if bliss is the fastest way to enter the bioactive rejuvenation field encoded with our good fortune, the question really is, what is the fastest way to obtain bliss?

Pure Principle as a science

Pure principle is the straight-forward path to a spiritual practice based on solid scientific precedents. Your practice of choice, be it yoga, meditation or any other discipline, can incorporate pure principle to facilitate bliss through direct ecstatic communion self-generated in your body. Life's significance and what I refer to as the Lakshmi Effect, is the sustaining of a resonance which is shareable with all DNA. Lakshmi is the Goddess of auspicious wealth, fortune, power, luxury, beauty, fertility, and pretty much anything else your heart desires. Not only does she hold the promise of material fulfilment and contentment, but she grants access to her wisdom through your very own DNA. This wisdom can be engaged to transmute negative thought forms, invoke fractal spacetime, and create the sacred stillness of phase conjugation. Countless people down through the ages have revered and celebrated Lakshmi. Meditation and ceremonial ritual are offered in the hopes of producing a resonance with this great Goddess. After all, a resonance which is shareable with all DNA is how we learn to activate the human soul through bliss and evolve. And the fastest way to obtain bliss occurs in resonance with an Aha moment. Every Aha moment has its bliss Portal. Understanding the practical application of resonance itself, shares a valuable aha insight.

Remember when you first wanted to learn yoga? If you signed up at your local studio for classes, you accessed the living resonance of yoga's morphic field. If only for one hour at a time, you were surrounded by a collective energy which supplied layers of appreciation and deep insights from which you could energetically draw. Now on the other hand, if you were isolated in your attempts to figure out basic asanas, or postures, you would have likely had a much longer, shallower, understanding of yoga. All elements of life have an aperture of ripening resonance which you can take tap into, by consciously connecting to its morphic field. In so doing, the benefits which have already been established, will energetically be picked up by the intelligence of your cellular biophotons as you become entrained, or resonate, with the information held within its field. To resonate, literally means 'return to sound'. It is from the Latin root word resonare. When two objects become entrained, their energies interact and amplify each other. Resonance however, only occurs when the first object is vibrating at the natural frequency of the second object. Grandfather clocks, similarly tuned tuning forks, or two friends coming together create an amplification of one of the many background frequencies in the environment. Resonance is the cause of sound production in musical instruments. Like the Woodwind instruments, in which the source of the vibration is the reed or wooden strip, so too, you, are the source of the vibration which amplifies the resonance in your conscious perception. How pure or clear are you, as the instrument through which vibrations resonate? Resonance which is shareable with all DNA, follows a similar principle best understood by considering nature's fractals or even Russian stacking dolls. The idea is that so long as the ratio or form is constant, then the scale can expand or contract at will. When we get right down to it, the question becomes, "does it serve and apply to all life"?

So, what exactly describes, in a practical mundane example, that resonance which is shareable with all DNA? Well, lets consider for a moment your thoughts. How many thoughts running through your mind would you share, unedited, with the world? Now consider how many of those thoughts would benefit the entire planet? Can you isolate one thought that would be of utility to Oneness or All-That-Is? If you find one that serves the All, hold onto it. Meditate on this, your shareable resonance, and you will find the portal has welcomed you as a descendant of Lakshmi. It doesn't take too longer to figure out that it needs to be based in universal principles such as Love, light, Joy, compassion etc. and extend far beyond your known community.

Many paths to bliss

There are many paths to join or 'yoke' our awareness to bliss and catalyze our own sacred interface in the field of consciousness, including AcuLomi Temple meditation, tantra, kundalini, yoga, or appropriately engaging plant medicine such as ayahuasca and so on. Each path forms the frequency domicile of related order to guide corresponding revival of illuminated perception and connection to who we really are.

Freedom is one component of Bliss but, it must be claimed. What is freedom? From where do we claim it? Sacred space, the birth canal of freedom, is created through the union or 'yoking' of the Observer's awareness with Consciousness conveying pure principle. The resulting bliss moment is suspended as stillness to attain liberation. If only for the moment, liberation provides the cosmic area code (which is a specific frequency) for conscious union with the blissful Spirit. This is freedom.

AcuLomi Temple meditation practices induce Yogaha's through awareness of posture (asana), awareness of breath (pranayama), control of subtle forces, cleansing the body-mind through focus on pure principle, visualization inducing frequency, chanting of mantras and mindful stillness. These are simply techniques which encourage the unfurling of our dormant potential. AcuLomi stimulated YogAha's awaken greater awareness of ourselves and the ways and means through which we feel connected. As such, YogAha is a process of self-discovery. This leads us to self-mastery and self-realization.

The philosophy and alchemical workings of John Dee, as summed up in his Monas Hieroglyphica, the Chymical Wedding of 1616, is structured after the inner spiritual transformation of an "elaborate Hermetic allegory" and is therefore, according to Teresa Burns and J. Alan Moore (Burns & Moore, 2007, p. 01) the deepest subject of this work, rather than the mundane alchemical quest for gold. To open the gate of discovery and true understanding in our own personal journey towards bliss requires the catalyst of inner transformation. AcuLomi Temple Meditation provides this catalyst to activate both prophetic and supernatural passage.

Temple was a name which meant magnetic field which can become implosive enough to fire self-awareness...symmetry operations necessary to ignite biology and DNA. Even meditating on just the geometry of sacred space ignited in the fire of self-awareness attunes us to our fully conscious selves. Focus on this pure principle literally alters our DNA and functions as powerful portals between worlds, drawing in spiritual blessings. Like the portals, sacred space is deliberately temporary so don't get caught up in trying to hang onto the frequency or you will lose the opportunity; just like the metaphor of someone trying to grasp gold at the end of the rainbow, it will become nothing more useful than dried up leaves.

Psychophysiology of Bliss

Like prayer borne on smoke of the Peace-pipe, bliss too will yield its wisdom more readily to those open and receptive to its wafting essence rather than clutching at calculated entrapment. In this way, the psychophysiology of Bliss is like inhabiting a lightning bolt. It offers a brilliant flash of acuity in one aha moment should the environment be a suitable transmitter. In a more scientifically rigorous vernacular, a suitable environment would be fractal. An electric field of perfect compression to be precise. According to Dan Winter, (Winter, 2016, p. 02) the geometry of perfect compression is the solution to every mystery that ever existed from, the cause of gravity to the cause of consciousness, the cause of colour to the cause of perception, and the cause of transcendence to the cause of enlightenment. Measurement of bliss or enlightenment occurs as golden mean ratio in brainwaves. Because the Aha seed essence is fractal, it can be grounded, take root, and grown into new budding neural pathways offering exponential growth in our return to full consciousness. The domino effect is perpetual. Imprinting perception of the Aha moment is electrical and subjective.

You however, have free will to prescribe meaning to your perception, either from a place of ego, from the perspective of pure principle, or, as is more often the case, from a position somewhere in-between. The tug-of-war vies for control from that position somewhere in-between, jousting for determinative certainty, simply to spell out 'rest'. We seek sacred Stillness for the resonance associated with Pure Source Energy, however, enroute, we may be enticed to settle for rest stops along the way.

R- E -S- T implies *Release *energy *sustaining *tranquility.

Paradoxically, should the ego slip in and grab hold the reins to execute a sleight of hand reversal, perception will instead be lured toward the smoke and mirrored opposite *Resistance *engages *self-perpetuating *trauma. This subordination to ego ironically provokes a frequency which disallows free will to prescribe meaning to your perception. Instead, an auto-pilot repetition of convenient, compliant illusionary script will dictate both meaning and thus reaction. Really, it comes down to who is holding the reins; you, in alignment with pure principle or you, in alignment with ego.

Unfurling our dormant potential

Both alignment with pure principle and alignment with ego are determined by resonance. Resonance introduced the wave physics (Einstein's *spooky action at a distance*) that charmed and baffled the scientific community until accepted as either miracle or entanglement. Resonance simply put describes a harmonic fractal. As a practical exercise however, let's investigate alignment with pure principle by focusing our attention, aka meditation, on a loving thought or feeling. To increase our bioelectric coherence, do this exercise outside in nature if possible. Alternatively, just imagine nature while surrounded by natural materials such as natural fiber clothing, crystal, water, or wooden furniture. Developing coherence by focused intention, causes electric fields to compress becoming portals of sacred space. Attuning to this subtle life force energy that animates and connects all living things will keep us dialed in to our true nature, the Rainbow Light-Body. Intention can be a transformative and therapeutic tool when utilized with resonance as a carrier wave of consciousness.

The medium of powerful creation and healing

The energy of focused attention on shareable mindfulness, can be the medium of powerful creation and healing. What shareable creation or healing would you like to manifest?

The energetic frequency produced by pure intention becomes conscious force, or voltage. Intense, absorptive states of bliss lead to Samadhi, which is the highest state of consciousness relating to Kundalini. Also received as the Holy Spirit, this descending aspect completes the Greater Divine Circuit. The heart offers indwelling Source or Soul, a faculty endowing spirit, as a current, to move down into itself as a holy grail of implosive DNA. (Winter, n.d., p. 01) The pure electrical geometry of this kundalini experience, otherwise known as bliss, directs the mental, emotional and subtle bodies, into the self-aware magnetic wormhole or 'sacred interface'. It is not enough to intellectually follow the steps of meditation. It is the tangible, infusion of ecstasy with focused pure intention which gives rise to efficient charge distribution. A perfect echo then occurs electrically and sonically to commune with the collective unconscious.

Let's do it

Imagine being somewhere in nature, say a lush and verdant forest. As we step further into our imagined scenario, an earthy fragrance is stirred by the gentle flight of a meadowlark. Dense emerald moss lovingly nestles the tiny blooms and beautiful foliage along our path. A glinting ray of warmth transfers euphoric joy to the depth of our being. But what is that sense of enchantment that begs communion? Something deeply profound is stirring the gossamer disquiet of memory just out of reach. Melodic trills of the meadowlark offer diversion but that glinting ray of warmth has become kindling fervor. It is then we realize we are in the presence of a great and Holy Being. Every molecule of our body is drinking in the majesty of this moment. Enveloped in a love that can only be understood as a light so sacred it defies perception, our very body deliquesces to become both one with the all and nothing. The vastness of this 'no thing' is perceptible only as joyous spin too delicious to resist. Counter rotating fields of ecstasy become a playground of dancing potential. Flowing into infinity and radiating ✿ through lemniscate figure eights, (*Figure 2,*) the indestructible double Dorje effect make a fusion of opposites to invite the 'one and the many' of our balanced collective consciousness. This moment alone sanctions the fulfillment of any desire or wish offered from your heart. In resonance with the All, perceived only through love, what is your wish?

So, how was it?

Did the simple act of conscious observation during prayerful affirmation of pure intention, animate and actuate coherence engaging Love? A system of education and meditation which introduces enlightened and blissful experiences, enable the ego and mind to dissolve through frictionless spin. The vehicle of entry into this sacred space, pure intention, converts visualizing and feeling the movement of body/mind flowing as a radiating figure-eight, into contraction of the golden ratio pattern expanding in counter-rotating fields. The infinitely contracted and infinitely expanded selves become One during the activation of meditation. Acknowledged since ancient times as the 'Harmony of Apollo', the psychokinesis of steering plasma with one's mind is enabled during coherent intention. Coherence happens in response to sound harmonics coming from the heart.

Let's take a moment to test-drive this resonance idea. Again, feel your focused attention on a 'wish' or intention, based in shareable loving thoughts or feeling. Now, let's add in a specific visual. We will use the Chintamani stone (*Figure 3)* or, "wish fulfilling gem" of Tibetan Buddhism. The symbol of triple dots, (circles or rings) produce an energy symbolized by wispy whorls of smoke and flame and will attune us to the resonance of sacred space. Visualize, feel and intend, with conscious awareness and purpose, the Chintamani having absorbed your wish. Notice any additional descriptive frequencies such as tone, pulse, colour etc. In this way, the consumed perspective of biology can unpack memory, or 'pressure waves' into a 'Oneness' experience.

Author William Henry has said that like light itself, even just the image of sacred art such as the Chintamani stone changes our DNA, alters our consciousness and attunes us to our future selves. (Henry, 2017, p. 02) The greatest mysteries are within our own self as a fractal of truth. If you want to understand the human body, look to the cosmos and if you want to understand the cosmos, look to the human body. The gnosis resulting from true contemplation is not to be confused with hypothetical philosophies but rather, nudges the terrain of theosophical alchemy of the human perception. Once this alchemical transmutation has occurred, holographic fractal nature becomes a self-evident expression of DNA. In other words, we will see and understand evidence of integration with the higher planes of existence. We will see and understand electromagnetic fields of Oneness as found in the Holy Grail. What was once high mystery will instead become your Temple of Transformation. This divine light of Consciousness which dwells within everyone is the glory which ancient secret doctrines referred to as the 'Blue Pearl'. Your Temple of Transformation is the catalyst which activates the Blue Pearl within you. The scientific characterization of 'temple' describes a plasma projection, or, 'stargate'. New applications with computational analysis of DNA, RNA, peptides, and proteins have advanced deeper insights of governing phenomena. Ever-increasing computational power only validates the internal signatures penetrating the 'Observer Effect'.

Outwardly, the Temple of Transformation can be catalyzed by a series of techniques that lead us to consciously connect with ourselves and with the life impulse at the center of all creation. As YogAha describes access and understanding of these techniques, there is no dogma or belief system attached to it. YogAha simply presents the unfathomed witness to the wisdom carried in our very own DNA. In practice and then feeling the effect of that practice, our internal Observer reveals the location of its volume control button and focusing lens. If we unmute our internal 'Observer', focus the mind and heart, we will develop mental peace and deep insight. This is YogAha.

Chapter Two

The Observer Effect

Observation affects quantum systems. Period. Beautifully, elegantly and simply proven. We have the 'Copenhagen Interpretation' and the double slit experiment, we have the 'Schrodinger Cat' phenomenon, we have the Heisenberg uncertainty principle, we have the butterfly effect and many other interpretations of quantum weirdness. Never mind inquiring into what kind of observer is necessary, need it be a human, another cat, or an extra-terrestrial, because any single observation provides the permeable event horizon receiving and transmitting its impressions… I know right; it's just weird. Beautifully magnificently Weird. Consciousness is simply expressing itself! And the memory of this accumulated totality is stored non-locally, available to the All. In comparison to linear, limited states of three-dimensional experience anyway. But once you have navigated quantum foam and become the 'All', the backdrop called weirdness, pretty much just falls away.

Scientists have found that being absorbed in an activity quietens the 'thinking cortex' which then releases our questing creativity. While routine performance of task-oriented detail performed via our prefrontal cortex has been found to inhibit creativity, love and passion take us beyond the limitations of the mental body. Beyond our mental bodies intellectual death grip of paradigm inducing perceptions is the land of the adept. Here one's heart intellect gives rise to our rightful endowment of creation. Concede completely to something you love, and you'll notice the stillness and space has suddenly becomes alive and self-aware. This is what entering sacred space feels like. Creation occurs in the moment of surrender: allow your fertile ecstasy to unveil nature exalted.

'Feeling' is the lodestar pathfinder

Feeling creativity is innate and must be obliged if we are to know freedom. 'Feeling' is the lodestar pathfinder. The form and ratio already exist. But focused attention on the feeling aspect of surrender will evoke the nameless and 'unseen helping hand" from within your own consciousness to cast a bridge into sacred space of creation. This bridge is the harmonic sacred interface, referred to as the sovereign God-Spark. It exists between the physical and the subtle worlds in the field of consciousness. It is a bridge of light made up of tiny energy packets called photons. Light, remember, is a form of electromagnetic radiation that shows properties of both waves and particles and the perfect host for bio-holographic transmission. This Wave and Particle conundrum is a tangled hierarchy within the immanent self-reference of a system observing itself. The biophoton light in the sense receptors of our own body, seamlessly communicate with the photons of the sacred interface. You are literally the 'light of the world', just like it says in the bible. When we obey its command of 'take no thought', we disable the ego stream of thoughtform activity. The reason for clearing your thoughts and emptying your mind in meditation is to raise above thought to be able to merge with the sacred interface. This is the meaning of the single eye or third eye of the pineal gland. Revered by mystics and shamans throughout all ages and all cultures, the third eye is considered to be the organ of supreme universal connection. Ayurvedic philosophy speaks of it as the Ajna chakra. Ancient Egypt refers to the symbol of the Eye of Horus which depicts precisely the pineal gland in the profile of the human head. But this third eye is only the relay point for receiving and exchanging information. You must filter the information packets carried by light and give them meaning. Are your filters clear as sunlight allowing the uptake of a clean stream of information or is the light refracted through a variety of conditioned measurements as left-over baggage? You will find your answer is clearly conveyed through your feeling. No amount of intellectualizing will bring you to the truth which your feelings already know. This clearing enables us to become centered and create the appropriate environment of sacred space. Yoga classes will often begin with the instruction, or reminder, to become centered or find your center. This is the kindred antecessor to becoming self-aware, self-organizing, negentropic perfected fractality required for phase conjugation if we just knew it. Finding your center might casually imply a connection with your spirit, but allow yourself to dwell on your innate goodness, and you might discover a portal straight through the heart of the sun. Your center is that subtle field that exists everywhere and nowhere. It gives you access to the best you possible. Where you connect to your higher power or Goddess, God, All-That-Is safe place, that is always available to you and offers renewal and inspiration. It also allows you the safety to feel the highest good in the world. This is a resonance with golden ratio perfected recursion embedding within the sacred interface. And created in an instant by 'feeling into' that very specific shareable aka, fractal, frequency. It may be joy, it may be compassion, it may be love or even bliss, but it must be shareable with all DNA. http://www.bioactivefield.com

How do your feelings register and express compassion? Compassion and loving kindness are the active aspects of wisdom. Can you remember when you received and conveyed compassion through the kinesthetic feeling sense of your vital energy? What does this state of compassion feel like in your physical body? What does this feel like in your emotional body? What does compassion feel like to your mind? Remember these feelings so that you can recreate the frequency at will and automatically be directed back to the safe and shareable sacred space. Yoga takes the view that our person is much, much more than a body. Quantum science disciplines agree.

Quantum objects are said to be transcendent waves of possibility residing in a domain of potentiality. When subjected to measurement however, these quantum objects will be triggered to behave as a particle, in physical space and time. The Observer Effect, as we well know, reflects what the double slit experiment so elegantly established. The scientific embrace of causality, determinism, and the notion that reality is "out there" somewhere, can now be put to rest. Having eternally blurred the line between the observer and the system being observed, Erwin Schrodinger said, "Subject and object are only one. The barrier between them cannot be said to have broken down as a result of recent experience in the physical sciences, for this barrier does not exist." Quantum physics also allows nonlocality, where no signal is required for communication. This quickly opens the door to entertain the vast but simple solution that leads us home, to ourselves. Downward causation describes Consciousness as the ground of all being. Mystics, Metaphysicians and Yogis knew this all along. While traditional conservative science was struggling to move ahead on one leg while stuck the mud or primacy of matter, quantum physics showed us that we must seek the harmony already flourishing in consciousness. The etheric body is an energy template that consciousness nourishes. This formative field is made of what the Hindus have known for millennia as prana (Sanskrit), and what the Chinese call Chi/Qi. Theosophical literature refers to the etheric body as the etheric double, a duplicate of the physical body in every way, though existing in a higher frequency domain invisible to normal human vision. Through meditation, you can experience the etheric double and begin to prepare for the deepening of your awareness. The field of consciousness contains the All, the 'other side', the potentialities of every level and scale. Consciousness expresses through us and through the All. We don't have consciousness, rather, consciousness has us. But its all good as we are one with the All. I remember hearing that Jesus said he is in the Father and the Father in him and that he and the Father are one. Well, consciousness means that it couldn't possibly be any other way. Resonance is not exclusive to particle and matter but also refers to thought, behaviors, emotion and ideas. Just about anything which vibrates will entrain in sympathy with another. Resonance creates and sustains a morphic field. As consciousness expresses itself through form, every form creates an energy resonance within and around itself. Sympathetic resonance increases the intensity of that vibration. This is the intelligence of information bearing form. Each independent form contains information specific to its unique quality, reflected as form. In an article found at http://www.spiritualresources.info, Yolanda Zigarmi Martin writes, "Simply being aware that there IS a field of resonance built by a form or an idea allows you to 'step into' that field and resonate with its history and characteristics, all of which have been added to over time by countless people and situations. This represents a large body of information available to you at your convenience and totally free of charge."

The act of 'feeling' into that field, is a skill available to every living being. Your sense of intuitive feeling can bridge the synapse between the physical material worlds with that of the subtle. We all naturally have access to the bio-energetic bridge between space-time and time-space. Our DNA provides a permeable network co-functioning between space-time and time-space. It is the instrument through which our "morphic fields" communicate with our physical bodies. All of them. According to the yoga tradition, every one of us have five bodies. From the Vedic era Sanskrit text Taittiriya Upanishad, we learn that each kosha, or "sheath," is made of increasingly finer energy. From the densest material body to the subtle most anandamaya kosha, or bliss body, most people would seldom sense this level of consciousness existing within themselves. Just knowing about these layers helps you begin to tune in. Many yoga texts will describe the five sheaths as being grouped into three. The physical body and vital force are called the sthula sharira, the "gross body." The mental body and intellect are called the sukshma sharira, the "subtle" or "astral body." The bliss sheath is called the karana sharira, the "causal body." These are recognized in many different spiritual and cultural traditions as well. Plutarch, a Greek priest who presided at the Temple of Delphi, called them the soma, psyche, and nous, respectively.

With this new insight, lets go back to the sense of receiving and transmitting compassion. This time try to imagine what that feels like through your vital feeling senses? What does this state of compassion feel like in your physical body? What does this feel like in your emotional body? What does compassion feel like to your mind? Does your Celestial and Causal body provide feedback registered as a sense which you can distinctly identify?

Science and spirituality are united in this way and realized in phase conjugate (golden-ratio) negentropic charge collapse resulting from activating the sacred God-Spark. Both classified quantum revelations and arcane wisdom are disclosed through catalyzation of the sacred interface. AcuLomi Temple meditation and workshops teach the subtle nuances of this art for those students who are ready to gain access to the subtle anatomy of the Universe.

Access to the known and unknown throughout time and space, as well as the inverted antimatter properties and elements, yet to be officially 'observed and hence named, demonstrate that bliss and compassion are inherent qualities essential to our well-being.

The kinesthetic, feeling-based heart journey of AcuLomi Temple meditation, complementing the intellect-based gnosis roused from the subtle fields of consciousness arise in the electrical phenomenon we call mind or awareness, as the peak experience able to fully catalyze the sacred interface. AcuLomi Temple meditation system actively catalyzes the sacred interface of our sovereign God-Spark to engage Oneness as the field of consciousness. Through use of this education and meditation system, the Observer Effect of the observed, observing the Observer, contracts and expands generating a ripple effect. Basically, it is the equivalent of looking into God's eyes while also seeing through them -seeing what God sees- while at the same time, God's eyes are looking into yours…gazing cognizant at each other. The acknowledgement of this observation creates an event impact of astronomical proportions uniting celestial and personal kundalini activation. Meditation fundamentally prepares the Pineal gland to polarize celestial light of the electrical phenomenon known as the kundalini bliss experience.

Plasma embedding of bliss permits the holographic portals in our DNA to become the correct, aka fractal, environment to host 'ancestors' who can guide us in our return to full conscious awareness of the All-That-Is or 'Oneness'. After all, the plasma entities we experience as our 'ancestors' are in fact us. Plasma centripetal force with enough 'mana', or sacred life-energy force, to affect our star, the sun, has been measured during such experiments as when one million children singing together in Thailand was found to affect solar flares. ("One million children singing," Mar 16, 2011, p. 01)

Mana and phase conjugation demonstrate that we are a seed for centripetal negentropic force. And that return to order can be supported and rewarded simply by setting goals and then acting to fulfill them. The Reward Molecule called Dopamine for example is responsible for the sweet exhilaration we experience by showing up to yoga class, or by finishing that book or any number of accomplishments that we set our sights on. Every type of reward seeking behavior that has been studied increases the level of dopamine transmission in the brain. If getting that hit of dopamine will activate your bliss, then just set a goal and achieve it.

What is Phase conjugation?

Phase conjugation is the solution which allows the Holy Grail to be passed along. "I Am that I Am' specifically defines where one is all and all is one, where the inside is in precise relation and replication of the outside like a toroidal vortex smoke-ring turning inside out. Imagine an infinite number of Angels (precise wave angles) meeting, merging and dancing boundless potentialities into existence. This perplexingly vast amount of information sits waiting to be noticed in some impossibly small quanta. What optics has proven is that this conjugating, or charge, wave geometry illustrates the first tangible evidence of the God-spark- self-organization and negentropy. (Winter, n.d., p. 01) The volumes on this subject that Dan Winter continues so graciously to share with the world demonstrates that the Phase Conjugate or Fractal field generates opposing wave fronts like 'pine cones kissing noses', as he says, - which implode at the Planck sphere generating gravity, color, life, consciousness and bliss. Yes, the Bliss that the world's children are so desperately in need of can be found in a mathematical formula. There is no longer a need to risk overdosing on drugs or extreme sports to get your fix when bliss is available, naturally, any time you need a little pick-me-upper. This is the kind of healing that we can all use. Until now, our society has lacked the natural modality to recalibrate joy, happiness and freedom when life experiences present fear, pain or trauma. Instead, when overloaded by the demands of today's world, people have escaped into behaviors of restriction at best and often even a wide range of addictions as substitutes for their freedom, paying the price of deep stress, shock, loneliness, financial debt-loads or poverty. When our lives are consumed with minor distractions, misaligned demands, fears, guilt, prestige or pride, we become restricted, tense and feel trapped. Trauma and stress, produce acidic heat and inflammation in the body, which is recorded as shock in the subconscious mind. The mind stacks every such experience creating endocrine fight or flight hormonal response, chemical, and other neurological effects in our cellular memory.

We carry our mind and body and subtle bodies in the conscious field. Bliss enables communication with this field while commissioning the freedom to shut off fear and connect to the internal soul compass by mindful bliss.

There are many paths to achieve bliss, however an immediate contribution to society is through the AcuLomi Temple meditation system breaking through previously imagined pseudo forces of separation to align your internal soul compass with foolproof intuition, self-compassion through self-care, and relaxation to connect to inspiration.

Do you believe that you can have freedom? Would you like to experience Stillness? Have you ever wondered how the elements such as Fire, Air, Water, Earth or Plasma can communicate with you? Would you like to experience your ancestors via meditation or would you be interested in hearing what your very own DNA would say to you? Every Aha moment has its bliss portal…where do you wish to explore?

Can you see the benefits of feeling peace & happiness? Can you see the benefits of sharing that with everyone? How would people treat you? Do you see any benefits of being able to trust and rely solidly on your own self?

Bliss brings us to mindfulness and a sharper intuition. It trains your brain (aka neurological process) for gratitude, happiness and relaxation. In so doing, the bliss experience encourages inspiration to find and live your purpose, guided by dreams and desires. You are alive: what are you going to do about it? Only you have the answers in your heart for you, only you can heal your bodies, AcuLomi Temple however, can teach you how to access your bliss and freedom. There is great healing and freedom available via bliss. Conventional medicine has not yet given any attention to this long-ignored science. Understanding the field of consciousness as a potential to heal the frequency field of the human body is finally being taught in medical universities such as IQUIM (Quantum University) and at Dan Winter's Fractal U and Learn It live classes on line. The subtle energy of the human body and its innate power to heal has been sadly lacking in allopathic medical education and training. However, over the past decade, Quantum University has developed an education system that explores this new paradigm of Integrative Quantum Medicine. Both conventional Western medicine along with traditional medical science of conclusively established

Homeopathy, Ayurvedic and Oriental systems of medicine, are clearly defined by quantum physics and as such, must now reach into the realm of non-locality.

The new Integrative Quantum Doctor of the future will not only need to expand his or her knowledge of the subtle energy anatomy but must also be equipped with the latest technological innovations. Stand aside Star Trek, the age of miraculous interventions has already occurred. As we cross this threshold seamlessly, the marvelous and astounding are welcomed into our personal domains. The TheraPhi devise co-invented by master alchemist Paul Harris and Dan Winter permit broad spectral range of phase conjugate harmonics either in your home or at a clinic or spa down the road. Imagine activating plasma healing and rejuvenation fields to potentially trigger kundalini effects of bliss or even a shaman portal, simply by spending a few minutes of your day in the wonderful plasma field of a nearby TheraPhi devise.

Let's discuss how to practically apply these insights of utility our perseverance deserves. Yes, this technology is way overdue but kudos to us for hanging in there!

Regardless if it is lucid dreaming you are after or the ability to calm some turbulence on your next flight south, the coherence required to achieve engagement-with-the-subtle-worlds begins with understanding phase conjugation. Two familiar concepts will help you to identify the frequency of coherence. Relationship and Power.

First examine the relation between two signals or data sets. Let's use any recent conversation to demonstrate signals and data sets. What was the relationship between you and whomever you were speaking to? What was the relationship between what you wanted to convey and the perception that person received? The signals sent may have verbally relayed one message while body language disclosed an entirely different directive. Or, for a different example, how can you be certain that your interpretation of a frequency, say the absolute magnitude of the color blue, is perceived identically, the power or intensity of the hue correspondingly equivalent, by the next person? Fortunately for our personal relationships, data sets such as these rarely require absolute coherence. The coherence of consistent congruence in Physics or Optics however, maintain a fixed phase relationship, predictably in phase relationship with each other over a period of time. Now that would be the 'next level' communication I could get excited about, but it is also what happens when atoms move to a higher energy level and radiate their energy in phase. Perhaps remembering to intend that our Relationship and Power are 'in higher phase' next time we attempt those heart-to-heart conversations will provide the coherence we hope for. But like our conversation demonstrating signals and data sets, coherent phase conjugation waves are not exclusive to the linear operations performed in one domain such as time or frequency, but rather have corresponding operations, simultaneously, in multiple other domains. And they all require absolute precision alignment to generate fractal, negentropic opposing wave fronts. Hence the analogy Dan Winter favours, it's like 'pine cones kissing noses'. Incidentally, 'pine cones kissing noses' implode at the Planck sphere to generate such wonders as gravity, color, consciousness, bliss and that little thing we lovingly call 'life'.

'Pine cones kissing noses' is a great visual of immense utility toward grasping the theory, however, the mechanism is worth investigating a little deeper. We must also understand the wave physics of miracles and the divine sciences. Back in the day, Einstein talked about 'spooky action at a distance' but now it's all 'quantum entanglement'. Why quantum entanglement' has even brought discussions of Love in terms of Light into the labs of astrophysicists as unseen and mystical connections relevant to science. And these connections do exist in the subatomic world where Plasma healing tarries. And our pine cones kissing noses know all about plasma healing.

The pine cone with 13 spirals to the right and 8 to the left, demonstrates the fractal progression of Fibonacci numbers and the Golden Spiral. The phase conjugating golden spiral on the pine cone is exactly the path that a longitudinal or compression wave must take to pass thru the Planck sphere out the tip of the pine cone.

Two commonly known types of electromagnetic frequencies which are produced in waves are called transverse and longitudinal. Transverse waves travel perpendicular to the direction of the wave much like the arching effect we would achieve by flicking a long rope. The rope would form peaks and valleys or crescents and troughs as the motion travelled long its course. The mechanical disturbance of vibrations in a plucked guitar string is one example. There are many sources of transverse electromagnetic radiation ranging from the natural occurring source such as thunderstorms and the earth's magnetic field to man-made sources, such as overhead power lines and substations to house wiring, electrical appliances, and our favorite technologies such as wi-fi modems, computers, cordless and cell phones, It is well known that some forms of transverse electromagnetic waves break down the chemical bonds between the molecules in the cells of the body. These days there are numerous companies producing a variety of devices to protect yourself from dangerous transverse EMFs.

The transverse (up and down) EMF wave is recognized by the up and down signature as opposed to the longitudinal EMF. Longitudinal waves have a back and forth signature known as compressions and rarefactions. Rarefaction occurs where the density of the wave is lowest, and compression occurs where the density of the wave is highest. While electromagnetic waves can travel through empty space, the longitudinal compression wave reminds me of billiard balls or the Newton's cradle toy where the motion of each ball is induced by the compression of being struck and causes the direction of travel along the longitudinal wave. This longitudinal wave component, measurably, goes faster than light, by golden ratio multiples x C, and can pass through pretty well anything. While longitudinal electromagnetics have been referred to as scalar or torsional, it is worth noting the value of a more rigorously accurate description, since among other issues, a scalar vector has other meanings in physics.

http://theraphi.net/static/remoteconjugatingplasma.html

All of this is important to begin to visualize the mechanics and thereby understand phase conjugation for it is this golden ratio phase conjugate implosion of charge which causes gravity. It is this golden ratio phase conjugate implosion of charge which reaches a limit condition at the Planck sphere dimension, where the phase conjugate pine cone translation of vorticity converts the charge inertia from transverse to longitudinal EMF. In phase conjugation the transverse wave translates its vorticity as it travels down the phase conjugating golden spiral (think pine cone) and then emerges without inertia loss as a longitudinal EMF wave through the Planck sphere out the tip of the pine cone. Further discussion of this, with wave animations, can be found at http://theraphi.net/static/

remoteconjugatingplasma.html. Here is what you need to get out of this discussion; it is the longitudinal wave component which is most responsible for bioactive, healing / rejuvenation fields. Plasma rejuvenation such as occurs through TheraPhi sessions, is the holy grail of fusion research and the true wave mechanics of alchemy. For deeper study of this aspect, please see 'plasma implosion' at: www.fractalfield.com/alchemyoffusion

You will also discover and breakthrough to deeper understanding of how conjugate longitudinal interferometry creates the 'action at a distance', known as 'flame in the mind' and remote plasma containment for anyone interested in distance healing at http://fractalfield.com/conjugateinterferometryout/. Optical phase conjugation is a non-linear optical process, which is capable of time reversing the scattering process, and healing the distortions in a wave front which allow negentropy in our return to divine order. Phase conjugation occurring via TheraPhi is a vital and compelling phenomenon that can enable you to become the correct environment to have visitation from ancestors, have communication with your own DNA, travel the subtle worlds and commune with nature as do our most gifted shamans and medicine men and women. In summation, the amount of coherence in your aura which can withstand acceleration by phase conjugation into longitudinal supraluminal EMF will determine your ability to approach sacred kundalini transformations, as well as travel fully conscious through the subtle worlds of Oneness and the All-That-Is. Bliss is the fastest way to wellness. We must understand fractality to understand bliss or kundalini hygiene. This means that you must have shareable thoughts to allow your aura to grow. Developing a capacitive lifestyle that attracts living plasma charge is based on shareable loving thoughts, and as much as possible, create your home environment from natural materials including focus on nourishing your physical human temple with organic whole foods. Considering all relationships as a sacred vessel of intention will jumpstart and amplify your momentum. Look for relationship in any area of life that does not appear to be your forte. For instance, if you curl up into fetal position at the prospect of being required to employ mathematical concepts, make this your breakthrough area by reframing formulas as relationship. What relationship lies between the numbers? What relationship can be found by looking at the space between objects instead of the actual object itself? Scott Onstott, former university professor who moved on to design visualization software, is the creator of the Secrets in Plain Sight video series, an inspiring exploration of great art, architecture, and urban design unveiling the unlikely he unlikely intersection of geometry, mysticism, physics, music, astronomy, and world history. The following set of numbers will demonstrate one example of the relationship between the numbers and the fractals they represent: Scott calls this the Cosmic Sequence...27, 54, 108, 216, 432, 864, 1728, 3456 ("Cosmic Sequence," 2013, p. 01) Each successive term is double the value of the preceding term. The first term, 27, is equal to three cubed. Pythagoras said that three cubed represents the cosmos. Many of the bodies in our solar system resonate with terms in the cosmic sequence.

Chapter Three

The Fractal Field and Yoga

*I*n a playful and yet empowering way, the fractal field of inherent symmetry and balance seeks to advance the hygiene of bliss. Bliss does not come about by sloppy living practices any more than a powerful asana would be possible without careful attention to all aspects of yoga. Yoga embodies the fluid relationship between charge density and movement while developing those inner muscles for alignment of the rotating charge field which leads to stillness. Attaining stillness as a state of unity with the divine has been the goal of mystics from all tradition and is the underlying current of mindful yoga practice. Pure intention which implodes charge, and lights the flame of connectivity, bliss and even psychokinesis, describes the physics of blissful peak perception. This electrical geometry of charge in the brain, as detected by an electroencephalogram, (EEG) forms a golden ratio, conjugate, longitudinal negentropy/ rejuvenation. And isn't that the confirmation that we are moving in the right direction? A return to optimal wellbeing that naturally revokes, repeals and cancels the deleterious damages incurred before we understood the implications of sloppy living restores not only our health but also our return to full consciousness. The term negentropy has been bantered about since the 1940's when Erwin Schrodinger, gave his famous "What is Life?" lecture. As the science community continued to revisit the various energy conversions of a fully living system, divine organization of matter causing the increase of available energy in local systems brought physical structure and evidence to support what the metaphysicians and spiritual leaders had been saying all along. Consciousness is the top down view or 'downward causation' as Amit Goswami describes a new paradigm of science called "science within consciousness. Consciousness as the ground of all being is inseparable from all its possibilities. Submersed in this relaxed state of awareness creates the energy of happiness that supports order. Entropy and chaos however, lures the body/mind complex into a landscape that identifies with the elements of separateness. For instance, ego at the helm, will dictate a preponderance toward perceptions of separateness. Separateness generates the energy of unhappiness. So why do we do it? Why do we allow that mischievous prankster called ego to hold the reins of our existence? We all long for the connected assurance of coherent relationship. But what do we do about it? Most often it seems that actions taken to secure coherent relationship somehow end up causing entropic karma instead negentropy toward Divine Order. The question of the One and the Many, and the Many returning to the One, has been the focus of alchemical master's and noble seekers since the earliest recorded history. Did historical accounting really get it right or has there been deliberate disorganization, randomness and chaos continuously sprinkled into our timid and tenuous grasp of reality? The Monas Hieroglyphica (Latin, for 'one glyph') aka the hieroglyphic monad, is reverentially considered a Gnostic ascent to the One. Human kind's spiritual evolution has always driven the inner transformative process of true initiates and adepts to the stargate of our ancestors located within our own DNA. Here access to fully restored consciousness offers up angles of light with which to stimulate our hippocampus, the organ of memory, into hyperdrive. Mystical symbolic language has long been used to divert those people considered profane enough to treat this sacred study with irreverence or disrespect until such a time as the light reaching our planet physically did so at such a precise angle as to awaken the sleeping god-spark naturally. These mystics of old kept the secrets of the universe alive by shrouding truths in many a creative resonance or fractal abstracts. Mystical experience was evoked by rites of initiation which often included various ecstasy-inducing techniques such as sacred movements and dances, such as yoga. Chanting and recitations and enactments of sacred events including 'mystery plays', often in conjunction with periods of fasting and chastity. Individuals who achieved Darshan or 'union with the deity or the god, had become the correct environment for an ancestor to arise like a hologram, through DNA. The practice of Yoga has long been revered and deeply esteemed for its ability to create a subtle order in the life of sincere yoginī's and yogī's.

Yoga postures instinctually replicate the foundation of our existence naturally. Through balance we establish a deeper connection to the Earth, the Mother and Holy Goddess Creator. Even those people who approach Yoga only for the physical exercise will realize Yoga is a path of self evolution and of self-discovery that can guide us to the universal still point and connect us with our own inner divine being. At this point, meditation and yoga become synonymous. In depicting a beautiful balance of proportion and symmetry, yoga becomes an expression of Universal Law which finds its fullest realization in the human form. Allowing meditation and yoga practice to discover negentropy reinforces the ecstasy of bliss waiting to be activated in our own divine blueprint. This blueprint holds the fractal signature of Phi, the nautilus shaped letter of the Greek alphabet used in mathematics to represent the Golden Ratio equation on which our theories of beauty and symmetry are founded. we find fractals of the Phi principle echoed in the spirals of nature, crystalline forms and atomic-level structures. Phi is the foundation principle demonstrating fractal fields as perfect compression are the essence of bioactive fields, and as pertains to human benefit is available as the TheraPhi Plasma devise spoken of earlier. The pure physics is clearly outlined in Dan Winter's "Origins of Biologic Negentropy", however, TheraPhi scientifically proves the concept that broad spectrum / centripetal conjugate field effects rejuvenate and reorganize biologic systems, aka us human folk, by addressing pain and many health issues. The reorganization element is notably experienced in every aspect of life including emotional, intellectual, spiritual and of course physical wellness. Embedded in the totality of Consciousness is our intimate connection through manifold bodies or frequencies. These include the thinking mind or mental body, the vital body which we experience as feelings, supra-mental or intuition where we intuit our values, and the sensing or physical body. The Causal, Celestial, Etheric and Astral bodies as well, contribute wholistic consciousness of the All-That-Is as Oneness gives rise to the ground of being. The physical sensing body with all its non-stop stimuli is difficult to ignore. It encompasses a vastness experienced from the micro or quantum classifications up through the macro Newtonian world level.

Fluctuating between these worlds invites a forgetfulness of the underlying unity giving way instead to perceptions of linear separateness. Our noble emotions further create distractions and diversions leaving us vulnerable to the potentiality of ego arresting command of interpretations and meaning. Permitting ego to fabricate life's meaning, undermines our true values. Manifestation through the impression of separateness can bring about treasured lessons and insights when we can retain the intrinsic principle of connected wholistic Oneness. Should the knowledge of our unified consciousness be forgotten, then the experience of separateness will likely offer denigration of values as painful reminders to dig a little deeper. If you feel the pinch of this painful reminder, check in to your vital heart energy to reconnect awareness of the innate Oneness that we are, to guide you through the landmines of separation and return the wholistic peace and understanding that we are and have always been, connected to everyone and everything. We have actually never been alone. This is like lying next to someone who is asleep and having a dream or possibly nightmare. Within the world that is engaging their awareness you have no ability to interact or reassure them, yet you know, that physically speaking, they are quite safe, lying there next to you. Shifting the paradigm of isolation and separateness to Oneness and love requires inclusivity at every level. Transparent orientation to unity consciousness refreshes the dominion of love, beauty, joy and bliss prerogatives to elevate ourselves ever closer to the fractal resonance of the universal still point to connect us with our own inner divine being.

Bliss is fractal.

Chapter Four

Unity with the Divine

The purpose of yoga is to reach a state of unity with the divine. Contained within the Aha moment of vital supramental realization, this unity coherence has been the goal of mystics from all traditions. Learning to dwell in the heart and experience the bliss of union with the sacred power of all life speaks to the impulse proclaimed in the Perfection of Wisdom Sutra. "Form is empty.

Emptiness is form," Form is the only thing that the universe conserves by maintaining the ratio of length, area and volume of the golden mean (Phi). Scale is profane, but ratio is sacred. The language of shape is the language of magnetism which is the language of charge. Bliss and ecstasy are measurable charge using golden ratio in brainwaves. EKG (electrocardiogram) recordings, used to measure electrical activity and collect data on the health of your heart, show coherent bonds between the heart, the mind, and our DNA. This interconnected heart energy bond is greatly influenced by strong emotions. The phase-lock of this electrical geometry of charge which forms a golden ration opposing pair conjugation is a teachable skill inducing blissful peak perception.

The Holy Grail is in your DNA and needs only the appropriate catalyst to be fired from your heart because Bliss itself is fractal. The 'aha moment' in prayerful (focused) ecstasy and bliss achieved as a harmonic cascade called holography, establishes a connecting field of resonation with all frequencies. Herein lies the appropriate environmental resonance for the most ancient of ancestors to activate, as a portal, and appear in refined space and time.

Self-referral in the cell (immunity) and coherence are the same, metabolically and emotionally throughout all nature and functions of the universe found within DNA. The core concept that explores this new paradigm brings together traditional medical science with the understanding of vibrational/energy healing, including an enhancement of low frequency sounds to engage the spontaneous re-emergent order of negentropy.

Harmonics cascading in golden mean ratio, aligning right and left hemispheres all contribute to engineering the science of enlightenment as taught in Advanced Hygiene for Bliss:

How to Switch on KUNDALINI with Dan Winter

(This course can be found over at FractalU.com
www.goldenmean.info/consciouskids)

Bliss

If you have ever experienced Bliss it is because the electrical field charging your bodies self-awareness and self-sustaining perfect fractal embedding, radiated that charge. It's really not complicated in the least because all human interaction is about Charge. Even the qualities present in your touch have been measured by spectrum analysis to define exactly where bliss is detected in relation to the duration and intensity of an embrace. The charge radiance climax point is detected by harmonic Phi cascades indicating the moment bliss and euphoria are reached.

Because this important science illustrates negentropy, how we spawn an immune system, lucid dream, and even survive death, our academic curriculums have been negligent in ignoring this practical study. Both science and spiritual studies are remiss to have omitted subjects that teach bliss and peak experience as material which also explains the powerful gravity making nature of biological implosion as perfect compression. The chemistry of ecstasy need not be relegated to the domain of drugs, sex, rock'n roll. It is the imperative which offers itself as the alternative to drugs and the other escape mechanisms that are wreaking havoc all over this planet. The human condition and evolution potential are contingent upon these unalienable rights. Our survival depends on it. Knowledge of symmetry, the charge environment, the physics of embedding and fractal compression geometries which define life, form the Science of Hygiene as taught by Dan Winter. "According to Einstein and every spiritual tradition of Earth", says Dan Winter, - "the Universe is made of only a single contiguous unified field" understood as symmetry of charge. The harmonic inclusiveness experienced as 'force', allow us to perceive electromagnetic field effects in physical matter. Divine force is pure and perfect coherence. In the same manner that rustling leaves bowing to the wind allow us to perceive the motion and direction revealed by suspended particles in air currents, negentropy allows us to perceive the motion and currents of divine force. Like negentropy, bliss is the self-organized, phase conjugate divine force returning to Divine Order. May the force be with you, enabling you to discern the subtle energies of shareable electromagnetic waves for it is the only way out of chaos. Ostensibly, it is safe to say we all want out of chaos. I certainly desire peace and happiness and I am sure you do as well. Negentropy defines the path of divine order powered by divine force. Charge is the oscillation that makes electromagnetic photons wave certain characteristics, given as frequency, wavelength or energy. The condition we know as resonance acts upon the oscillator. So, if we take this back to our examples of relationship, just to keep it practical, we can identify charge in every interaction.

Using any recent conversation to demonstrate signals and data sets as charge this time, think of the relationship between you and someone you were recently speaking to. Conversations are more than they seem. As carriers of force that impact our neurochemistry, they activate networks holistically throughout our body (eight subtle bodies including our bodies of experiences within the four worlds of consciousness, in chapter 8 we will come back to this in more detail) While we are at it, let's get to the real meat of the question and ask, "Who is it that perceives"? Our heart 'reads' the energy, but who is it that perceives? Let's look again, a bit closer this time. What was the relationship between what you wanted to convey and the perception that person received? What emotional signals were sent, and which ones were received and how were they amplified by your perspective of the conversation? How would you like to attract a coherent blissfully satisfying relationship? Is that a Yes? All you need is the quality of grace. "OK, terrific, but what is the quality of grace", you may ask? Ultimately it is a resonance, and naturally, it holds a postal code in the field of feeling. Once you know the address, you will be able to return any time you like. Let's consult our nautical GPS, target the correct angle, and focus on this as a pure principle. Directions to this location will initially require a bit of mental extrapolation so 'get centered'. Being grounded is really slang for accelerated charge to your center, so do that too, get grounded. Find your still-point. You will need to remember that anyone who has learned to launch the kind of aura/ plasma charge field which is projective, coherent and most importantly, sustainable, will be already producing charge distribution efficiency, so be prepared for miracles once you get your resonance on. You likewise will require the qualities to perfectly match that cherished apple-ofyour-eye biologic form of charge sustainability to make your love relationship immortal. This can be achieved by maintaining the hygiene required to develop the skill to become centripetal / phase conjugate. "Yes, great, but what is the hygiene required to develop the skill to become centripetal / phase conjugate ", you now ask? The answer is found by reflecting often on pure intention, compassion, joy, gratitude and love until you feel these qualities alive in every cell of your being.

Just be kind to yourself and others until any remnant of poverty mentality and separation has completely dissipated into the light of love. Meditate on three and four-dimensional geometries until you are able to navigate implosive living charge inside out. And then learn to harness and distribute the charge of life force in your immediate living space by favoring natural and organic materials over manufactured synthetics. Reduce harmful radiation of electromagnetic polluting electro-smog.

Nourish and honour your temples with musical recipes for bliss entrainment, such as those that resonate to the harmonics of nature and creation. For example, play your music tuned the sacred geometric phi ratio, octaves of the Schumann resonance and Fibonacci sequence. Be mindful of your posture and breath, specifically learn the tetrahedral fire breath technique or learn to breathe into stillness by inhaling .618 less each time in a sequence. Learn the touch permissive geometry of pressure/

time to create voltage and put the E in E Motion (energy in motion). All emotion needs to be shared compressively, perfectly, without the heat of resistance. How are we doing so far, are we there yet? Focus on a shareable mantra to affect your charge radiance and distribution or trace a labyrinth.

Through perfect sharing abundance is created. Let's choose abundance! If your water supply is pumped from dams through pipes to water filtration plants and then to storage reservoirs where it must flow through more pipes just to reach your tap, then chances are it will need to be energetically charged to reduce the molecular cluster size and increase the spin density and solubility. The 'Superimploder' (the world's most powerful and proven magnetic and vortex water treatment) represents a breakthrough in water science as revolutionary understanding of fractal physics, life force and biologic rejuvenation. You should try it! (http://www.fractalfield.com/fractalspacetime/) Further to the simple steps you can take to powerfully impact your quality of grace would be to investigate enlightened design as described throughout 3,500 years of Feng Shui. Originating in Chinese astronomy, Feng Shui philosophy regards resonating frequencies that establish information and energy transfer in a flow throughout one's environment. Shape = energy = function is the accepted formula to suggest bio-resonant shapes generate electric and magnetic fields. And just to keep our momentum building, quality of grace will be further enhanced by attention to the quality of air surrounding you. Have you considered increasing negative ions by ensuring verdant trees and plants abound both inside and outside?

Moving water, be it fountain or the oceanside, nature sounds, sun-gazing and Earthing either formal systems in architecture or just spending time barefoot in nature; the whole spectrum of influencing the harmony of energetic information codes from the language of light will all amplify your attraction potential and charge distribution efficiency. With just a little attention to these details, the quality of grace will establish itself, literally as the essence of real science behind spirituality. The quality of grace provides the means to become more fractal, to gain inertia through compassion and emit brainwave frequencies causing peak perception/bliss. All this makes your plasma launchable. The 'E Motional' waves which transport our impressions and viewpoints through the course of any relationship, allow us to perceive the direction and currents of vital energy in motion. Most intriguing is the effect your emotion literally, physically produces upon your heart muscles, to create a specific correlation registered in your DNA. This correlation begins to explain the heart's ability to extract voltage from gravity. As Dan Winter explains at 7 Arrows of Shamanic Science, (Winter, n.d., p. 01) and based on the same physics as his 'pine cones kissing noses' analogy, this slip knot of perfect fusion was first detected clairvoyantly, as has so often been the case with science. Eventually confirmed by physics, but what your feelings knew all along, your heart has higher levels of intuition which can lead to more meaningful, insightful Aha's! Whether your heart has registered a loving message or a warning, it has responded through the physical muscle configuration and symmetry of the spiraling seven-heart muscle layer outside, tilted precisely to the axes of the tetrahedron, and the five-muscle layer inside.

Every time you elicit an emotional response to someone's touch, be it a verbal caress, or tactile embrace, your heart muscles respond kinaesthetically. The fire of life itself lies in the symmetry operations which make this self-organizing non-destructive implosion, self-sustaining.

Sustainability is the first requisite for creating sacred space. Scared space has charge distribution efficiency equivalent to the heart of the sun and the heart of hydrogen. Shamanic viewing has confirmed Anu, the heart of the sun, is a portal, both transmitting and receiving information on many levels. As a fractal within our tangled hierarchy, both the hydrogen molecule and your heart are likewise conduits of conscious transparency. The first element of the periodic table is hydrogen. 'Hydro' is defined as 'water' and 'gen' is defined as 'in the beginning' which depicts a most fitting label since it is the hydrogen atom from which all other elements are built.

Consequently, hydrogen, 'water in the beginning', is the building block for all material forms in the universe. This is a concept revealed to us from sources such as the ancient Book of Genesis.

The Greeks gave us the word, 'hydrogen' which was translated from the Hebrew texts around 150 BC. Ancient Babylonians revered the primordial goddess of the salt sea, they called Tiamat. Defining the chaos of primordial creation, Tiamat is referred to as the glistening one who mated with Abzû, the god of fresh water, to produce younger gods. Through a "Sacred Marriage" between salt and fresh water, they formed the peaceful creator gods/goddesses of the cosmos through successive generations. Our own DNA and heart communicates infinite (in-Phi-knit) encoded messages to and from the All-That-Is, including Tiamat herself. But what message is it relaying? Your every thought has impact on the All-That-Is and reciprocally is likewise affected. Becoming ever more responsible and accountable for the shareability of your thoughts, not only determines the hygiene of your personal environment but demonstrates the capacity to directly represent in our body, all the possibilities of the supramental archetypes of mental thinking—love, beauty, justice, good, and all that which we call godliness. Along with nonlocality and discontinuity, tangled hierarchy divulges the quantum signature of divine downward causation.

Consciousness and your free will to express divine order

What a delightful game our Great Creator is playing. The collapse of the wave function consists of possibilities that are not (yet) manifest. A paradox in the observer effect we can posit as a circularity, contains the whole 'chicken or egg' conundrum all over again. From our perspective here on a three-dimensional planet operating primarily with very basic alpha/beta frequencies is that an observer is needed to collapse a quantum possibility; but collapse is needed for manifesting the observer. More and more I am leaning to the whole 'let's get out of our paradigm and see this from above' scenario. There can be no collapse without an observer; and no observer without a collapse. This subject-object split arises co-dependently whenever there is a tangled hierarchy in its measurement. Self-reference brought about by the tangled hierarchy makes it appear dual. Polarized duality on the material level, has no apparent solution to the paradox. Consciousness itself offers the solution. Collapsing the possibility waves of both observer and the object from the transcendent reality that Consciousness itself is the ground of being represents a viable reconciliation. Taken one step further, from the position that in every event of perception you are actually seeing the neuronal activity going on in your own brain, the experience you have, and your brain's neuronal activity are one and the same. Identical images of brain cells and the universe abound and make for stimulating meditation focus. Focus on the pure principle of Consciousness invokes the silent hand, the self-organizing charge field effect of spirit, which sustains bliss. So, again, just to keep it practical, let's look at a few examples how we build this charge.

Waves of charge -the field effect of 'spirit'

Meditative focus on pure principle or any shareable thought or the optical spectra of sunlight, or the sound signature of certain gifted musicians and sound healers, or meditative focus on the geometry created by specific pressure in your touch would all support the path curve based on Golden Ratio for charge inside DNA to conjugate phases and achieve the implosive communion in the blood called bliss.

Now if meditation just isn't your cup of tea, a few minutes in the plasma rejuvenation field of the TheraPhi will welcome waves of charge as the field effect of 'spirit' to induce bliss. The film called Biology of Bliss discusses this in much greater detail if you are interested in learning more about biofeedback for peak perception. (Winter & Harris, n.d., p. 01 www.theraphi.net)

Besides transmuting negative thought forms, the golden ratio/phi charge brought about by vibrations and frequency of bliss affect the molecular structure and charge in your blood. The path of bliss follows a glorious Holy Grail within a Holy Grail as a cup which expressed internally is identical to the external fractal of turning itself inside out. Fractality is infinite compression. The real key is observed in the sequencing charge spin symmetry on the surface of a torus. The Torus is the only known shape in our known universe that exists with hyper dimensional geometries at all scales. It is the shape of all protons which defines all life. The physics of creating matter out of light, bliss out of charge and even steering your aura through lucid dreaming and death are found in focusing the correct sequence of these torus angles.

Navigating your plasma field is covered in length in the AcuLomi Temple Meditation system (Evans, n.d., p. 01) and lastly, on this subject, it is only appropriate to at least hint at Flame letters, the Enochian or Angelic alphabet and the John Dee and Shakespeare enigma.

The Torus is the only known shape in our known universe that exists with hyper dimensional geometries at all scales. It is the shape of all protons which defines all life and assists our enquiring minds to comprehend the invisible structure of space. Meditating on the torus flow provides an instant resonance not only with the wisdom of this form but also as an aperture to mindfulness.

Chapter Five

Sacred Space
- the real key

While we all understand reverential sanctity generally perceived in association with the hallowed and holy, the term 'sacred' defines a fractal charge environment. Think Holy Water. What has created the fractal charge which effects water in such a way as to authentically appoint this venerated label? Or, think Holy Man as the Shaman is sometimes called. The Medicine Woman too, is synonymously regarded as a Holy Woman. The deep meditative calm attained in focused shamanic entrainment creates a layered harmonic environment. This superposition enables the catalyst to act as a carrier wave through time frequency ratio as a transmission of data. The Sham (often spelled Shem) is the Song of the Goddess and the fiery Shamanic skill to direct implosive, conjugating, centripetal field physics can be taught. (Winter & Botte, 2017, p. 01) Implosive conjugating centripetal field physics can also simply be experienced if shamanic training hasn't yet been scheduled into your itinerary this year. The TheraPhi plasma device, depicted with remarkable accuracy in the Egyptian stone carving, is a phase conjugate, centripetal, negentropic charge field, meaning, your experience in the TheraPhi field will induce a rejuvenation effect through time reversal. Rejuvenation caused by time reversal follows the path of negentropy on the tractor beam of sacred divine order. Returning to full consciousness which has always been, always is and always will be, is you and me, the Be -er's of divine consciousness, expressing its Beingness.

The conjugate field is the fractal expression of Temple. Our own ancient 'Altar' or Shem Stone has always been as close as your thought. The temporal and sphenoid bone within the human cranium house the crystal palace. Here in our physical brain are waves converging at Planck's distance, length and time as the symmetry operations necessary to ignite biology and DNA. This explains why being with the TheraPhi feels like being in a sacred temple. It is sacred because the time reversal negentropy steers rejuvenation back to divine order! Temple is a name describing a magnetic field which can become implosive enough to fire self-awareness. Even meditating on simply the geometry of sacred space ignited in the fire of self-awareness attunes us to our fully conscious selves. The Shem implies connection to our Source, the Ultimate Being reality in which we all exist. Also known as a sacred stone, the Shem is created through personal and cosmic kundalini energy rising to ignite the fiery furnace frequency described in ancient alchemical, mythological and sacred texts. This 'Highward Fire Stone has long been sought after, causing wars and mayhem throughout history, despite its very essence being available to every living being. Not unlike the DMT (Dimethyltryptamine) that is produced by your own pineal gland by mixing an enzyme with an amino acid, the Highward Fire Stone likewise is a naturally occurring substance. Through correct hygiene and education, our return to full consciousness will include activating the hippocampus to remember this and many other jealously guarded secrets.

TheraPhi's plasma healing field technology is a powerful centripetal broad spectra phase conjugate field, both plasma/optical and ELF which will assist in the stimulation of sacred memory. The net effect of this device is highly stimulating, healing and rejuvenating to most cellular life. While all the frequencies and phase relationships used in the TheraPhi are available in Dan Winter's book, (Winter, 2014, p. 01) his discovery of the fractal/ conjugate - frequency signature of Hydrogen as the phase conjugate pump wave has been remarkable in solving other significant enigmas from the spiritually cosmic domain as well. The field of consciousness does after all, encompass the All!

This new Implosion Physics is so exciting because every single person can now access creations vast secrets. When a spark of charge within the fractal plasma rejuvenation field uses golden ratio geometries, the bioactive field becomes self-referencing and intelligently interactive. Basically, alive!

And in a way, we humans can communicate with it. Like a down-stepping of intelligence, this field enables reciprocal synergy between us and the subtle worlds. Reports now by medical professionals using the TheraPhi with clients, prove the frequency emission is as safe to use as a sunlamp.

Implosive capacitance equals sacred space

This Holy Grail of sacred space has a psychological component to be sure. Defining not only the mechanics which detail precisely how the inside is the exact replication of the outside, the great masters of ancient wisdom knew that the Holy Grail of illumination, peace, and joy, was brought about by compassion. Compassion for yourself and others. Compassion as implosion now takes on significantly new and fertile associations transforming our consciousness. Within the wisdom of ancient sacred texts was secretly coded knowledge of how the outer world mirrors our inner conditions. (Besant, 1911, p.

01) With the great Hermetic epithet; "As Above; So Below, As Within; So Without" came the promise that each of us can transcend ordinary consciousness, align ourselves with the forces around us, and directly participate in creating our individual perception of the "outer world". The Essenes, for example, taught that the events of the world around us mirror the beliefs that we each hold within us, and that the collective thoughtform could be modified to correspond with new perceptions, new technologies and that the world will change accordingly. The real key to understanding Essene wisdom was held in the science of compassion. Compassion holds the fractal environment of charge specific, non-destructive implosion effects, that begin in our minds and transfers to our bodies and extend into the cosmos and unified Oneness. The Essenes suggested that events of the world around us, notably reveal the beliefs held within. Knowing the love our Earth Mother has for each of us personally, compels our behavior to likewise extend our caring service in love to protect her children (the All) that we go beyond mere tolerance, to join in resonance with her love.

The benefits exponentially raise our light quotient quite literally.

Light is what's called an electromagnetic wave. A photon is the basic unit of light and the force carrier for the electromagnetic force. An ion is an atom that has either gained or lost an electron, causing the atom to become either negatively or positively charged, respectively. A positive ion is positively charged because it has more protons than electrons, while a negative ion is negatively charged because it has more electrons than protons. Although Democritus gets credit for information regarding the atom back in 460bc, Lucretius and Euclid described light properties. Skipping forward to Heron, Ptolemy, and the Bible, written in Alexandria Egypt under Greek direction, we find the story of Adam and Eve as the story of nuclear fission, and ionic bonding. Saving the whole conversation regarding Enki and Enlil's genetic stairway to the stars for another publication, we have Bible(KJV) verses literally stating that God is not a man, rather, God is light. Thus, Jesus is the son of light and since we are created in Gods image and likeness, we too are light. According to the hidden meanings revealed by Bill Donahue, this means that God is an intelligent light messenger particle photon... Not a human being, but light. (Donahue, n.d., p. 01\) The scripture clearly identifies God and Jesus as light, or photon. Scientifically, the scripture is accurate, in the view that they are entangled photons, to say that the two are actually one.

We have recent experiments of physicists having entangled particles such as electrons and photons, as well as larger objects such as superconducting electric circuits. In China, for example, a team of physicists sent quantum particles from a satellite to ground stations separated by 1200 kilometers, to achieve 'spooky action' now at a recorded distance. Sharing the same existence is not new to metaphysicians however. When one understands the scripture that reads, 'I and my father are one', or "When you see me you have seen the father", we can easily accept that as entangled photons, they are in fact, one. But the idea was always that we get to the father through Jesus. What is the mechanism which allows us to entangle with God?

Photon A (us) must join/entangle with photon B (Jesus) in order for us to become one with God (photon C). Now joining A with B will reverse the polarity of B thus 'sacrificing' photon B. However, the good news is that photon A is now in good shape to be accepted by God. (photon C) What we don't want to miss is that Photon B (Jesus) had to take upon itself the original characteristics of photon A, (You and Me) to facilitate becoming one with us. Only by us first receiving the light called photon B (Jesus) into ourselves is the possibility of meeting the heavenly photon C even achievable. By this quantum entanglement, the Jesus photon sacrificed itself to become one with us. Because we as photon A absorbed the Jesus photon B, thus making the Jesus photon take on our characteristics- hence photon B (Jesus) no longer exists-, the God photon C must accept and exchange polarity with us to reunite with the sun, photon B (Jesus).

You see, because the God photon must stay one with the Jesus photon even though the Jesus photon is now you and me, the God (photon C) changes polarization to stay one with Jesus. And there you have it, God now becomes one with you and me because Jesus is one with us. The end.

.... Or is it perhaps, like the new moon, a return
to yet another .... beginning?

In the beginning was the word...we all know that, right?
("John 1:1-14King James Version (KJV)," n.d., p. 01)

The word brings us right back to creation, shamanic
navigation, potentiality and light.

Chapter Six

Word, the frequency signature

Waveforms based on harmonics of the golden mean flowing on the in-breath and out-breath of pulsating polarities, converge together as the original sound - the 'word' as it was translated from the original ancient sacred text. John 1:1 "In the beginning was the word and the word was with God".

Word, often related to as sound, is a translation from the Greek word "Logos" and refers to one's mind, reason, or wisdom. This fundamental key-note or colour depicts an Eternal weaver, alchemist, speaking words which bequeath the endowment of qualities. Beginning with the logos of ever increasing harmony that is the Monad and ground of all being, we find Consciousness. Nothing is outside consciousness. Therefore, consciousness is unitive. The domain of non-local potentia that encompasses all reality, exists within consciousness. What we call objective empirical reality is within this consciousness. The one becomes many through self-referenced fragmentation into tangled hierarchies of self-iterating information.

Space and Time are the great masters of illusion. The real trick is to distinguish between consciousness and awareness. Within the immanent self-reference of a system observing itself there is a tangled hierarchy. The beautiful rose pattern of electrical charge called gravity will communicate the role of human minds once symmetry is better understood. Mind can affect matter non-energetically because they share the same essence. consciousness is not mind; they are different concepts. it is not a message transfer (from a sender through a channel to a receiver) but a communication in consciousness. … a universe based in consciousness, logically and coherently resolves some of the major paradoxes of physics. everything is made of consciousness. Everything that the Creator wanted to communicate to man, pre-existed as the light of all mankind.

Non-local consciousness is a creative discontinuity leaping from moment to moment and event to event. This discontinuity is the quantum jump that is the essential component explaining creativity within self-reference. Creativity within self-reference provides the freedom to prescribe a new context. The self of self-reference and the consciousness of the original consciousness, together, actualize self-consciousness and describes some fundamental wave operations within physics.

The conversion from light to sound wave, for example, slows down the stored information, making it easier to manipulate. Sound is a name for stored pressure, just as voltage and love are also names for stored pressure. Sound waves, also known as compression waves, are made when atoms in stuff vibrates. Simply put, sound waves require a medium to travel. Solids, liquids, and gases transmit sound as longitudinal waves, but photons or light, move along a transverse wave. Even though radio waves can transmit information about sound, they are a completely different kind of energy, called electromagnetic energy. Electromagnetic energy is the same as radiation or light. This type of energy can take the form of visible light carrying packets of information thus relate to the roles high energy cosmic rays have played in our evolution.

Sacred Geometry conveys the blueprint of Creation and the dawning convocation of all form framing the energy patterns and ratios of Oneness. The sudden quantum leaps found in human development duplicate inherent proportions of balance and harmony. Those great masters of illusion, 'Space and Time', reflect though Nature the forms within sacred geometry. The only trick initially, is to boldly draw the distinguishing feature between consciousness and awareness. The Knower/Seer, the knowing/Seeing and the known/Seen play such a role. To understand how mind can create matter out of light, we need only to understand Sacred Geometry as love or pure principle. Waves of charge which have 'spirit', are those which nest into fractal or rose like patterns. Because of their symmetry, they begin to participate in the charge implosion called

'Life'! Understanding these electrical principles at the core of all life, instructs and advances hygiene for bliss and the sacred kundalini energy driving enlightenment. The symbol of Kundalini energy rising is the serpent which itself informs the very action of expressing the universality of energy, as the basis underlying all manifestation.

Meditate on these principals so well that you can store the patterns of wave pressures in your memory. This wave symmetry shapes the muscles of the human heart, is the slip knot geometry of ANU, Quark, Hydrogen, and the heart of the Sun! All esteemed matter composing the universe is made of nothing but stored pressure. Understanding the role of mind among waves, is needed to be able to share sacred space identical to the symmetry design of gravity. Understanding this fractal role within Nature, just makes it applicably functional and easy. For example, issuing electromagnetic fields that are identical to those found in nature, by using biomechanical simulation or TheraPhi field exposure, effectively achieves negentropy within biological systems. Effects of force field-enhanced expansions on the mind, perception and consciousness document exceptionally high cure rates for myriad conditions.

"And the Word was made flesh, and dwelt among us, (and we beheld his glory, the glory as of the only begotten of the Father,) full of grace and truth." (John 1:14 KJV)

Oneness, Trinity and the Physics of Consciousness

Forming the 'silver cord' called Sushumna (or Sutratma), which is one third of a triple thread extending from the 1st Aspect of The Godhead, is considered the Will of God. This is the channel through which the Monad influences the Soul with its purpose in being. The will-to-be, the will-to-do, the will-to-love, and the will-to-self-determination in the human being relate to the energy coming through the Sutratma. This particular thread of buddhic/intuitional matter on which the permanent particles of each incarnation are strung like pearls, is our channel to the Monad. In order to infuse the Life Principle into its lowermost reflection on the physical plane, this higher self of the soul is said to extend its life-force through the 4th chakra of the etheric body thereby animating the physical heart of the 3-dimensional body. Having this life-thread anchored physically in the heart, the vascular system acts as a distributing agent of this vital energy.

Life energy from the Monad and Soul flow via the central channel Sushumna, enlivening both aetheric and physical correspondents including Ida, energy of love and wisdom (the Consciousness Thread) and Pingala, energy of intelligence informing creativity (the Creativity Thread). If you have ever been startled during meditation or during astral-travel while asleep, you will at once understand the sudden and serious cardiac arrhythmias resulting from the rush of life-thread energy returning through the Sushumna anchored in the heart.

Connecting the atomic trinity -Atma, Buddhi and Mana, is the life-self or separated spirit called Jivatma. This seed of consciousness guides the vibratory wave from the Will aspect Ātma atom, the Wisdom /Buddhi and from the Activity-aspect called Manas.

Thus Ātma-Buddhi-Manas, the Monad in the world of manifestation, is formed.

Here is the mystery of the Watcher, the Spectator, the action-less Ātma, boldly drawing the distinguishing feature between consciousness and awareness. The Seer the Seen and the Seeing describing the sacred geometry of mind creating matter out of light. that his influence is well-nigh imperceptible, later with ever-increasing power

As the optical, dielectric and magnetic principles of phase conjugate systems are established in matter, echoing of the mighty cadence of the Sun, so too does the ether of space surrounding the Monad vibrate, in resonance with the fractal three-fold nature of the sacred trinity. Nature, nurture and creativity.

Sacred geometry of love

Aspecting the trinity is the positive and negative emanations from the one, which form two sides of the triangle whereby its base is the resulting abstraction of potential in which the objective of creativity is conceived. Duality and polarity resulting from the first cause produce an infinite source of energy due to the tension between two poles. This tension establishes itself as the force aspect within creation and evolution. The three qualities of matter, Inertia, mobility and rhythm, that form a triad, naturally produce a septenate 7 by its own internal relations, since it's three factors can group themselves in 7 ways and no more. The life of the logos flowing into matter manifests in these 7streams or rays. Similarly, out of the three aspects of consciousness as the universal self, arises activity of existence in willful bliss, and cognitive wisdom. Pythagoras said that three-cubed represents the cosmos. The intra-dimensional doorway though which matter manifests as 3-D reality must follow specific ratio patterns. This pattern naturally expresses the aesthetically seductive Phi, universal Golden Mean stellated dodecahedron design, of the greater cosmos.

That which is Below corresponds to that which is Above, and that which is Above, corresponds to that which is Below, to accomplish the miracles of the One Thing" -Hermes Trismegistus

As Aristotle said, "The whole is greater than the sum of its parts." From the Platonic Solids to Metatron's Cube, unified Oneness revealed in geometry provide a portal to the inner workings of the Universe itself. Just pull on one thread and we find it is attached to all life… The short cut is to simply be the love thread connecting the Great Goddess to the All-That-Is… And then, become the still point simultaneously receiving and transmitting that love. Affecting and being affected both, coils the braid of this high frequency vibration into extra-dimensional realms. Personal meditation on the pure principle of sacred geometry enlists the means or method to invoke the wisdom of Form and the compassionate action of Love. Like Dorje, Vajra, (the Sanskrit word meaning both thunderbolt and diamond), the diamond as a symbol of the Self epitomizes the union of extreme opposites - of matter and spirit.

Jung wrote of "quaternity," or fourness, in connection with the lapis, and drew, as a symbol of the self, a set of four geometrical diamonds (squares rotated by 45 degrees) The term diamond is another word for a rhombus used to denote a square tilted at a forty-five-degree angle. Male and female squaring the circle of hypercubic dimensions (* remember you must double everything to arrive at the appropriate resolution;) and found also in the Hebrew letter He in our DNA. The genetic equal of the

Monad and many facets of Hieros Gamos embody the ultimate alchemy of forces which harmonize opposites of the One. The sacred marriage of inner hiero-gamic unions, between the human being and the divine (the Inner Spirit) represent the unification of all life expressions. Pull on one Thread and find it is attached to all life. It is said that all the most powerful ideas in history go back to archetypes. This is particularly true of geometry. Archetypes are visual forms that energetically imprint patterns in our psyches. Universal archetypes are created by the patterns of Sacred Geometry. Harkening back to the original model recognized in the collective unconscious, geometry and mathematical ratios as harmonics and proportion found in music, light and cosmology, provide insight into the deepest mysteries.

The square root of 2 embodies a profound principle of the whole being more than the sum of its parts. Distinguishing integration synthesis and growth as well as the hallowed reconciliation of polarities by spanning both perspectives equally, the root of two leads to greater unity and higher expression of cardinal truth. Onward in our bearing toward understanding basic geometric concepts, we encounter the square root of three, eminently recognized in the Vesica Piscis. The Vesica Piscis is formed by the intersection of two circles and the overlapping spheres whose centers exactly touch. This symbolic intersection represents unification between equal individuals. Consider also the spirals and toroid, fractals and recursive, indelibly etching their immortal signatures into our awareness. Converging into a singularity we find angles are the angels of divine code and divine symmetry.

> *If you only knew the magnificence of the 3, 6 and 9, then you would have a key to the universe. – Nikola Tesla*

Angles, the angels of divine code

The divine symmetry of everything and nothing push the boundaries of a deeper philosophical truth. Diverse feathers ungroup. Among his many insights, Nikola Tesla gave us this wee pearl, "The day science begins to study non-physical phenomena, it will make more progress in one decade than in all the previous centuries of its existence." Resembling a vortex which allows energy to bend back, perpetually re-entering itself, is the geometry which heralds a zero-point convergence at center. This action of turning inside-out to continuously refresh and influence itself forms a torus. This geometric shape suggests the self-reflective nature of consciousness itself. Toroidal energy fields are known to exist around everything under and beyond the Sun. From universal scale right down to the atomic, these frequency converters figure heavily into the esoteric study of Sacred Geometry. At www.goldenmean.info/life, you will find a more sophisticated outline of the molecular geometric as the skeleton and the life force/divine spark of the conjugate/fractal/implosive /negentropic 'field' they embed. The two things that allow consciousness to reside inside a material existence, is electricity and magnetism. Word, Light and Life unite to create a synergy. Synergy is what happens when one plus one equals three, ten or even a thousand ... The seer, the seen and the seeing synergistically reflect though Nature the forms within sacred geometry emanating more than the sum of its parts.

Who is it that perceives again? Our heart reads the energy but where is it that the perceptions are received? Beyond our physical body lies our aura, an etheric body, emotional body, mental, body. And then we continue expanding into our astral, etheric, celestial and causal bodies. These bodies are all ours with which to receive and transmit information. Likewise, throughout our physical bodies are receptors that have never been given their due credit. Innate intelligence connects the heart and brain in function as well as all other organs and receptors.

Chapter Seven

Zero Point

Spending time in nature to still the mind is easily the most refreshing path to the zero-point energy field. Ensuring we receive a strong dose of those peace-teasing negative ions along the way, Nature has our back. Every thunderstorm offers an organically sensual invitation to step outside and expose yourself to the newly purified air. The zero-point energy field beckons likewise from the singularity where the laws of physics no longer apply. Exalted by a divine sanction of power, the sacred being, or realm/field, is understood to be at the core of existence and to possess a transformative transcendent, domain. Within our own personal zero-point is access to our sub-atomic essence, biology's DNA radio, the collective mind. This fundamental characteristic connects us directly to the great Oneness. The invisible lifeforce within matter/energy ignites transcendent, transformative bliss by attracting fractal charge information of this domain. Meaningful access to zero-point energy awaits our understanding of charge attraction by conjugate fractality. Having covered the slightly more rigorous explanations earlier, let's examine this principle through common, every day experiences. Recently a friend sent me an excerpt from Hilda Charlton who was relaying an analogy from her travels. She said to imagine sticking your finger in a glass of water to see if it's hot or cold. You put a tiny part of yourself into the vessel, and when you bring it back out, you've gained all the experiences that minute portion of your body had. Now, we know that inner peace leads to global peace, and likewise our zero- point energy science has established that impossibly minute frequency that enters charge compression is our access to the all -that- is. A human mind, operating in Beta range frequency, might only retain a tiny fraction of who and what we are, however, using zero-point energy we have biologic recollection attributes that range throughout a broad spectrum of the conscious field. Memory, as the retained and sustainable spin symmetry therefore, makes available the whole, anytime we choose to enter the still point. Centering our essence into the still- point of awareness enables coherent communication with the conscious field. In the Bhagavad Gita we find reference to inducing this still-point through balance of the three gunas - — sattva, rajas, and tamas. It is said that personality and the mind are governed by these gunas. Prayer helps to form the sattvic guna. We bless our food for the nourishment of our bodies, and thus catalyze a potential to receive. However, when we prayerfully bless our food with the intention of ceremonial ritual of a sacred offering, the frequency is amplified and resonates as pure peace. This is what is meant by Prasada. Prasada is the sacred food offering, where Sattva is light and pure energy. Milk and fruits are naturally sattvic. Love, kindness and compassion are light and pure. With awareness, we can take away any negative energy to a great degree. Awareness serves as the Observer Effect magnetising the centripetal coherent plasma force which phase conjugate dielectric hopefully creates in your aura. Being the cause and mechanism of consciousness, this precisely explains why DNA is based on Golden Ratio and fractality. As a shape capable of producing the perfect fractal, the stellated dodecahedron can cause charges to scale, materialize and implode. efficient distribution of charge. Only the Golden Ratio allows for constructive interference heterodyning of wave addition and multiplication. Rajas is active energy. It gets things moving, perfecting charge distribution for living plasma and memory-is the grail mystery key. Tamas is stability which also holds the potential for inertia. We need to maintain balance so that stability compresses to still-point of the three gunas - — sattva, rajas, and tamas.

The Holy Grail

> *"... the Holy Grail is most concretely, the science of how biology uses fractality and self-similarity to create the wave agreement that produces immortality. It is a nice test for being pure and shareable - and really does teach us the physics of how to get our DNA on fire with Bliss..." -Dan Winter*

The fastest, simplest way to produce a blissful peak experience is a skill we all have. Imagination! The frequency induced by simply by imagining, play-by-play, a scenario of sharing a loving exchange has the power to turn your world inside out. The informed-formation of the holy grail is identical between the inside or the outside, thereby solving the problem of separation. There is no separation, never was, but we knew that...in our highest truth anyway. The song within the blood, or sang rael, is phired from your heart because bliss is fractal. 3 6 9 the sacred marriage two cubes tilted at appropriate angle to form the diamond. And fractality is the key to infinite compression. Only the golden spiral charge compression trajectory allows phase velocities to interfere or heterodyne recursively constructively. Thus, the holy grail of fusion can be demonstrated by compassion. An old Zen master once said that compassion was no different than reaching back for your pillow in the dark. It is just a normal human characteristic, something we all do, no biggie! Just know that compassion is learned when the little picture inside your heart becomes so self similar that it is fractal to the shape of magnetism in someone else. That perfect compression is the fractal attractor which, like the jellyfish drawing the outside in, transport themselves through the eternal cosmos.

This recursive turning inside out becomes the implosion and the electrical sensation, aka the rush of bliss. And this is how the sacred and the divine can be created and understood. The highly celebrated Greek Key or labyrinth is a two -D shadow of this three-D model turning inside out.

Rennes Le Chateau of Grail fame is the same golden-ratio, plasma projecting pent geometry as the Hydrogen atom. Now pent means being true to yourself, so follow the magnetic lines of rose symmetry to nourish your home space. In this way, biology's DNA radio could certainly be at the helm of 're-penting the collective mind'. Repeatedly draw the form of a rose, ad infinitum, and this practise will open a portal of potential, whereby your meditative journeys always find their way to bliss. What condition outside can be represented inside? Recall health and bliss. In the neural network, there is no difference between sensory data entering the network from outside or the traces which operate inside the network. The outside is simply reiterated on the inside, thereby deconstructing the distinction between outside and inside. The synapse between the two frames of reference collapse. Think Ganesha phenomenon. Dr. Dan Burisch coined the name "Ganesh particle" during his work on the Lotus Project. Dan Winter says it would more accurately be described as the Ganesh Phenomena. Formerly Lotus, (then coded as Star Flower 1),was an investigation into life's evolution of higher forms dependent on genetic programs that come from space. What began as the 'seeds everywhere in the Universe' Panspermia hypothesis, unfolded as a symbiotic polyphyletic origin (derived from more than one ancestor). For example, eukaryotic algae are polyphyletic because chloroplasts have been secondarily transferred to new lineages by the permanent incorporation of a photosynthetic eukaryotic algal cell into a phagotrophic protozoan host. Mitochondria is known as power house of the cell whereas the Plastids are known as the kitchen of the cell. Mitochondria produces energy in the form of ATP whereas Plastids manufacture food i.e., photosynthesis. Understanding the relationships of evolution becomes the revolution. Instead of clinging to the conventional constructs intended to restrict creativity, the energetics and principles of optical phase conjugation capture a friendly generalized model. A complementary behavior exists between this science and a simple concept referred to as Oneness. These evolutionary jumps in consciousness are an active force in creation. At the heart of this force we find tangled hierarchies along with a blueprint or archetype that is present in consciousness. This blueprint gets activated as soon as the appropriate ingredients and correct conditions are there. Consciousness then chooses to 'collapse' the necessary DNA, RNA, cell boundary and supporting proteins. The principles of optical phase conjugation supply the field out of which this collapse can occur.

If we want to orbit the spiraling spin path to zero-point in the blood, we ride the holy grail. This heart-within -a-heart shape, informs the fractal of perfectly self-contained, self-embedded compassion. We could zoom in to infinity and still see the same heart-within-a-heart shape. Holding thoughts of compassion, align the magnetic field torus/donuts that surround the heart in such a way that the nested dodeca icosa perfect embedding self-knots. At the core of all relationships is love. This love remains pure despite the many layers of pseudo-meanings and false filters which free-will may experiment with. Love is the root of all creation, all being and all phenomena. Love is the fractal of Divine magic manipulating natural forces.

Continuous creation within the intricate web of life pushes forward the complexity found within the biosphere, to perfectly match species diversity to the other elements of our living world. Communication and control are two required activities within and between cells to maintain homeostasis. Normally, it is thought that both these functions are achieved through biochemical and neurological means. Biophotons act as subtle energy carriers. This coherent light source is thought to be another arm through which both control and communication are achieved. Coherent biophotons as a control signal, are proposed in acupuncture theory also. Coherence is a property which occurs when the phases of the signals are related precisely, such as in a laser which gives the laser beam its unique properties. It is tempting at this point to think biophotons are to Qi energy (as modeled in Traditional Chinese Medicine), as prana is to Ayurveda and Yoga, the seed of all cosmic energy, permeating the Universe. This dynamic exchange between Qi/prana and biophotons communicate to create the sacred interface. The photons in the body likewise, take part in biocommunication and signaling.

Hydrogen, who are you?

Water. Life. Star fuel. With an atomic weight of 1. 00794, Hydrogen is the lightest of all known elements and will form both positive and negative ions more readily than any other element. Not only is Hydrogen the most abundant element in the universe, it is also the only element that can exist without neutrons, says every school text you encounter. But let's talk character, personality, purpose and expansion. Hydrogen is a phase conjugate pump wave as determined by its structured form and the climax form of coherence. Charge distribution enabled frequencies make Hydrogen the basic building block of our entire world. Think Planck frequency. This is the frequency that just happens to be everywhere in everything and is one example of being shareable with all DNA. It speaks to the God- spark or the resonant energy that is everywhere and, dare I say, nowhere -at center. Hydrogen is our Champion and best friend. This magnificent atom represents the supportive structure needed to receive the flowing spirit of love. Likewise, the outpouring of love needs the structure as much as the structure needs to receive its cascading abundance.

Dan Winter shows that" the fractal structure of hydrogen is precisely the proof that golden ratio constructive 'implosive' charge collapse is key to the creation of matter and the subsequent outpouring of energy from it. Turning compression into charge by acceleration is hypothesized to be the core wave mechanism of phase conjugation, self-organization and the centripetal forces of gravity, life force, color, and perception."

It's all about the angle of those tilted building-blocks on the path out of chaos. http://theraphi.net/the-path-out-of-chaos/ (Winter, 2016, p. 01) And what a gas we have with Hydrogen. The primary form of hydrogen is that of molecular hydrogen. Molecular hydrogen gas, or H2 has been shown to exert a wide range of therapeutic effects including anti-inflammatory, anti-obesity, and anti-allergy benefits. Well over 500 peer-reviewed articles demonstrate positive potential exists for essentially every organ of the human body simply by drinking hydrogen rich water. 150 different human disease models show that H2 reduces oxidative stress as a selective antioxidant.

The hydrogen ion is the H+ responsible for the pH of the water, referred to in the scale indicating acidity or alkalinity. The 'p' refers to the German word 'potenz' or power. This p is in reference to it being an exponent. Diatomic hydrogen rich water is also known as alkaline ionized water. The H+ ion coming from the self-ionization or auto-proteolysis of water, wherein H2O splits to form the proton H+ ion and OH– ion called hydroxide. Since the H+ ion is attracted to the negatively charged oxygen of other water molecules, another form called form H3O+ ion (hydronium ion) is brought into play. A water molecule can both pull a hydrogen off another water molecule, or reverse the reaction thus behaving as either an acid (a molecule that produces H3O+) or a base (the produced OH– can neutralize the acid), which defines water as amphoteric. Pure water is neutral, pH7, because for every H3O+ ion created, an OH– ion is created. The concentration of the two different ions is the same. No wonder Grandma was committed to drinking her of milk of magnesia brew…it scores a whopping pH of 10. Beware the many misnomers and quick fix solutions surrounding this topic though. Alkaline ionizers raise the pH of the water by consuming the H+ ions in the water, not as a direct result of adding H2. Just to be clear, molecular hydrogen, also referred to as dihydrogen, contains two protons and two electrons making it a neutrally-charged molecule. It is a tasteless, colorless, odorless, non-metallic highly flammable gas, and very explosive above a 4.6% concentration by volume. It is this form of hydrogen that has been shown to exert the wide range of therapeutic effects. To produce Diatomic hydrogen rich water, the H+ ions in the water must be consumed, thus making the water more alkaline. Methods of producing hydrogen water such as bubbling or infusing, which simply add pure hydrogen gas to water, do not change the original pH of the water.

Mystical properties of water

Known as the blue planet, our beloved home is bequeathed its shimmering distinct status so richly honoured by the vast presence of water. This sacred water is said personify the shining Goddess, Tiamat. Known as Mother Goddess, the supreme queen of the universe and all creation, the saltwater sea, "she who bore them all", Tiamat is the universal mother who gave life to all creation in her womb, the salt water. As the cosmic dragon, Tiamat existed before any of the other deities for she was the primordial chaos that contained the abstract, formless elements of the universe. As Tiamat had markedly ancient roots, the various manifestations of and references to her remain particularly complex. These ancient roots are intricate and include all regions of the cosmos that relate to other aquatic constellations like Aquarius, Pisces and Eridanus, for example.

Water remains at the heart of all creation and facilitates the esoteric and mystical conveyance of subtle information. Sharing the common heritage of being united by a common bond with water is the epitome of holism and Oneness. Not only does it connect all of life, but life cannot exist without it. Spiritual and mystical experiences throughout the ages have confirmed that communication between elements, relays and translates vital information. Our subtle bodies recognize the need to match the same golden-ratio, plasma projecting pent geometry as the Hydrogen atom. Water is the infinite continuum of life in which all living creatures are sustained and contained.

Dynamic water, when it is alive and energised, performs the roles which initiate and operate all processes of life. The most important function of biological water is to facilitate rapid inter-communication between cells and connective tissues, so that the organism can function as a coordinated whole. The function of biological water plays a wide variety of roles in life processes, from macromolecular structure and function, to cells, tissues and organisms. Being of a both Yin and Yang nature, an essential unstable reciprocity exists as a control function between extremes. For example, we all can relate to the energising effect of moving, circulating water in comparison to the water is effectively dead. Water is the ideal medium for processes because it is a dynamic medium. Shape and form of the bifurcated unsymmetrical hydrogen bonds make water unstable and unpredictable. As the guiding law of the Universe, this preponderance to change is the guiding impetus of the Universe. The instability and unpredictability of life create a necessity for creativity. Necessity is the mother of invention. Water flows naturally, energetically in spirals and vortices, and is constantly changing its state. When it is restricted from this natural movement it becomes stagnant and the vibrating energy centres no longer fulfills the coherent exchange of information with every contact the water body makes.

Imprints of all energetic transmissions are retained as the memory of water. Through water, quantum coherent organisms invariably become entangled with one another. Each being is implicit in every other because we are all entangled. Benefitting oneself occurs in direct relation to the benefits experienced by the other. This has been understood throughout history and explains why water has always been regarded as sacred. As a "conscious organism", it has integrity, independence, cohesion, and the subtle qualities that drive life and evolution. Consciousness expresses itself through water. As a medium of communication, water likewise is an honoured medium of consciousness. To understand the properties of water, is to understand the secret of the sacred everlasting relationship. Our attitude toward water reflects human potential. Are we driven by an insatiable desperation for artificial technology that loudly proclaims human supremacy over Nature or do we respond to the sacred bond of Oneness instructed by water and its pulsating movements?

The hydrogen bond in water is both electrostatic and covalent, or electron sharing. Water is an example of a polar molecule; the oxygen end has a slight positive charge whereas the hydrogen ends are slightly negative. This polarity explains why some substances dissolve readily in water while others do not. The properties which molecules of water exhibit, result from their hydrogen-bonded lattice. Hydrogen bonds have only about 1/20 the strength of a covalent bond, yet even this force is sufficient to affect the structure of water, producing many of its unique properties, such as solvency, cohesion and adhesion, high surface temperature, high heat capacity, high heat of vaporization, and varying density. Hydrogen bonds are important in many life processes, such as replication and defining the shape of DNA molecules. Many exquisite yet seemingly counterintuitive anomalies exist in water's domain. For example, the combined facts that oxygen feeds fire and hydrogen is explosive might lead us to assume that water could be combustible. Here again is another beautiful analogy providing insight from Mother Nature.

Within the framework of an endosymbiotic theory and exploring signals exchanged between the properties of individual atoms when they combine into molecules, lies the potential for evolutionary allegory. Evolutionary, because it points back to the repenting fractal schematic, where being true to yourself is found in the model of Oneness. It is the old 'do unto others as you would have them do unto you' scene. Working together in symbiotic harmony, rather than at the expense of other. Reciprocating coefficient collaboration for the highest good of each other and therefore, the All-That-Is of Oneness. Just like any single person entering a relationship, unique properties modify in the presence of 'other'. How Mother Nature combined explosive hydrogen with oxygen, which feeds fire, into life sustaining water, gives us a hint. Combustion usually has three requirements: 1) fuel, 2) oxidizer and 3) heat or source of ignition.

In this example, hydrogen is the fuel and oxygen the oxidizer. Despite being mixed, they still require a spark or other source of heat to ignite the extremely rapid combustion that results in an explosion. While the process of burning is found in the oxidation of hydrogen or combination of the hydrogen and oxygen molecules, the combustion product resulting from the oxidation of hydrogen, is simply H2O or water. Regardless if the state is gaseous, liquid or solid, water is already the product of combustion. The reaction releases a large amount of energy, mostly in the form of heat that causes the water vapor to expand rapidly to a large volume. This rapid expansion of gases is what normally would cause the explosion. So too in our personal relationship example, when the sacred union encounters clashing perceptions of inflated ego or deeply submerged id, the fermented 'baggage' offers itself as material for combustion. In this sense, the sacred union has opportunity to increase its purity.

Distillation, the sixth major operation in the alchemy of transformation which comes about in the agitation and sublimation of psychic forces, is the product of combustion. Meditation on Nature's life force reveals exquisite potential in our return to fully conscious relationships. Consciousness seeks to express this power of higher love flowing harmoniously, as coherent visions of Truth. Water, like love and truth, is an infinitely complex subject. The properties of water, truth and love, flow in and morph according to the various elements they are combined within. Like atoms combining to make molecules, water, truth and love will also react by combine the elements of awareness. Expanding our awareness into the state of Oneness can likewise be catalyzed by combustion. Naturally expressing the three requirements of fuel, oxidizer and a source of heat or ignition, Oneness represents an elevated or purified distillation of awareness. The degree in which you successfully achieve Oneness, very much depends upon the degree in which your 'filtration system' has purified your living water. The quality of your internal environment (such as food or thoughts), and external environment (such as noise or air quality), stamp your field with vibrational signatures. The vibrational signature is retained and integrated on may levels. These vibrational patterns are contained within the water of our bodies 37.2 trillion + cells, for example. The well-known research of Dr. Masaru Emoto demonstrates that the molecular structure of water literally changes from these energetic stamps. Our scientific world has established proof that water is deeply connected to our individual and collective consciousness.

Our bodies are composed of at least 70% water. This percentage reflects similarly to that of the ocean surface of Earth. Blood and sap are really variations of water and while hemoglobin and chlorophyll are very similar, the notable significance is scale. Chlorophyll contains oxygen, carbon, nitrogen, hydrogen as does haemoglobin from the blood except that hemoglobin contains iron in place of chlorophyll's magnesium. That said, both iron and magnesium are metallic atoms. Despite the striking similarity between blood and chlorophyll, plants are 'producers' in that they make their own food using energy and materials from their environment, while animals are 'consumers' that cannot self-produce their food. Relying on food grown amongst environmental stressors, pesticide-ridden crops, and air pollution all lead to a rise of acidity in the body. This trajectory of increasingly higher acidity in our diets lead to unhealthy bodies and the preponderance of a host of diseases to follow. Add in convenience foods, sugary drinks, and the resulting intolerance disguised as allergic reactions, and you will find mainstream eagerly responding with manufactured chemical pharmaceuticals to embed a deeper more sinister miasma.

This miasma describes a contagious power that has an independent life of its own which misleads us into treating what began as a simple issue, instead as a specious cause of chronic disease. Acidity in our bodies, regardless of cause, opens the door to an entire plethora of illness and dis ease. Placing focused attention on your food before you eat, through prayer, a quick mantra or affirmation, also helps to prepare your body to receive your intention, regardless of whatever components may be presented as a meal. Simply chewing our food slowly and thoroughly and staying hydrated will help to alleviate much of the acidic burden.

Ironically, it is well known that many people are chronically dehydrated. Undoubtedly, some of the positive results in the hydrogen rich water health studies came about simply by an increased focus and attention, to drinking more water consciously. The poet, philosopher and scientist, Johann Wolfgang von Goethe (1749-1832) referred to water as "the ground of all being." Austrian 'Water Wizard', Viktor Schauberger (1885-1958), likewise viewed water as the product of the subtle energies that brought the Earth into being and is itself a living substance. But we have to actually engage that water, drink it, bathe in it and honour it, to receive this blessing.

Water dissociates to form protons and hydroxides describing the self-ionization or 'auto-proteolysis of water. The Hydrogen bonds in water's structure, permit cohesion and adhesion, where molecules stick together or to other substances necessary for transporting nutrition and waste. Because water molecules are more attracted to each other than the air above, a high surface tension is created. The high heat capacity permits changes in water's density without disrupting its form. Witnessing the relationship hydrogen has with oxygen in producing the third component, water, reveals the elegant Fibonacci pattern of fundamental mathematical expressions of phi golden ratio. This relationship also parallels the wisdom metaphorically, in successful personal union. Wave patterns remember information and perfect wave compression provides a way through the wormhole. The point is attracting the aha moment of charge to open that bliss portal in seeing the phenomenon from a philosophical, spiritual, and sacred geometry perspective and return us to full consciousness.

Bliss is the condition produced by radiating charge to infinite sustainability. This requires perfect fractal embedding that facilitates becoming self-organizing and self-aware. DNA enveloping itself in long wave folds, based on Phi multiples will enable ensoulment, lucid dreaming and time travel. Bliss creates the warp-drive for quantum acceleration to wellness. Additionally, bliss provides the literal experience of turning inside out like the holy grail to rule out separation while speeding up the evolution of your genes. Successful yoga, meditation or spiritual practice will attract waves to center themselves inside you. This establishes more clarity, focus and power. Such practices provide an appropriate solution to concerns like attention deficit disorder and addiction. Our DNA has contained the fractal potential of Oneness all along. AcuLomi Temple meditation with TheraPhi training has opened the door for DNA to speak back, clearly and concisely in all languages. Access to exploring All-That-Is, as the subtle worlds of Oneness, is contained within DNA. The organic natural production of the messenger molecule Dimethyltryptamine (DMT) is self-induced by the focus of the pure principle, Love. Activating this feeling in the meditative state, supports the means of accessing any of the subtle worlds. Just think for a moment what happens to your focus when you are in love. Your focus becomes an inexhaustible supply of power. Now carry that reference point into any desire or goal and you have the fuel of the gods. Through the continued practice of disciplines such as yoga and meditation, our return to full consciousness hastens exponentially. The greater truth of who we humans are, has always been with us, both within our DNA and all around us, as the heavenly cosmos. These truths, preserved in mythologies, and sacred but obscure texts, are revealed to humanity from time to time at the nexus points of evolution. Humanity is once again at a nexus point of opportunity. Meditation and training sessions in TheraPhi reawaken our connection to the All-That-Is.

Pure Principle, ANU

The problem of cognitive dissonance arising from the disparity between science and accepted spiritual beliefs can be overcome by the certainty of a shared frequency. This shared frequency is found in the embrace of Oneness. The All-That-Is, or Oneness, is a celebration of life at every scale and is found in the spin of every molecule of matter and anti-matter. It holds the potential for clashing dissonance to be replaced by coherent alignment as the experience of peace. As proposed in the Self-Aware Universe, by Amit Goswami, (Goswami, 1995, p. 01) only a theory of consciousness, rather than one of atoms, can reconcile this fundamental rift: Consciousness affects the spin of particles and thus the environment. Although quantum science offers solid evidence to support Consciousness Theory, (Goswami, 1995, p. 01) religious doctrine or spirituality has thus far venerated disparities. And yet, the practice of a system which engages insights from both religion and science, reveals that it is not humanity who are engaging Consciousness, but rather Consciousness that engages humanity. Moreover, Consciousness IS the All-That-Is. The notion that somehow humanity has superior intellectual capacity to express consciousness has created many great rifts breaching the blueprint of peace. Consciousness expresses itself through All-That-Is without regard for the abilities and limitations of the human mind. The gaping disconnect has been found in the limitations of the human mind to perceive the multitudinous expressions which are united as Consciousness.

Consciousness is, that field of Oneness. Consciousness is not limited by humanities inability to grasp its full scope of function. Contrariwise, it has been humanity that was limited by the belief of separateness thus resulting in disconnection from the All-That-Is or Oneness. Through a system of employing relevant analytical information prior to specific meditation, the gap produced by beliefs of separation finds that a bridge has been rendered, allowing life to be experienced as more fully consciousness beings.

Searching for an answer compatible with bases in science, religion, and intuitive certainty will help dispel the confusion which has impaired previous scholars' best intentions and progress. More specifically, a holistic approach permits logical enrichment of intuition to engage higher levels of neurostimulation by engaging hemispheric synchronization, resulting in validation of the concept of 'fractal Oneness'. All historical eras have demonstrated pockets of knowledge suggesting that adepts and elites transferred an underground version of the Consciousness Theory through a select lineage. This knowledge reconciled both religion and science in the Hermetic tradition, understood as the cryptic system of alchemy. These pockets of knowledge over time became diluted and vague in direct parallel with the cosmic journey of Earth through the galaxy. Time and space offered their own constraints and deviations from explicit cognition of the myriad worlds which collectively refer to the One and the Many. "Have you also learned that secret from the river; that there is no such thing as time? That the river is everywhere at the same time, at the source and at the mouth, at the waterfall, at the ferry, at the current, in the ocean and in the mountains, everywhere and that the present only exists for it, not the shadow of the past nor the shadow of the future."—Hermann Hesse. By assembling many views into One, or the "consumed perspective," we can define the very foundation of E Pluribus Unum, or "From many, One." (Cicero, 1560, p. 01)

If Oneness is dissected to ascertain the sum and content of its parts, we fail to capture the conscious essence or Essene of operations, the golden mean's holy grail. Therefore, only a holistic approach can offer both logical and spiritual satisfaction. The word Essene is thought to derive from the Aramaic word Assaya, which means healer, and is also associated with the Egyptian word for Therapist. Healer in any language implies balance and optimum homeostasis of body, mind and soul, which is the true fount of wellness. A notable phrase in the Hermetic system of alchemy, derived from the Principle of Correspondence, states "As above, so below…" (Three Initiates, 1912, p. 01) Offering solution to this paradox, through "phase conjugation," is the mechanization of negentropic propagation of gravity and mind. The art and methodology for obtaining a unified solution for every scale of life is found through perfect implosion of the golden ratio. Perfect Implosion describes centripetal non-destructive charge compression. As well, superposition through fractality depicts harmonic inclusiveness on every scale, which can be observed in both religion and science. Registered on all levels and scales of life, this phase conjugate (golden-ratio) negentropic charge collapse can be brought about consistently and repeatedly during the practise of specific meditation when accompanied with relevant analytical data to produce the frequency resonant to bliss. The science of both classified quantum revelations and arcane wisdom support the findings disclosed through catalyzation of the sacred interface. These findings provide transport across the synaptic gap imparting communication between subtle worlds by appropriately connecting the proverbial dots of awareness.

Arcane wisdom describes Anu as one of the names of Brahma, given to signify the most atomic of the atomic, the immutable and imperishable heart of the Sun, the heart of hydrogen, and the Ophanim sigil or 'seal' of truth. (Beyer, 2017, p. 01) Anu has been documented in ancient sacred texts, theosophical literature, prophetic writings, mythology regarding the cosmos, studies of human anatomy, and scientifically documented evidence—all of which introduce key concepts and patterns required to understand the "sacred interface" catalyzation process. Anu (in ancient Akkadian, An, meaning "sky, heaven") is the earliest identified Sky Father deity and describes the shape or formation of the human heart, the heart of the Sun and Hydrogen. (Griffith, 1896) This structure holds in formation, 'in formation', manifesting as wave patterns that evolve ad infinitum, perfecting towards coherence. It is also the superluminal, or faster than light, phase-conjugate harmonics of natural biologic origin which allow the survival wisdom and evolution of deoxyribonucleic acid DNA. Composed of fractal antennas of two structural characteristics, electrical conduction and self-symmetry, Anu describes the shape of sacred space. This perfect fusion operates through an implosion of the golden mean turning inside out. Efficient charge distribution is key.

The human heart represents the Anu in seven layers of muscle to provide seven spins on the outside and five spins on the inside. (Winter, 2015, p. 01) As such, a perfect recursion model is observed. Simple human emotions of the heart are based on the magnetic field braiding DNA. The resultant sonic, harmonic cardiac rhythms, go on to program the thymus, immune system, and can be measured by EEG, or electroencephalogram, which is a test that detects electrical activity in the brain. Fractal wave patterns create perfect compression and distribution of charge and spin, and fractal phase conjugation tends towards coherence, thereby producing the hologram effecting longitudinal "everywhere-at-once" properties. Fractality also signifies infinite compression, whereby self-similarity creates an inner structure as an identical scalar match with the outside, as seen in a pinecone or fern, for example.

Given the basic understanding that the Pineal Gland, or single eye, functions as the conduit between human beings and the universe, there exists yet another subtle although essential element between the layers of matter and antimatter which yields simply to our beckoning. (Donahue, 1998, p. 1) It is the world between an electron's orbit where calculations of quantum foam evade description. To fully catalyze this living element wherein greater consciousness awaits, specific magnetic resonance is a key feature achieved through a variety of combined effects. Availed through the system of workshop and meditation, all components of creating shareable thoughts, specific spin patterns and coherent intention, teach psychokinesis. An experience of deep bliss occurs during successful steering of plasma with the mind. Further insights have been obtained by observing these effects during AcuLomi live activation meditation. Evans, S. J. (2015, April 26-May 17). *Meditation Engaging our beloved God-Spark*

The meditation itself is the teaching device to ensure the carrier frequency can be duplicated at will. The subtle frequency comprising information contained in the name of that live activation meditation 'AcuLomi Temple', describes the self-similar conduit or mechanism in the activation process which occurs during the meditation it is named for. Broken into three parts, the first element named is 'Acu' to specify accurate or skilled manipulation of energy flow or Qi. The second element,

'Lomi', is a Hawaiian word which metaphorically indicates peristalsis, the wave-like kneading type of action required to move energy effectively. The third element in the name is 'Temple', which conveys the area overlying the temporal and sphenoid bone to suggest that the Temple is within.

The self-similar mechanism is also found as sound traveling in liquid, which is referred to as a phonon wave. When the heart sounds travel through living cells, the phonon wave leaves eddy's in the liquid current which literally impact DNA braiding. The selection process for which codons replicate directly responds to embeddable compression of heart harmonics. Expressing compassion for example, is an alchemical rendering of biological transmutation turning base emotions into a shareable fusion of Oneness. Heart harmonics create the embeddability of the golden mean during moments of bliss and compassion. Tilting the angle of the phonon wave which literally forms and sustain our Being, causes a sound shadow to be cast most noticeably in the temple area of the skull. The brain waves within the Temple, converge at Planck's distance, length, and time, when a focused intention i.e., to be responsible, generates pressure resulting as emotion. (Winter, 2015, p. 01) Focus on such a pure principle is the straightforward process which creates the spin path to implode charge. This is the nature of a bliss or eureka moment. Discovering a shareable thought in service to all life creates the holy grail of shaktipat. Shaktipat transfers the impulse to awaken or activate the Divine force or God-Spark that otherwise remains resting as potential. From the Sanskrit 'shakti', meaning psychic energy and pāta, which means to fall, this descent of Grace is often conferred upon a student to trigger a kundalini experience. Kundalini exists in potential like a room in which electricity is readily available. Like the light, kundalini is only experienced when the switch is turned on or activated. Although kundalini often remains dormant, a shaktipat impulse transferred through meditation can cause Kundalini energy to ascend from the base chakra. Traversing along the spine pathways to the crown chakra causes an awareness of one's True Self or possibly the attainment of degrees of realization.

AcuLomi Temple's system of education and meditation begins as a guided tour through cosmic and human chakras alike and is included in Chapter 13 of this book. Breath and focus on pure principle directs the spin frequency for navigation which enables the alignment of seven apertures during the initial stage of this Quantum Kundalini experience. Next, a sequence of sound patterns opens and maintains the channels between the multilevel awareness of the physical body, the subtle bodies, and the greater cosmic body—which provides expansive gnosis of implied Oneness. No longer restricted to theory and philosophical principles, a system of education and meditation combined can open the door to experience Oneness first hand thus presenting Pure Principle, ANU and illuminate the sacred interface between the subtle worlds.

Chapter Eight

Routing

$\mathcal{A}$ system of education and meditation which self-refers as a microcosm resolves the illusion of separation. Not only does such a system present ancient scientific practices such as astrology, alchemy and sacred geometry but also mirrors quantum physics and esoteric schools of thought alike. Corresponding to patterns in nature as the defining structure of universe, both inner and outer Cosmos describe Divine Order as a balanced harmonious system. By catalyzing the dynamic interconnectedness of sequential steps within the mind/heart, or knowing/feeling, a journey through seven chakras of our heavenly cosmos and the inner private kundalini rising through the seven main chakras of the human body can be navigated. The Sanskrit word Chakra speaks of a spinning wheel of energy which opens in similar fashion to the aperture through which light passes in an optical or photographic instrument which determine the cone angle of a bundle of rays that come to a focus in the image plane. This analogy is especially pertinent as it also implies the simultaneous pineal related activity as an essential component to successfully catalyzing the sovereign God-Spark. The outer seven celestial apertures open to permit the light of cosmic awareness as Supernova 1987a in the large Magellanic Cloud, in constellation of Mensa, and traverse a direct route through the constellations of Hydrus, Dorado, Reticulum, Horologium, and Eridanus to the luminous blue giant in Fornax, a region just below the constellation Orion, called Delta Fornicis.

These seven apertures are represented in the human form as the seven

as normal alert functioning. ("Beta waves," n.d., p. 01) This allows for mindful retention of the experience during meditation instead of the more common experience of forgetting in dream-like state of oblivion. This pulse-triggering creativity emanates from each atom within the universe as a complex arrangement of standing waves creating itself to the fractal beat of Anu, hydrogen, the heart of the sun and human heart alike. This expansion is much like a joyous spherical ripple radiating conscious receptors and receivers throughout time and space which instantly and continuously communicate with the All-That-Is. Taking heed of the Taoist notion that there is 'only one moment', (Tzu, 2008, p. 01) meditation can access the portal to the greater life lived in the moment of mindfulness. The humble acceptance of physical limitations juxtaposed against calm inner consciousness of infinite and eternal seeking, inverts to become outward heart-opening which gives and receives the energies of Love and Faith. Having the duality of a rotational pulse/pause to create perceived movement, such as the perceived passage of time, or the division of cells during meiosis, collectively contribute to embody minds and senses as the event horizon perceiving reality as 'solid'. Like Nassim Haramein's holofractographic model (Haramein, 2015, p. 01) perpetuating the dual torus manifold creating a feed-back loop of information transfer between infinite potential and finite form, specific frequencies of activation are henceforth generated at the event horizon. The torus can be utilized to represent the infinite spirit whose center is everywhere but whose circumference is nowhere. The outside perpetually coming back to the inside precludes separation. When included in meditation, esoteric practices and various techniques long advocated to trigger awareness of the subtler states of consciousness allow higher degrees of perception. Additional means of heightening perceptions from the event horizon include engaging a 33-45-degree raising of one's angle of sight or holding of one's breath during conscious breath-work. Breaking from established patterns of behavior in this way induces inner creativity, which encourages a quantum jump. Both the uncertainty of moving beyond ego and relinquishing control, by mimicking symptoms of death-like stasis, assist in prompting the physical vehicle to willfully cede that etheric essence back to spirit, thus laying the groundwork for a transpersonal experience. The third-dimensional experience of limitations is tangibly employed and appropriated both practically and profitably.

Remember the Zen saying, if you die before you die, then when you die you will not die. (Eriksen, 2012, p. 01) What that means is, you die to the lower self in meditation. You shut down the physical left hemisphere to ensure that during your meditation you will dwell in the right hemisphere. As Bill Donahue writes: "God is looking for empty vessels to fill. (Donahue, 2012, p. 01) He is looking for people who have died to the self and wish to be filled with His Spirit. He is looking for vessels willing to be filled. However, before He can fill them, they must be empty. Empty of pride (ego), lust, arrogance and bitterness, empty of those things that will defile the oil He wishes to give. Emptiness is achieved by taking no thought in meditation. Empty thyself and the lord (wisdom and knowledge) shall fill thee". ("Biblical allegory," n.d.)

Scientific technology such as bio feedback devices which measure such abstract content, concepts and criterion support the utility of meditation and education for the ability to effect realms of both subtle and physical bodies. Results documented from Heart rate variability (HRV) of Veda Pulse analysis can offer ongoing meditation participants individual comparison models for coherent analysis. Veda Pulse is a hardware and software program performing pulse analysis for meditation as Biofeedback - visualization and evaluation of effectiveness of techniques such as breath training (pranayama, qigong) and visualization. ("Veda-Pulse," n.d., p. 01) Heart rate variability measures change in the time intervals between adjacent heartbeats and is directly related to the body's interdependent regulatory systems and ultimately, their efficiency and health. Developing heightened awareness during meditation increases improvement in the supportive areas such as eating better, deeper rest, and recovery periods as well as overall stress reduction. This improvement then is measured in heart rate variability.

Made up of two components, autonomic nervous system addresses both the sympathetic and parasympathetic systems. Where the sympathetic nervous system is analogous to the gas pedal in a car, the parasympathetic system can thus be likened to the brakes in a car or the 'rest and digest' system. Heart rate variability is indicative of responsive and appropriate parasympathetic activity. For example, during inhalation, a branch of our Vagus nerve allows for an unimpeded sympathetic system. During exhalation, the Vagus nerve inhibitory action returns to slow the heart rate down to ensure homeostasis and optimum performance. This mechanism accelerates the benefits of meditative breathing. The additional coherence and breath training made available through bliss activated meditation further measures phase conjugate perfect implosive caduceus as golden ratio, self-organizing compression/collapse to guide and program heart rate with breath to achieve the precise frequencies to perfect collapse/implosion of conjugate wave rejuvenation. Theraphi.net ("TheraPhi," n.d., p. 01) provides all links and research data. Also see fractalfield.com (Winter, n.d., p. 01) for the frequency equation from Dan Winter providing an entirely deeper meaning of heart coherence. Humanity, is but one example of the routing synopsis or general survey along the path which consciousness can impel and enliven the embodiment of a Temple of Living Light which interconnects as Oneness with the Cosmos.

Chapter Nine

Kundalini

*P*ure intention, perceived uniquely from the individual viewpoint as a single point of light, hails as a beacon navigating a route. The energetic frequency produced by pure intention moves as a constant upward current or force. As the intensity varies according to flowing states of consciousness, the conscious force, or voltage, is a signal which returns the call for attention. Intense, absorptive states of bliss (samadhis), can only alert the guide like the beacon until an answer is received from above as the downward current of higher Kundalini. The higher Kundalini is also received as the Holy Spirit. This descending aspect completes the Greater Divine Circuit. The higher Kundalini, called Shaktipat in Hindu Kashmir Shaivism, (Qazi, n.d., p. 01) descends to open the Sacred or Mystic heart-center. The heart offers indwelling Source or Soul, a faculty endowing spirit, as a current, to move down into itself as a holy grail of implosive DNA. (Winter, n.d., p. 01) The pure electrical geometry of this kundalini beacon alerting the intellect and emotional body, the physical and subtle bodies alike call out, as did the ancient sacred texts, as a means to actively direct awareness into the sacred interface. Pure intention is superconductive longitudinal wave mechanics which informs space as zero resistance resulting from a shareable wave, otherwise known as bliss, the self-aware magnetic wormhole. Meditation provides experience in generating the specific frequency referred to as the kundalini beacon by bringing together two planes of reality. However, it is not enough to mechanically follow the steps of meditation intellectually. Pure intention elucidated within the education and meditation combination renders efficient charge distribution. The perfect echo then occurs electrically and sonically to commune with the collective unconscious. Add the simple act of conscious observation during prayerful affirmation of pure intention, to animate willful choice and actuate coherence engaging Love and Faith. A system of education and meditation utilizing protocol which introduces enlightened and blissful experiences, enable the ego and mind to dissolve through frictionless spin. The vehicle of entry into this sacred space, converts visualizing and feeling the movement of body/mind flowing as a radiating figure-eight, into contraction of the golden ratio pattern expanding in counter-rotating fields. The infinitely contracted and infinitely expanded selves become One during the activation of meditation. Acknowledged since ancient times as the 'Harmony of Apollo', the psychokinesis of steering plasma with one's mind is enabled during coherent intention. Coherence happens in response to sound harmonics coming from the heart. Effects from the 'Harmony of Apollo' in the form of magnetism has been acknowledged by Hubble Space Telescope News. During the late 1980's, talk about Supernova 1987a from Hubble scientist George Sonneborn (NASA, p. 01) fulfilled the Biblical statement in Matthew 6:22 which says, "...if your eye be single your body will fill with light". (Donahue, n.d., p. o3) The cosmic kundalini inducing Harmony of Apollo' as Supernova 1987a can be traversed in meditation to effect pineal activation.

Exercising the Pineal gland by meditation is essential to effectively polarize the cosmic light now effecting the Earth. This galactic beacon has aroused authentic heart-opening to receive Divine light coming upon the earth from the universal eye. Theta waves, inducing reception, completes the circuit, thus prompting the subtle adamantine particle into action. The adamantine particle, or Vajrasattva, is regarded as both matter and anti-matter. (Abzu, 2012, p. 1) This Sanskrit term implies a diamond essence, or Adamantine Being, representing the esoteric aspect of Bodhisattva purification and healing. Citing consonant, the fractal nature of the universal template provides authentication of the Kundalini beacon presently engaging the planet and all aspects of frequency.

Chapter Ten

The Science of Love

*L*ove, the magnetic power of pure and infinite potential, pervades and precipitates our life-force. The science of Love is now acknowledged as an essential aspect of study in many Astrophysical and Quantum physics labs today. Cosmic values are reflected in the conscious pursuit of a collective Oneness, which invites further investigation into the patterns revealing universal harmony of Divine Order within and without. Pervasive and elementary throughout the Universe, love is no longer exclusive to conversations of religion or psychology. When scientists began to validate a fundamental platform made from the energy connected to human consciousness, significant strides were made to include Love as integral to the equation. From the Quantum Double Slit experiment to the Global Consciousness experiment (Dr. Strauss, n.d., p. 3) to (Dunn, 2011, p. 1) Teleportation (Nelson, 2014, p. 1) to spectrum analysis of the magnetic field produced by the heart, Quantum physicists have rediscovered tools and mechanics to measure and quantify the effects of love. This new scientific blueprint has since been used to understand ancient systems of healing and cause a paradigm shift in approaches that reconnect love and spirit to physical matter. The shape of a rose for instance, contains the in-form-ation to define the perfect charge compression of a bioactive field. Fractal phase conjugate negentropic non-destructive compression occurring as the still point within or the 'sacred interface', is precisely the conjugate geometry of the place of power which already knows you as whole and complete. The sacred interface is called upon for it can provide access to the Divine blueprint of the subtle fields. This sacred interface access point is unlocked by the distilling process which renders bliss from engaging pure principle. Demonstrating exactly how the nodes in the hologram get their multiple-connected, everywhere at Oneness expression, entanglement occurs not only in the subtle fields between you and the sacred interface, or between the Healer and healed—but throughout All-That-Is. Opening to the higher expression of your Archetype/Ascended Master, which is a specific frequency not unlike a cosmic zip code, occurs by first acknowledging the limitations of three-dimensional intellect. Literal engagement of 'feeling' is required to step out of third-dimensional limitations. The sacred interface has a dwelling place between the left and right hemispheres of the human brain where it can be called upon to unite polarities as One. From the King James Bible, in the book of Acts, chapter 7:48 "The most high dwells not in temples made with hands". ("KJ Book of Luke," n.d., p. 01) 1 Corinthians 3:16 "You are the temple of God. ("1 Corinthians 3:16"Know ye not that ye are the temple of God, and that the Spirit of God dwelleth in you?" For the temple of God is holy, which temple you are". King James Version (KJV)," n.d., p. 01) The electrical arc between brain synapses is the electrical charge within the brain which effects the physical change. Meditation allows an awakening that places the typical pursuit of material gain, or three-dimensional concerns such as the pursuit of material gain deep on priorities the backburner of priorities. Gaining access to the subtle anatomy of the Universe through meditation joyously avails access to the known and unknown throughout time and space, as well as the inverted antimatter properties and elements we have yet to officially name. Through use of an education and meditation system, the Observer Effect of the observed, observing the Observer, contracts and expands generating a ripple effect. Basically, it is the equivalent of looking into God's eyes while God's eyes are looking into yours…gazing cognizant at each other. The acknowledgement of this observation creates an event impact of astronomical proportions uniting celestial and personal kundalini activation. Meditation fundamentally prepares the Pineal gland to polarize celestial light. The universal pineal activation has already taken place as described by considering Supernova 1987a as the Pineal which many ancient sacred texts and science documents concur. Just what effect this incoming light has in the form of magnetism on the human brain is receiving much attention around the world. Supernova 1987a was first seen from Earth on February 24, 1987, hence its name. (Gov, 1994, p. 01) It occurred in the Large Magellanic Galaxy about 170,000 light years away. Although it is thousands of years old, Hubble Space Telescope News was not able to document the event until the light reached Earth in 1987. Interestingly, on December 27th, 2004 Dr. Chris Burrows of the European Space Agency, said of Supernova 1987a, "This is an unprecedented and bizarre object. We have never seen anything behave like this before". Jason Pun of Goddard Space Flight Center Greenbelt Maryland, says "This is the first time we can see the geometry of the explosion and relate to the geometry of the large glowing ring around the Supernova. George Sonneborn of NASA Goddard Space Flight Center in Greenbelt Maryland said, "The wave of energy from the exploded star is now invisible, but it is beginning to shine brightly in ultraviolet emissions". Sonneborn speaking to a meeting of the American Astronomical Society said, "The immense energy of the collision probably will begin to glow in visible light upon the earth." The gas is expected to soon glow at thousands of degrees causing a final burst of light that will be visible on Earth in 2005. (Gov, 1994, p. 01)

Phil Plait also writes on Dec. 27, 2004(Plait, 2012, p. 01)— "The Earth was rocked by a cosmic blast so epic its scale is nearly impossible to exaggerate. Several satellites were blinded by the event. Whatever this event was, it came from deep space and still was able to physically affect the Earth itself…". Phil Plaits was referring to a remnant of a supernova known as magnetar SGR 1806-20 discovered in 1979.

This is not simply a celestial astronomical event. This is cosmic Kundalini of universal order. A system of education and meditation provides training to utilize the magnetic array of these photon packets now dispersed throughout the planet. Employing a system of meditation and workshop as training to develop the ability to focus on pure principle creates the needed spin path to non-destructively compress charge. Galactic clusters such as Field Galaxy NGC 4555, ("Field galaxy NGC 4555," 2004, p. 01) hold a probability distribution of undergoing experiences such as the stars mentioned above going supernova in countless years past. It is conceivable that Star Nations currently unknown to Earth dwellers saw these events and provided descriptions of these events to Earth humans recorded as visions, mythologies and other means, long before that light ever touched the earth. Much research has been gathered and organized by Bill Donahue of Hidden Meanings to suggest that Galaxy NGC 4555 (Donahue, n.d., p. 01) was a galaxy of immense importance to our ancestors. Effective education and meditation utilizes many current events from around the world and insights from the world's leading critical thinkers such as those of Donahue's, instrumentally, as visual assistance for catalyzing and activating the sacred interface space to access the subtle bodies of sacred space. (Donahue, n.d., p. 1)

The Covenant of the Heart, as catalogued by Coptic Christians in Egypt over two thousand years ago, in the book called IEOU, is a Kundalini beacon used to provoke vigorous investigation of the cosmos. ("Book of IEOU," n.d., p. 1) The number 4555 is reverentially bolstered as a keystone principle. This number was allegedly given by Jesus to the Coptic's as part of the key to the universe. The instructions were to hold it close to you. IEOU also proposes other instruments to augment and accelerate activation of the Beloved God-spark, such as the symbol 8, light filtered by crystal, and a galaxy in the sign of the Virgin. Bill Donahue's research shows Galaxy 4555 to have sharply defined features and a very bright center. The book of Isaiah also shares the covenant. In chapter 7, verse 14, it reads, "Behold the Lord himself shall give a sign, a Virgin shall conceive..." ("Therefore, the Lord himself shall give you a sign; Behold, a virgin shall conceive, and bear a son, and shall call his name Immanuel.," n.d., p. 01) The great and blazing electromagnetic radiation in the heavens has given a sign in Virgo and the Virgin has indeed conceived. The constellation of Coma leads us by way of the shepherds as well, revealing the Star of Bethlehem. There was a traditional prophecy, well-known in the East, carefully preserved and handed down, that a new star would appear in this sign when He whom it foretold should be born. (Perdue, 2011, p. 01) Even Shakespeare understood the truth about this constellation description, which has been so long covered by modern inventions. In Titus Andronicus, he speaks of an arrow being shot up to heaven to the Good boy in Virgo's lap. Thomas Hyde, an eminent Orientalist (1636-1703), writing on ancient Persian religion, quotes Abulfaragius (an Arab Christian Historian, 1126-1286), who says that Zoroaster, or Zerdusht, a pupil of Daniel the Prophet, predicted to the Magians (who were the astronomers of Persia), that when they should see a new star appear it would notify the birth of a mysterious child, whom they were to adore. (Bullinger, 2007, p. 01) It is further stated in the Zend Avesta that this new star was to appear in the sign of the Virgin.

Disseminating intrinsic design within the allegories from the book of Daniel of the Old Testament are three stories outlining our pending quantum leap to enlightenment, which connect Galaxy 4555 to our Pineal gland in a celebration of Cosmic Kundalini. As the first story is told, the fourth or spirit man is manifest only after three people [Shedrach, Mesach, and Abednigo] are cast into a roaring fiery furnace which had to be heated seven times. ("Daniel KJV," n.d., p. 01) This can be understood as a direct reference to both the Constellation Fornax of the heavens being heated seven times by significant magnetic light advancing through seven constellations, as well as the Fornix in the human brain being activated upon the rising of conscious light through seven chakras. Both actions generate the manifestation and give rise to the fourth or spirit man. The three figures of Shedrach, Mesach, and Abednigo embody the natures of physical/earth, emotional/water, and intellectual/air. When they ascend to the Fornix (furnace) via meditation through the Pineal gland, they are joined by the fourth which is spirit/fire, or Divine intellect which fans the Divine spark of the soul. Both Fornix and Fornax translate into the English word furnace.

Stedman's Medical Dictionary locates the Fornix at the part of the hippocampus responsible for memory and connected to the Pineal gland via the stria pinealis. (Stedman's Concise Medical Dictionary, 1997) So too, the constellation Fornax runs a straight line to the cosmic Pineal Supernova 1987a. ("Fornax Constellation," n.d., p. 01) Stedman's dictionary also refers to the Fornix of the human brain as "Delta Fornicis" because of its geometrical Delta shape. In the constellation named Fornax, amidst several spectacular galaxies, is the bright blue-white giant star called Delta Fornax, which points down as the human Delta Fornix points up, creating a sacred geometric form of the Star of David. Consciousness orchestrates mysterious and amazing coherence on all levels of being and not being. Meditation, when coupled with relevant education, can facilitate experiential expansion through this connection between Fornix and Fornax, allowing focused attention to fully perceive community, country, planet and solar system as well as corresponding micro levels of cell, molecules and atom.

Transposing this journey of matter and antimatter energetically into conscious observation of personal and cosmic Kundalini movements, collapses the coherent superposition to lock in a new context of feeling and knowing. Distilling bliss out of pure principle elaborates a context richness that serves as the foundation for a system or chain of reasoning. The collapse of the wave function is a consequence of non-linearity. This result demonstrates that the wave function collapse can occur in both microscopic and macroscopic systems, as above, so below. Collapse through conscious observation brings about the subject-object differentiation and leads to the primary awareness of I-am-ness that Amit Goswami called the "quantum self. "Heart and mind shift identity to embrace the ever-expanding quantum-atman, comprehending a new self-identity. "Atman is our quantum self, our inner self, an identity taken by consciousness when a creative quantum measurement takes place in the brain". – Amit Goswami (Goswami, 2014)

Potentiality has become self-aware of inner growth potential. On the quantum level of energy exchange, coherence becomes aroused as the sacred interface stirs. A cosmic pendulum timekeeper signals to its Pineal counterpart below. The time is at hand and creativity, the drive from the collective unconscious, ensures that our shareable wave engages all DNA in our return to full conscious awareness.

Dissemination of this intrinsic design is found flowing from the water jar of Aquarius, and Eridanus, the animating force found adjacent to the constellation Fornax. On the banks of this great river of life is Horologium, the constellation marking order in the seasons and cycles, yet another marker of conscious design. Literally translated from the Greek word orologion, "that which tells the hour," and corresponding to the term Horae (from Greek mythology, the Horae were goddesses of time), "those embodiments of the right moment— the rightness of Order unfolding in Time." (Aquiliana, 2014, p. 1) The Horae were daughters of Zeus and Themis and said to live in a cave on the river Eridanus. Themis was the prophetic goddess of divine law and order who presided over the most ancient oracles, including Delphi. She was specifically identified with Gaia

(Earth), particularly in the role of the oracular voice of Earth. Inscriptions found in the vestibule at the ancient Oracle of Delphi further compel meditating on the covenant to engage the pure principle conveyed: Gnothi Seauton ("Know thyself"); Meden Agan ("Nothing in excess"); and the letter E, a capital epsilon. ETA is the 7th letter of the Greek alphabet and means the Sun. (King, 1908, p. 1) Plutarch's essay "On the E At Delphi," the only known literary source on the meaning of E, proposes various explanations, which serve only to tease the intellect like a Zen koan, a riddle intended to dissolve the ego and facilitate emptiness. The meaningful E from the holotome alphanumeric system of notation referred to as the auric key (2520) is the first and lowest numerical sum which is divisible by all eight basic numbers. As the quantum wave of divine intellect expands, an echo reverberates to provoke generations down through the ages. The whispered conundrum taunting generations past implies there was not one, but three E inscriptions to tantalize the temple. E, epsilon, 5, times three. 555 and hahaha in the Thai language. e (the base of the natural logarithm and equal to 2.71828...; = 2+1/2! +1/3! +1/4! +...+1/n!) Consciousness has a profound sense of humour. "E pluribus unum" translates from Latin to English as "from many, one." Ea was also referred to as Enki, in Akkadian and Babylonian mythology. The main temple to Enki is called E-abzu, which means house of the cosmic waters. Specific meditation combined with relevant analytical information can demonstrate the reflection of the human temple also revealed as the two pillars of King Solomon's temple Jachin and Boaz, within the human brain temple.

Several ancient stories reference the three fives from Plutarch's essay. (King, 1882, p. 01) The first story speaks to the fiery furnace and Kundalini undulations in both cosmic and human forms. Immediately after the furnace story, a hand without a body writes on the wall, "MENE MENE." In Hebrew language, these words translate to "number number," meaning the kingdom is numbered:

Daniel 5:24. ("Daniel 5:24," 1995, p. 01)- Then was the part of the hand sent from him; and this writing was written. 25. – And this is the writing that was written, Mene Mene, Tekel, Upharsin. 26. - This is the interpretation of the thing; Mene; God has numbered your kingdom and finished it. Tekel, you are weighed in the balance, and are found wanting.

Hebrew Gematria calculations arrive at the numerical value of 4555 for mene [m=40 e=5 n=50 e=5]. Both Daniel and Plutarch's E times three suggest "Your Kingdom is numbered." The number 4555 also plays a prominent part in the Book of Ezekiel 1:1-2 (Book of Ezekiel 1:1-2, n.d., p. 01) as it speaks of UFOs and aliens. Because intelligent light Beings in Galaxy 4555 would have witnessed these events thousands of years ago, they could then foretell such mysteries to the inhabitants of an earlier Earth long before that light touched the Earth, therefore affecting the destiny of Earth.

The 4 of 4555 denotes a tesseract, a four-dimensional hypercube. Known also as a space warp or wormhole, the tesseract may facilitate connecting one area of space to another. This is said to be possible through the bending of the structure called "pacha," which is the continuum expressed as the three dimensions of space plus one dimension of time. NGC4555 has shared its frequency as a master tuning fork of the whole universal body. Having the capability of communicating to other bodies, and even other lifeforms, conscious Oneness as the All-That-Is exists as potential to visit, experience and expand awareness through engaging the sacred interface during heightened meditation. A growing body of evidence indicates the dominant form of matter in the universe is dark matter which interacts with itself and alleged 'normal' matter through gravity. (Cain, 2013, p. 01) Gravity happens when waves agree to meet in such a way as to achieve non-destructive compression. Fractal geometry of self-embedding or self-similarity is the only geometry that enables this gravity-making to occur.

Based on the Golden Ratio fractality, DNA forms the perfect design to fabricate gravity fields.

It is the process of perfect self-embedding that permits DNA to bond to it's larger electrical environment producing conditions which trigger bliss, euphoria and peak experience.

Within inside every cell is a fractal antenna capable of responding to a wide range of frequencies. The structure of the DNA molecule performs as a fractal DNA tesseract or a four-dimensional hypercube having sixteen corners. This geometry called a hecatonicosachoron, is considered a gateway across dimensions. The interesting parallel is that it is comprised of basic hexagonal and pentagonal geometry. The hexagonal seven spin outside/five spin pentagonal is inside of Anu, heart of the Sun, hydrogen and the human heart to match this form and reveal how DNA tesseract creates magnetic scalar waves. Dr. Konstantin Meyl's book, DNA and Cell Resonance (Meyl, 2011, p. 01) show hydrogen electrons surrounding the hexagonal and pentagonal shapes of the DNA literally spin not solely around the hydrogen atom but around the entire molecule that makes up the pentagons and hexagons. This spinning of the hydrogen electron cloud causes the creation of vortexes. These vortices are the generators of scalar waves throughout the human body whereby the DNA can behave as a transmitting antenna as well as a resonant receiving scalar antenna. Through this work, it has been determined that the human body exhibits massive collections of DNA tesseract gateways made viable through meditation.

Activating the pineal through meditation provides fully conscious access to realms obliviously passed by otherwise. Theoretical physicist Fritz-Albert Popp, PhD, determined how the DNA of living cells store and release photons. It was Popp who keyed the term biophotons to differentiate what others call "higher-dimensional light" and said, "We now know, today, that man is essentially a being of light." ("Biophotons," n.d., p. 01) DNA communicates via these biophotons, and has the capability of communicating to other bodies, and even other lifeforms. The sacred interface permits access to this fractal antenna bridge that directly connects humanity to all ancestors including those who seeded this very planet. As a fractal antenna interacting with the vacuum/aether/zero-point field as consciousness, effecting change in DNA through bliss, results in an expanded consciousness. Author and researcher Vincent Bridges, called this "Angels in our DNA". ("Angels in our DNA," n.d., p. 01) Meditation generates a greater interaction between our DNA and the torsion and/or scalar forces in the vacuum and as such holds the key to reclaiming God-given right to create, alter, and inform the collective Oneness.

Nobel Prize winner Luc Montagnier ("Luc Montagnier," 2008, p. 01) and his team suggest DNA emits its own electromagnetic signals that imprint the DNA's structure on other molecules (like water). Emitting electromagnetic signals of its own construction, ghost imprints replicate

DNA. This teleportation mechanism is not reliant on the usual cellular processes, ostensibly functioning just like a holographic computer, using endogenous DNA laser radiation. An education and meditation system has been scientifically proven and explained as vibrational behavior effecting DNA. (Baerbel, 2005, p. 01)

Having studied the research of Manfred Clynes, (Wicherink, 2008, p. 95) Daniel Winter saw conclusive evidence that demonstrated love to be Golden Mean related and went on to produce the equations that prove it so.

Universal consciousness of the universe creates through the loving non-destructive interference bending of light into fractal structures of geometries that allows the waves to stand and interfere eternally centered.

Daniel Winter was a member of the Heart Coherence Team that developed a heart/brain biofeedback system (Wicherink, 2008, p. 01) to measure the coherence between the heartbeats (Electrocardiogram ECG) and the brainwaves (Electroencephalogram EEG) of an individual to measure human emotions such as compassion, empathy, love, anger and frustration. A cascade of Fibonacci series of harmonics is created as thoughts and emotions attune to love, thus linking the energy of the heart and mind to DNA.

Quantum entanglement and teleportation

Entanglement and Teleportation through any field is not limited to the quantum internet of our DNA. Quantum physics has established that the fundamental building blocks of the universe, such as subatomic particles, can exist in two or more places at once. Evidence for an entirely new conveyance of medicine in which DNA can be influenced and reprogrammed by words and frequencies not only validates what metaphysicians have said all along, but as well provides a bridge between quantum science and spiritual objectives as Entanglement and Teleportation. The sacrifice, resurrection, and ascension of biblical entanglement, plays itself out in quantum teleportation. Biophoton light is stored in the DNA molecules of an organism's nuclei. This potent web of light constantly released and absorbed by the DNA is a communication network vitalizing Oneness while performing regulating principals for all life processes. Biophotons are weak electromagnetic waves in the optical range of the spectrum which create light. All living cells of plants, animals and human beings emit biophotons. Light broadcasting DNA is not only responsible for the construction of the physical body, but it also serves as data storage for communication. Russian biophysicist and molecular biologist Pjotr Garjajev and his colleagues explored the vibrational behavior of DNA. (Baerbel, 2005, p. 1) By modulating certain frequency patterns (sound) onto a laser-like ray, these scientists influence the DNA frequency and thus the genetic information itself. Language and the basic structure of DNA-alkaline pairs are shadows of different flows of energy of the same structure as demonstrated by Dan Winter and other notable scientists. Each letter is a precise angular strip or slice of the vortex. Fire letters are seen as the cellular alphabet of our DNA. (Franckena, 2017, p. 01) Vincent Bridges ("Angels in our DNA," n.d., p. 01) discovered the Hypercube symmetry in Ophanic letters to confirm in principle- phase conjugate implosion among letter vectors reveal Human languages are a direct reflection of our inherent DNA. The top down view of DNA is the same as the top down view of a dodecahedron. Nature as biology speaks in forms and shapes as in-form-ation to inform creation. It is the form that delivers the message as a donut photon of light. Light waves are electromagnetic energy. In a unified field, light moves into a circle and spins into a torus donut, or a photon of light. Spinning light waves align to a symmetrical geometry to create matter. Wave patterns remember information. Everything is made of waves. They are perfect energy conductors because they are perfect patterns. Platonic solids are the shapes from which the light waves create matter. Golden Mean ratio permits adding and multiplying of waves and is the distance between the rungs of the DNA ladder or helix. DNA genetic material is mechanically connected to sound waves of the heart through the 'slinky-like' formation. Coherence happens in response to sound harmonics coming from the heart and provides the context richness of DNA. The nature of what makes a wave sustainable is what makes it sacred. Golden ratio phase conjugation is wave geometry of perfect quantum tunnel. DNA attracts electromagnetic energy into itself. Projecting the Phi spiral onto the face of the tetrahedron creates the Hebrew alphabet. These same angles rotate the torus such that a nesting can occur in relation to the symmetry of the Platonic solids. Golden ratio perfected fractality as seen in recursion and embedding called phase conjugation, is proven to be negentropic, self-organizing and self aware.

Russian linguists established that the alkalines of our DNA follow a regular grammar and have set rules just like spoken human languages. (Baerbel, 2005, p. 1) Living DNA has been consistently found to react to language, and sound frequencies. This scientifically explains why a meditation system including relevant analytical information has significant reproducible effects on all fields of the human body, including the physical body, etheric body, emotional body, mental body, astral body, etheric template, celestial body and causal body as it conveys the science of love. Entanglement and Teleportation principles used in meditation, catalyze the sacred interface. Expressed in the King James bible, in the book of John 14:20 ("John 14:20," n.d., p. 01) it says," I am in my father, you in me and I in you". Just as Quantum physics has established that the fundamental building blocks of the universe, such as subatomic particles, can exist in two or more places at once, so too the existence of a bonded-grouping will behave in duplicate pattern. The bonded-group refers to every individual's physical expression and antimatter duplicate existing as does the superposition of photon or light. Light is coherent electromagnetic energy that has the property of superposition. Darkness exists simply in the absence of such light. The education and meditation system seek to find those places where light is absent, has been resisted or, not accepted. The concept of nonmaterial duplicated bond-groups, subtle energy bodies of light, "Mana" or "inner fire" of Indian, Tibetan and Chinese philosophy speak of the essential light of man referred to by the famed alchemist Paracelsus. ("Paracelsus, p. 01) A single unit, or quantum, of electromagnetic radiation is called a photon. Just as waves in an ocean are the result of energy moving through the water, photons consist of electrical and magnetic fields propagating through space. To allow light in via meditation, a wave offering must be accepted. This happens by first quieting the intellect and all its desires, which might require throwing a proverbial bone to three-headed Cerberus. The Temple, via right hemisphere of the brain, provides rite of access by disallowing or negating the desires of the intellect through meditation. Kundalini or movement of electrical energy henceforth rises through seven chakras or nerve centers in the spine to arrive at what the Taoists call the Crystal Palace, located between the pineal, pituitary and thalamus of the brain.

The right hemisphere of the Temple brain is activated by the frequency of kundalini energy which, like voltage making a cell membrane permeable, allows entrance via the Pineal Gland. As the electrical energy ejects from your Pineal Gland (single/third eye or seventh seal) it travels straight to the Fornix lighting the furnace within as a portal to the higher worlds of Oneness. Noted by Stedman's Medical Dictionary (Stedman, 2000, p. 01), the Fornix of the brain or "Delta Fornicis" is thus named Delta Fornix, because of its triangular or Delta shape. Likewise, in the heavens is the constellation Fornax, which is also noted to mean furnace, whose bright star is called Delta Fornax. This important correlation is discussed in later segment 'Journey Inward'. When the energy in the body is raised to the point of the hippocampus through meditation, it touches the Rams Horn. In the hippocampus is an organ called Ammons Horn. Ammon is an Egyptian Deity whose symbol is the Ram. The Shofar is the Rams Horn which is blown in the temple at Yom Kippur. Yom Kippur is the day of atonement or At One Ment, the point of enlightenment. The Ram or Aries represents the head in the study of Astrotheology. Thus, Ammons Horn is the Rams Horn. The Shofar is blown to evoke a physical manifestation of the power that is accessed through kundalini energy activating the Fornix but can only be channeled by the photon within. Quantum entanglement and teleportation are cognitively experienced in awareness of willful surrender which implies separation from thought to find unity with All-That-Is. As electromagnetism results from the interaction of photons with charged particles, the answer is revealed by considering the process of collapsing the wave to a particle and receiving the light. Photons as visible light waves, appear when an atom has been stimulated by heat. Through the act of meditating, solar energy rises to the Pineal causing heat to stimulate the atom and the photon appears. (Miller, 1993, p. 01) For example, the Biblical sacrifice can be defined as quantum entanglement where God and Jesus are described as light. For this example, allow atom to represent God in religious terms and Photon to represent Jesus or the Son of God. Removing an electron from one atom and putting it into another, produces positive and negative ions. Positive and Negative are represented here by the polarities Male/Female or Adam and Eve. God is the light out of which Atom and Eve represent ionic bonding. Quantum entanglement can likewise be understood using the description of Jesus coming to Earth to sacrifice himself for humanity by viewing God as photon 'C', Jesus as photon 'B', and humanity as photon 'A'. Although the first proof-of-principle demonstration was reported in 1997 by the Innsbruck4 and Rome group, Albert Einstein famously dubbed it "spooky action at a distance" in the 1940s. ("Quantum Entanglement," 1935, p. 01) Quantum entanglement requires that one photon be sacrificed, so that two other photons can merge. In this example, the scripture of John 14:6 ("John 14:6," n.d., p. 01) states Jesus as saying, "…no one can come to the father but by me". The A photon cannot get to the C photon except through the B photon. The idea is to transmit A (humanity) to C (God the Father). Photon B (Jesus) is invited into one's heart and entangles with A (the photon comprising the human state). Human becomes one with Jesus which overturns the original state. (As the Bible says it is no longer I who live but the Christ in me) Photon B (Jesus) is now part of the human, therefore photon C (God the Father) must change polarization to remain an opposite of Photon B (Jesus). The opposite of photon B (Jesus) now is A (human). Photon C's (God the Father) polarization changes to A (human). Thus, humanity become one with God and move into the realm of light. C's polarization ended up the same as A. A and C became one. A (human) is the photon inside that has become eternal by entanglement with photon C (God the Father).

Light was brought into order of matter through the harmonics of sound. Thus, the material world was created. A distinct change in a macroscopic observable phenomenon is brought about only by the entanglement and teleportation causing change in knowledge about the system.

The analogy of the Bible story is true. God and Jesus are entangled as one. Jesus must be sacrificed to become human. God must always stay one with Jesus however, now Jesus ceased to exist in order to save humanity by becoming human. Therefore, God changes polarization to become entangled with humanity which is Jesus in the human state. The sacrifice of photon B Jesus, becoming photon A, humanity, enables entanglement whereby humanity becomes one with God, photon C. The opposite of B now is A. God's polarization therefore changes to become one with A. Thus, the Holy Trinity is expressed as becoming one with God. This story of the Holy Trinity as related down through the ages in every culture has always been to share the meaning of the catalyzed photon.

Reality is created by observation. Quantum entanglement of evolution requires that human photons receive information regarding the higher state of light. The photon light now reaching Earth from cosmic kundalini activation of sources such as Supernova 1987a and Eta Carinae can enhance, catalyze and potentize meditation. The catalyzation takes place through meditative focus on pure principle. The molecular gas pouring out of Eta Carina at 1 and a half million miles per hour is a precursor to a key component of DNA which is catalyzed through meditative focus on pure principle. We move out of the human body to the realm of light to fully grasp the consciousness of One. Multidimensional frequencies outside the range of humanities perception permit evolution. Matthew 5:14 ("Matthew 5:14," n.d., p. 01) Jesus says, "You are the light of the world". Instruction or guidance from the sacred God-Spark interface is achieved by reaching the state of willful surrender, which is separation from intellectually driven thought through meditation. Oneness or 'unity of all things' is the central teaching of this activation.

The Harmony of Apollo as recorded by the ancients' also express the Holy Trinity as quantum entanglement and teleportation. Everything is a law of correspondence.

The frequency of this sacred Trinity is known as the Harmony of Apollo. Apollo, Hermes and Zeus create Root Three, the relationship of geometric patterns. Zeus had two sons named Apollo and Hermes. The findings of David Fideler, a specialist in ancient religions, philosophies, and cosmologies, shows "the Logos represents the heart or Anu of the cosmic pattern and the source of existence, its emblem is the sun, the source of life and light."(Fideler, 1939, p. 39) Whereas the early Christians personified the Logos in the figure of Jesus, the Greeks represented the Logos in Apollo, the god of geometry and music. Another representation was Hermes. [Ibid, p. 46] Apollo, Hermes and Zeus together create a geometric pattern of the harmony of angels or angles in relationship to geometry that matches perfectly the pattern of Hour Glass Nebula. The formula for Root Three or the controlling ratio of the perfect equilateral triangle is 1.7320508. In the above diagram, Apollo 1061 represents point A to A, Zeus 612.5674 represents B to B and Hermes 353.666 represents point C to C. Hermes is the 'eye' representing judgement or the judge yet provides for the hermetic sealing of Karma that results from kundalini energy activating the pineal or 'third eye on fire'. Hermes in Greek is also known as Egyptian Thoth who carries the Tetrahedron as a display of the photon which is a reference to the speed of light according to Nassim Haramein And R.A. Rauscher ("Quantum gravity," 2014, p. 01). The formula of multiplying Zeus times Root Three (612.5674 x 1.7320508 =Apollo 1061) or Hermes times Root Three (353.66 x 1.7320508 =Zeus 612) represents the activation of the Fornix of the brain 'on fire'. The Fornix is described in Stedman's Medical dictionary as a subterranean cave located directly in the center of the brain. The Oracle at Delphi was likewise said to be a subterranean cave located directly in the center of Earth. The equilateral triangle is said to be delta – shaped. A polyhedron composed of only equilateral triangles is known as a deltahedron. The delta triangle recognized as a connection to the sacred trinity and because it has long represented the concept of the Deity in geometrical form. In the Ineffable Degrees of Masonry, the sacred Delta is presented as the symbol of the Grand Architect of the Universe. The Oracle at Delphi sat upon a delta tripod to deliver her oracles and prophesies. The Oracle of Delphi represents the Fornix receiving electromagnetism from the celestial Delta Fornax. In the Oriental legend about Queen of Sheba (or the seven chakras) who was attracted to Hiram, the pineal gland of the brain. Allegedly King Solomon became so jealous that he plotted the death of Hiram. Hi-Ram / Aries the pineal gland, threw his jewel, the energy of creation, down a deep well. The jewel was found and placed on a Delta or triangular altar, which Solomon then had erected in a secret vault beneath the Temple. Not only were anatomically correct descriptions of the human brain written into ancient Greek mythologies but likewise, precise descriptions of astronomy pervade the mythos of ancient lore. The practice of meditation engages yet another relevant analogy of the Sacred Trinity expressing itself as photon packets of information, which is composed of

1 - the individual physically as third density Matter,

2 - the individual as anti-matter

3 - the individual as the consciousness that encompasses both, the all and nothing.

The Universal Law of Correspondence basically says that our current reality is a mirror of what is going on inside us. Our reality is a result of our inner most dominant thought and as such effects epigenetics as described by author and scientist Dr. Bruce Lipton. (Lipton, 2012, p. 01) Established and substantiated by Dr. Lipton, that neuroscience acknowledges the subconscious as controlling 95 percent of our lives, further means, gene activity can change daily. Ultimately, human thoughts and perceptions become a self-perpetuating situation. Understanding the Principle of Correspondence enables gleaning of insights to come from studying the monad to understand the archangel or study of the cosmos to understand the human form. Certainty derived in meditation accelerates the manifestation of creating wellness in all areas of life through the expansion of awareness.

5th century AD. Greek philosopher and mathematician, Proclus, (Editors of Encyclopedia Britannica, 1999, p. 01) considered the cross-sections of a torus by a plane parallel to the axis of the torus and dubbed this concept with the word hippopede, a device for hobbling the front feet of a horse together. Bill Donahue of Hidden Meanings (Donahue, n.d., p. 01) has provided decades of compelling data to show that the authors of Greek mythologies link the hippocampus, human's organ of memory, and ancient sacred texts to demonstrate NGC 4555 to be the galaxy of their origin. Moreover, Eta Carina personifies the 7th Angel of the Book of Revelation, and Supernova 1987a is the Cosmic Kundalini or Gods single eye on fire. The Book of Daniel ("Daniel," n.d., p. 01) establishes Fornax the furnace as Fornix through Shadrach, Meshach and Abednego. The book of Daniel further connects the Pineal through its tale of Daniel in the Lions den. Daniel also solves the code for galaxy NGC 4555. In the Book of Daniel, a hand with no arm writes "Mene Mene" on the wall, which means your kingdom is numbered. The Greek and Hebrew values of Mene is 4555. Those who came from another galaxy as recorded both in the Emerald Tablets and the Bible, arrive from their home galaxy NGC 4555. Documents of witnessed UFO landings on Earth in the Emerald Tablet and in the Bible, such as in the Book of Ezekiel, include two specifically detailed descriptions of extra-terrestrials. If a very distant hydrogen cloud emits Lyman alpha radiation then this spectral line will be red shifted from the ultraviolet into the blue, green or red region of the spectrum. The energy would flow through chakras which are nerves or resistors in the spine. The Pineal Gland or "Third Eye" is described in the King James Bible. From1 Kings 7:21-22, "And he set up pillars in the porch of the temple: and he set up the right pillar and called the name thereof Jachin: and he set up the left pillar and called the name thereof Boaz. And upon the tops of the pillars was lily work…" Solomon's Temple represents the human mind. Two pillars named Jachin and Boaz have been well established as the gateway to the Holy of Holies. In the Hebrew language, Jachin means strengthened, upright, firm and stable. The Hebrew name Boaz means strength, power, and source. These pillars symbolically demonstrate spiritual energy of fire and water emphasizing synchronous forces of the left and right brain hemispheres united in creation. Uniting the two hemispheres activates both the pineal and pituitary to form the Third Eye. The lower nature must be relinquished through meditation to induce the ascension of kundalini energy through the seven energy portals or chakras representing the shekinah glory of God which manifests in the temple as the secretion of amrita, a yellow/golden fluid from the "land flowing with milk and honey". As the kundalini energy advances through the fornix/furnace, (the burial vault of Christ) the stone is symbolically rolled away to affect the return of Christ consciousness whereby the opened lily or lotus flower atop the pillars represent an awakened individual. This is also the cave of Brahma. Ahi-Ram, the temple builder, means 'exalted snake' or Serpent Grail. This is the kundalini that ascends through the seven chakras rising along the spine to activate the Crystal Palace, and thus be met by the descending spirit of photon carrying its packet of transformational information to merge into One, as the star of David implies.

"Where the skull divides, there lies the Gate of God"-The Taittireeya Upanishad ("Upanishad," n.d., p. 01)

A system of both education and meditation catalyzes the sacred interface to establish the activation of the Pineal gland's 'third eye'. As a portal to the All-That-Is, the Pineal activation has been held in highest regard down through the ages. Recorded as individual and cosmic events dependent on specific angles of light non-destructively compressing phase conjugation as a shareable wave to effectively communicate with all DNA, pineal activation reveals itself as the key. For example, allegories from the book of Daniel, lead us as an intentionally conspicuous device designed to attract attention to a specific information. Conveyed through this apostolic text, the story of Daniel in the Lion's Den relates yet a third relevant covenant. In this biblical narrative, the sacred metaphor and the importance of the Pineal Gland is expressed both universally and human in design. For example, in Astrotheology, which is the study of religious systems founded upon the celestial observation of activity in the heavens mirroring the patterns as fractal expressions in the human body, the Sun is eminently referenced as Leo (the Lion) after it travels along the ecliptic representing time. Here Leo is exalted as it intersects space as the Spring Equinox thereby transcending the illusion of space-time. As referenced above regarding the book of Daniel, the Lion is said to lay down with the Lamb. Astrotheologic wisdom figuratively denotes solar energy as rising to the Ram-Aries constellation, during which time we Passover, or transition, into spring and all that is renewed. Mirrored below the heavens in the fractal expression of human form, the same information is replicated and occurs as the sun or fire passing through the solar plexus to eventually enter Ram-Aries which is the human head or otherwise referred to symbolically as the lamb renewed or transfigured within. When the fire of the solar plexus rises through kundalini ascending to enter the Pineal, which is a region in the brain, both become the domicile of the Sun. The Lion of Judah has prevailed to open the seven seals or constellations/chakras and thus has "laid down with the Lamb."

Chapter Eleven

Pineal Gateway

$\mathcal{F}$ acilitating freewill and securely ensconced amidst two tiny structures called the suprachiasmatic nuclei and the epiphysis cerebri, are the bodily calculations of time. The pineal gland is responsible for producing melatonin, which not only influences sexual development, but also regulates the sleep cycle in the human brain and body. More specifically, the Pineal gland is responsible for converting amino acids into serotonin, which is then converted into melatonin during the darkness of night. The pineal gland also produces pinoline, which stimulates the dream state when it reacts with serotonin. Moreover, using Calcite microcrystals, the pineal gland can become a sensitive monitor of the Earth's magnetic field.

Calcite micro-crystals consisting of calcium, carbon and oxygen produce bioluminescence, connoting light without heat, ranging in the blue-green light spectrum. Frequency waves such as those in the green, blue and violet range produce higher emotional energies and temperament, while the lower infrared band of frequency waves can adversely affect the disposition and health of the human body. Using Scanning Electron microscopy and Energy Dispersive spectroscopy, Calcite micro-crystals have been found to exhibit piezoelectric properties, associated with electromagnetic energies within and around the human body pertaining to extra-sensory perception and energetic sensitivity.

Meditation as an 'energy therapy' utilizes magnetoreceptors, photoreceptors and optical signals pertaining to the Ajna chakra and the Third Eye. Positive and negative charges unite to culminate in light production, and the properties of a magnetic field developed through establishing relations between the pituitary and pineal glands refine and entrain harmony as a standing wave. Through this method, the Kundalini energy swells through each vortex, amplifying fusion at each successively heightened node. The Pineal gateway detonated through meditation for the Super-Nova of mystical experience, initiates personal advancements.

The Pineal symbol has been passed down through the ancient mystery teachings of all of Earth's mythologies and creation mysteries. In Ancient Egypt, it was symbolized by the Eye of Horus, the sun god, as a reminder that activation of the pineal occurs when divine photon or sunlight signals the rise of kundalini. The gland remains dormant until activated by specific frequencies. The sacred sun disk represents enlightenment and connection to Divine Intelligence. The DNA serpent of kundalini energy must rise to meet the descending photon or spirit fire to activate the 'all-seeing-third-eye of the pineal. Thus, the two systems denoting "as above, so below," become navigational systems. Or, as the Gospel of Philip states: "The Lord did everything in a mystery, (Isenberg, n.d., p. 01) He said, 'I came to make the things below like the things above, and the things outside like those inside. I came to unite them'." The Holy Grail cup within a cup formation of DNA literally describes this inside exactly as the outside concluding there is no such thing as separation.

Taoists refer to the Temple area—between the two brain hemispheres, and between the pineal and pituitary—as the "Crystal Palace" that appears as a "thousand suns" when activated. (CHIA & THOM, 2017, p. 01) During the height of this illumination, an intense opiate-like production of dimethyltryptamine (DMT), called the 'White Drop', Amrita or, 'nectar of the gods' is released and descends to the heart center. This organic natural production of DMT can be self-induced by the focus of pure principle in a meditative state and is the positive supportive means of accessing the subtle worlds through bliss. Fractionation of personality however, can result from using external sources of DMT such as hallucinogenic mushroom and plant extracts. This extraneous dependency leads to debilitation of the sacred God-Spark interface instead of the intended holistic activation by light induction. Distillation of pure principle into Bliss sustains coherent centripetal steering of the tornado vortex which is the vehicle of psychedelic transportation through the subtle worlds. Certainty develops in relation to the degree in which implosive capacitance or 'attention density' can be derived from pure principle. Further, certainty seals the experience in the Beta frequency enabling full recall of all that takes place during such journeys in the subtle worlds.

Healing patterns amplified in the sacred space of implosive capacitance create a centripetal force which requires grounding and hydration thereafter to integrate the plasma projection experience of entanglement and teleportation or transfer of information. Thus, the pineal gateway offers a tangible practical bridge between spirit and matter.

Chapter Twelve

Gnosis

ystically acquired knowledge of spiritual matters or 'gnosis', facilitates freewill and implies a type of knowledge that is derived from authentic personal experience and encompasses the whole of a person. The Gnosis of antiquity implied direct mystical experience and consequent enlightenment through experiencing the Divine. The workshop and meditation system, in an ever-expanding body of gnosis develops neurological pathways enhancing intuition and deduction in quantum leaps of conscious creativity to access subtle planes of existence. These corridors of exploration become successively more tangible with every encounter. The very nature of consciousness holographically reinforces fundamental concepts.

The symbols used in the ancient writing of Coptic Gnostic text IEOU, ("IEOU," 2005, p. 01) remain in today's technological societies. According to ancient lore, IEOU names the identity of God: I represent the symbol in electricity for current. E is the symbol for Electron. O is the symbol for OHM. U is the symbol for internal energy. Thus, internal currents and electrical resistance are necessary as we focus our receivers to listen for signals and magnetism through the universe. There are more similarities to the Coptic IEOU in IOEO. For instance, the amplifiers of microwave frequencies in radio relay systems employed in the search for extraterrestrial radio signals. These are also known as Klystrons, which modulate the velocities of emitted electrons. IO and EO are the beam current and voltage, and the efficiency is how well the DC power supplied is converted to RF power, or radio signals, which in this instance are those that SETI is listening for. There are many ancient references saying that God is Light. From the King James Bible, John 1:5. ("John 1:1-5," n.d., p. 01) "This then is the message which we have heard of him, and declare unto you, that God is light, and in him is no darkness at all." In the Divine Pymander (II: 8-9), ("Divine Pymander 11:8-9," n.d., p. 62) the Mind of God also is recorded to have said: "I am that Light, the Mind, thy God ... and the union of these is Life." If the image and likeness of God is Light, then it follows that Love must also be Light. Invisible subatomic electrical power and human beings are made in the image and likeness of God. The Coptic approach to God was a quantum, subatomic approach which duplicates the journey of Moksha (Sanskrit: मोक्ष) or "spiritual liberation." In Moksha, the soul is compared to a drop of water. Liberation is compared to the water droplet merging into the vast ocean which represents the Supreme Soul of Great Creator. The individual soul is compared to a green bird that enters a green tree or Supreme Soul of Great Creator. The individual soul only appears to have merged but still retains its unique identity. Many spiritual practices and rites of passage are aimed at liberation and consider moksha the goal of life. Liberation as understood by and achieved through meditation leads to freedom within the Oneness of All-That-Is. This Universal dance called spiritual liberation culminates as ascension through the cosmic eye to reclaim full consciousness. Many of the other-worldly meditation experiences are an impetus requiring the maintenance of open pathways from the brain frequencies connecting Beta to Alpha and beyond. Once the door to higher realms has been opened, the three-dimensional experience of life on earth retains the knowledge that so much more exists all around. Know or unknown, seen or unseen, once that personal awareness has expanded, the magnetic attraction to move further into the light will not be denied. Traveling through the specific resistance at each chakra, the electrical energy carries the chrism or Holy Christ oil energy from the solar plexus up the spine. Upon reaching the apex of the pineal gland itself, the alchemical 'wedding ring of fire', (electromagnetism acting upon the optic thalamus) activating gnosis or the inner sight. The energy continues building with the oil, until it passes through the anterior pillars, Jachin and Boaz, where it then culminates in the third ventricle of the brain, or the Holy of Holies. Otherwise known as the fornix of the brain, or the vault or cave of Brahma or Christ. Arriving in the cave like structure of the brain, the electrical energy ignites the oil. This is the passage of kundalini, the journey of the prodigal son, Samadhi, Nirvana, enlightenment or the death of HiRam. The stone is said to be rolled away to receive Christ consciousness.

Observe yourself in relationship to the universe expressing and exploring itself. Just as sound waves do not become sound unless they enter an ear and sunlight is not perceived as such unless it enters an eye, "You are a function of what the whole universe is doing in the same way that a wave is a function of what the whole ocean is doing, however, trying to define yourself is like trying to bite your own teeth."- Alan W. Watts. ("Allan Watts," n.d., p. 01) The value of attaching meaning and its context richness to perception leads gnosis to inform Consciousness and the conscious field. Mystically acquired knowledge of spiritual matters referred to as gnosis conveys, exponentially, more than the sum of its parts.

Principles of the Journey

The Law of Correspondence, "As above, so below, as within, so without, as the universe, so the soul", is the reminder that expressed within the individual, is the map of our cosmos. From the Hermetic Philosophy called 'Kybalion' originally published in 1908, ("Kybalion," 1908, p. 01) we are taught, "The Principles of Truth are Seven; whomever knows these, understandingly, possesses the Magic Key before whose touch all the Doors of the Temple fly open. Having laid out the premise that the Temple is noun, verb and adjective of consciousness, which may be accessed through the mind and heart, the first Principle of Mentalism, that "All is Mind" is understood to imply consciousness. The Seven Principles of the Universe as taught by Hermes Trismegistus greatly augment the direct experience gained through exploration of the subtle worlds. They are;

1. Principle of Mentalism: "All is Mind"
2. Principle of Correspondence: "As is above, so is below. As is below, so is above."

3. Principle of Vibration: "Nothing rests; everything moves; everything vibrates."
4. Principle of Polarity: "Everything is dual; everything has an opposite, and opposites are identical in nature but different in degree."
5. Principle of Rhythm: "Everything flows, out and in; the pendulum-swing manifests in everything; the measure of the swing to the right is the measure of the swing to the left- rhythm compensates."
6. Principle of Cause and Effect: "Every cause has its effect; every effect has its cause."
7. Principle of Gender: "Everything has its masculine and feminine principles."

Contemplating the seven principles above, will prepare a fertile place like soil for planting. Seeds of insight will become imbedded where relevant analytical data germinates during the various meditative journeys. Blossoming as compassion which is sharable with all DNA, sacred space is thus catalyzed. Seeking balance between the two cerebral hemispheres or two natures is necessary to receive the higher knowledge which exists as frequency. The uptake of that information, requires receptors resonating at the complimentary frequency achieved by entering the fornix. Emotion and logic convey awareness to this frequency specific 'feeling'. Feeling is a sacred interface of kinesthetic gnosis merging with the 'All-That-Is and knowing it. Emotion is simply a carrier energy transporting your awareness to the furnace or Fornix where you may choose to remove the dross by entering sacred alchemical transformation of the Refiner's fire and Crucible.

Stria Pinealis is the medical name for the connection that runs from the Pineal Gland of the brain into the fornix. Mythically it is the fire that travels to the furnace to ignite it. The furnace is recognized cosmically as the constellation Fornax. Supernova 1987a is the cosmic 3rd eye or Pineal actively participating in the tantric dance of our cosmic kundalini.

Acknowledged and viewed by scientists around the globe, Supernova 1987a ignited as the liquid fire travelling to the constellation Fornax, igniting the long heralded coming of the great light upon the earth.

On a practical level, such meditation that activates kundalini energy assists us to rise above any thoughts contained in turbulent emotion. By proverbially placing the pineal stone upon the delta alter, we leave the ego behind and cross over into the promised land of milk and honey. The chosen land of milk and honey is the higher mind arrived at by first driving out the lower mind or those biblically metaphoric Canaanites. Once the lower mind has relinquished control, sacred transformation can occur by renewing the mind. The Gospel of the Holy Twelve ("The Gospel of the Holy Twelve: 82:26:" n.d., p. 01) 'When Jesus therefore had received the vinegar, he said, "It is finished". And he bowed his head and gave up the ghost. And it was in the ninth hour'. The ghost he allegedly gave up represents the death of ego. Meditation immersed in the state of pure principle creates the frictionless spin to dissipate any influence from the ego mind. The sacred interface is here, between physicality as matter and anti-matter, yet encompasses them both. The wave of charge that rises and falls yet remains stationary stores inertia to become mass whereas the wave of charge that rotates is negentropic creating an interval effecting the very definition of time. Through meditation, the holy grail of wellness is found when this wave becomes centripetal and implodes as bliss. Flowing through the lemniscate pattern of figure-eight radiation and contraction, as inflow and out flow of breath, serves to reinforce the expansion into counter-rotating fields. Initially, this may feel like a psychedelic experience from the 60's, but with a little consistent practice, the 'inner psychonaut' will fully command navigation with ease. Prior to meditation in AcuLomi Temple workshops, this science about how the natural world works, is intellectually developed to provide explanations. Having met the intellectual and mental resolution, the mind is then freed to delve fully into the experiential 'feeling' quality of meditation without the dispersions of self-doubt eroding that subtle boundary of creative freedom. Discoveries may replace existing hypothetical explanations, refine or incorporate logically coherent explanations of phenomena. A specific meditation model coupled with relevant analytical data represents the current understanding of science while providing criteria for evaluating analysis to interpret novel data. The proceedings of this science evaluate, and communicate information that is progressive, knowledge- and solution-directed. As such, engaging in these practices afford collaboration, reflectiveness and openness to share innovative ideas. The results derived in developing these skills not only nourish life, but also develop and use models representing relevant testable features of scientific explanations and applied design. By employing a unified theory to meditation and enlisting self-similar fractality as the premise for substantiating findings, the principle hologram theory allows meditation (not defined by dimension within a light field) freedom to interpret the vector function. This methodology provides compelling evidence that supports the monistic idealism of the consciousness down model described by Amit Goswami. "In searching for the fundamental basis of physical reality and the nature of the mind, Goswami has defined consciousness as, the agency that affects quantum objects to make their behavior sensible. Amit Goswami, PhD proposed a theory of consciousness, rather than atoms, as the fundamental reality of the material world". (Miller, 1993, p. 01) A paradox-free meditation, likewise affirms consistency and coherence. Utilizing known celestial mapping as the backdrop for inner navigation satisfies validation of findings which perfectly bridge the scriptures of sacred texts with Astrotheology incorporating the human body and astronomy, to describe the Universal body.

The journey which Supernova 1987a has traversed through the cosmos, matches the physical description and behavior of the activated pineal gland of the brain. By drawing a straight line from Supernova 1987a, which starts in the constellation Mensa, passes through Dorado, Hydrus, Reticulum, Horoglium, Eridanus to conclusively enter Fornax is the precise duplicate pattern which occurs during the ascension of kundalini.

The principle significance of correlating the path of Supernova 1987a (the cosmic pineal) to the constellation Fornax is illustrated by correlating formal descriptions of the physical elements.

Familiarity with the layout of this design enables the meditator to recognize landmarks and more accurately gauge resonance patterns. By having learned prior to the meditative experience that a promontory marker defines sides formed by the optic thalami that are limited above by a delicate band of white fibers, will identify the stria pinealis, (the word stria means a line…in this case from the pineal) which runs along the junction of the mesial and upper surfaces of the optic thalamus to join the anterior pillars of the fornix. Understanding the principles of this inward journey allow for a context richness in decoding the individual landmarks along the way.

Beginning in the Megallanic Cloud in the constellation Mensa expresses the exploration begins at the Lord's table. Megallan Ferdinand was an explorer that the celestial body was named after as well as a mountain in Africa. The next constellation closely located to Hydrus, representing serpentine Kundalini energy flowing through the spinal fluid is Dorado, which means 'the fish of gold or sword fish'. The fish plays a highly significant role in ancient mythology regarding both religion and DNA as a connection to God or spirit. Jesus is Biblically portrayed as the fish and often refers to having come with a sword. Hydrus, the water snake affords gnosis of compressed wisdom. The lesser but intriguing water snake is a fitting tribute to the cosmic dance of ritual blossoming. "Hydrus was the protogenos of the primordial waters. In the Orphic Theogonies, (Meade, n.d., p. 01) Water was the first being to emerge alongside Creation (Thesis) and Mud. The primordial mud solidified into Gaia (Earth) and with Hydros produced Khronos (Time) and Ananke (Compulsion), the protogenos of inevitability, compulsion and necessity. The mate of Khronos, like him, was an incorporeal serpentine being who twisted circling around the whole of creation. These two in turn caught the early cosmos in their coils, and split it apart to form the god Phanes (creator of life), and the four ordered elements of Heaven; Fire, Earth, Air and Sea, or Water." The constellation Hydrus is positioned right at the mouth of the long celestial river, Eridanus, denoting rivers flowing into seas or oceans. Hydrus has notably endured more redesigns than any other constellation. Undulating along its ratified path of newly allotted stars from neighboring constellations Horologium and Reticulum, this dynamic region of outer space reflects the gossamer design of inner space. The celestial map charting its course of rapturous Kundalini has enjoyed the unswerving ambit of an arrow straight through these constellations. Enroute to conclusive combustion in Delta Fornicas, Supernova 1987A's explosive departure defines the path travelled by cosmic and human kundalini energy alike. This stellar yoga meanders along its serpentine path through the constellation Hydrus, relaying the photonic torch from Dorado, the Swordfish and Mensa the Table, to Reticulum. with its net-like pattern. Heavenly mirrored to replicate arachnoid as the net or veil, Reticulum emphasizes separation of the outer part of the brain Dura Mater, from the inner Pia Mater. Thus mystically, we are entering into the most sensitive sanctum. Symbols of individuation flowing through the spiral channels of Sushumna seek creative crescendo. Sushumna is a term borrowed from Hindu philosophy which is associated with the energy of kundalini. Kundalini is said to uncoil and enter sushumna through the Brahma dwara or gate of Brahma at the base of the spine. Just as negative and positive forces of electricity flow through complex circuits, so too does prana shako (vital force) and manas shako (mental force) flow through every part of heavenly bodies via extra-dimensional nadis. The nadi, which means 'stream' include the seven main chakras forming a network of subtle channels through which the life force (prana) circulates. The human brain is thus a fascinating duplication of galactic activity expressing the greater conscious pulse. This cosmic star map follows seven constellations igniting the fuse-line from Supernova 1987A in the constellation Mensa to its defining crescendo in constellation Fornax. The human brain map likewise provides stria pinealis as the same fuse-line to correspondingly conflagrate, or catch fire, sevenfold connecting the pineal gland, through the chakras, before consecrating the Fornix.

The mysterious maestro of consciousness, or the Great Creator of pure source energy, is quantifying precise celestial transformation as human evolution. The cosmic fish constellation Dorado is reminiscent of the furnace analogy in the book of Daniel in that the Dorado constellation resonates in accord with the return to a four-fold nature. The ancestor-god-fishman, "Oannes" [Enki/Ea/John/Nimrod], dating back over 5000 /7000 years to ancient Sumerian/Babylonian times respectively, comes out of the water to facilitate a renewed connection to the hallowed but invisible place of origin of our DNA. Like Daniel, this mythological tale is about rectifying the covert domination of human nature by 'louche', meaning derivatives of the lower instincts/emotions such as fear and greed. the return to full consciousness or the four-fold nature of mankind remains dormant until the 'furnace' is heated seven times. This means the fire of kundalini must rise up through the seven chakras, pass through the Pineal by casting the proverbial net to the right in order to reach the [Delta Fornix] furnace.

Passing the cosmic firelight through seven constellations signals the physical, intellectual and emotional natures as pledged in dedication, to the fourth, or spiritual attribute, initiating the return to full consciousness.

Spirit, as such, is said to appear in the furnace. The fire is said to be heated seven times, denoting ignition intensified at each ascending chakra. Likewise, in passing through the seven constellations, the celestial fire is heated seven times. In so doing, the invoked fourth or spiritual attribute, aka the sacred God-Spark interface, becomes available to elevate the physical, intellectual and emotional natures. Having issued forth in graduation of the first level of brain-mind activation, into the second level experienced within the cosmic fish constellation Dorado, dynamic escalation into the third level is summoned. Coming up out of the water denotes the first elevated stage of consciousness achieved through meditation. It is above the physical or lower mind. So it is, that the fishman "Oannes," comes out of the water to coax, educate and galvanize the repaired connection to the exalted Source we strive to reclaim through meditation. Swept along in the stream of kundalini to be recalibrated seven times in the rising and refining forces of each nexus point along the way, awareness of a greater consciousness becomes evident. Identifying with Hydrus, as compassion in the Life-Giving Waters, describes the key electro positions of the brain mind as divided into 5 symbolic elements. These identify the levels of activation during meditation which follows relevant analytical preparation:

1. EARTH: The Lowest. Physical, brain, lower mind
2. WATER: This is the first elevated stage of consciousness achieved through meditation. It is above the physical or lower mind of intellectual identification.
3. AIR: This is the next elevated stage achieved through meditation. It is above water and attained through the absence of thought. Separating from thought initiates the reclamation process.
4. FIRE: This is the highest level of the brain mind achieved through meditation which produces the fifth stage, the New Mind.
5. NEW MIND: Achievement of Christ consciousness, or Krishna, or compassion of Buddha consciousness through meditation.

The principles of the journey lay intellectual traction and maintain holistic cognition throughout the process.

Observing the Observer

Take no thought in meditation. Be as an empty vessel, for this is when the key will activate your new mind. Let go of all thoughts. Transit through the zero-point of the synapse is a literal crossing over which transcends intellectual concepts. This passover is analogous to the transitional state of "becoming." As in the exchange between two nerve cells passing impulses by diffusing neurotransmitters, this same action occurs within the synapse interfacing the sacred space of the God-Spark. The word synapse is derived from the Greek words syn (together) and haptein (to clasp). At the hub of the synapse lives eternal conscious potential. Compassion is the requirement for creating a phase conjugate or 'shareable' intention, and the next phase is only accessible by releasing desire, which is synonymous to an act of faith. Letting go is the essential component for crossing the synapse to be actualized; however, you must be ready to pick up the frequency imprint on the other side. Autonomy, out of which the manifest form of perceptions can emerge creatively, as unconditioned acts of perception within the All-That-Is, do require their own life-breath. In other words, for your perceptions to manifest they must be set free. Imagine your idea or perception of the potential you wish to manifest as a small rubber ball held in your hand. The act of setting your perception free is no different than releasing that ball… you just open your hand and let it go. However, just before it hits the ground you grab that ball right out of mid-air. Now you can once again feel the ball in your hand, perhaps you notice more detail or other subtle nuances about the ball previously ignored. Each time you release and reclaim that ball, your awareness of it sharpens. You get to know it better. As your mind becomes receptive to the subtle fields of information and the many levels of consciousness interacting with that ball of perception, Implicate Order begins to unveil Oneness as the holographic template of all existence. This methodology of negentropic navigation, observe the action of cosmic creative intelligence amplifying the feedback of new meaning. As such, infinite expansion and contraction of the pristine plasma in a quantum wave evolves. Engaging the elements as directed above, spark new circuits, exhibiting the cosmic power in the sacred God-Spark interface. Observe your experience from a third-party like perspective to hold the conscious awareness of both your matter self and anti-matter self. Photons are light quanta. There is an information transfer between matter and light during the act of observation. Photons transduce from virtual (nonordered) to normal (ordered) photon energy through photon/antiphoton pairs. The subtle worlds opened by this process tune out petty desire for the coherent or shareable Divine blueprint. Restoration from your divine blueprint directs a flow of awareness by the light and phenomena within you, for this IS you, and this is your path to that divine blueprint as the observed, observing the observer.

Bill Donahue of Hidden Meanings (Donahue, n.d., p. 01) applies this methodology to decrypt the biblical story of Jesus walking on the water. True teaching is an awakening of consciousness. Bill teaches that when you rise to the second level of meditation you have arrived at the emotional body expressed as water. By rising beyond the emotional body to meet Jesus in the air (as we are instructed in 1Thessalonians 4:17) ("1 Thessalonians 4:17," p. 01) implies that the mental thoughts are beginning to disappear. Thessalonians said of rapture, "Then we who are alive and remain shall be caught up together with them in the clouds, to meet the Lord in the air" or in the realm of no-thought. The realm of no-thought is the 3rd level of meditation. The fourth level corresponds with the Baptism of Fire as recorded in Matthew 3:11 ("Matthew 3:11," n.d., p. 01): "I indeed baptize you with water unto repentance: but he that comes after me is mightier than I, whose shoes I am not worthy to bear: he shall baptize you with the Holy Ghost, and with fire." Notice that John the Baptist represents the lower meditation states of earth, water, and air. Then Jesus to come, represents the higher states of fire and the new mind. As it says in Psalm 11 ("Psalm 11," n.d., p. 01), "In the Lord I put my trust: how you say to my soul, flee as a bird to your mountain"? In this way, meditation facilitates the ascension to that higher place of the mind.

The human individual expresses three aspects, Physical, Intellectual, and Emotional. The fourth however is spirit as the sacred interface or Beloved God-Spark, which comes into existence during meditation when the 7th seal is opened, and the state expressed as fire stimulates the pineal gland. Cosmically, Eta Carina (the 7th Angel) and Supernova 1987a (the 7th seal), has already become activated and testified to the baptism of water and fire. The meditative process follows rising from Earth into water, through air into fire. Just as water and fire change states to become steam or mist, these quantum changes in the brain mind are achieved during the meditative state.

Recognizing the hippocampus as the place of memory in the human brain by ancient and modern-day authorities alike has ordained Pegasus of Greek mythology to be the vehicle for the return of all great prophets heralding in the time of peace. Likewise, in the heavens is also an organ of the cosmic brain which correlates to the memory. It is the white horse constellation called Pegasus. Poseidon, god of the sea, was the father of Pegasus, god of earthquakes and horses and brother of Zeus. Pegasus of the human brain is connected to the function of memory. The memory organ of the brain is the hippocampus, which translates to mean Sea Horse. To the Goddess of Memory named Mnemosyne, Pegasus is considered sacred. Mnemosyne was considered one of the most powerful goddesses of her time. It was believed that memory distinguished humankind from the other creatures in the animal world. Hers was the gift that allows reason, predictions and anticipation of outcomes, emphasizing the very foundation for civilization. She was also given responsibility for naming all objects, and by doing so gave humans the means to dialog and converse with each other. Initiates were taken to the spring of Mnemosyne to drink so that they would remember all they might learn from the oracle. In Stedman's Medical Dictionary, the Hippocampus Major or Cornu Ammonis is described as 'a white eminence.' (Stedman, 2000, expression H) The Hippocampus of the human brain is a White Sea horse associated with memory. In the New Testament, Jesus is said to return on a white horse at the time of our ascension and return to Christ consciousness. He returns to you when you return to him in remembrance of the parallel and subtle worlds. In the hippocampus is an organ called Ammons Horn. Ammon is the Egyptian deity whose symbol is the Ram Head. Bill Donahue says, "So we obviously do not need more religiosity to solve our problems. We need more RAM." (Donahue, 2012, p. 01) Through mythology, the Earthly, limited three-dimensional plane can know the touch of the infinite creator and the nerve-center of our origins. Once the ego is thrown into the fiery cauldron of transformation, freedom from this taskmaster of pseudo-authority restores harmony with all nature, and the hologram portal to our ancestors will become available through our DNA. The action of confronting fear, removes the veils of separation to instead be understood as an illusion, thus transcribing an important shift to the quality and source of the meditative experience. Unlike the alchemical first stage of Calcination (from Latin 'calcinare' - to burn lime), where we were alone in our battle with the ego, after renewal by fire, we sense another force assisting us: it is our Beloved God-Spark waiting to observe the observer.

Solar Principle of the 8

Hermetic knowledge of the seals (chakras) and Supernova 1987a, speak of a shared kundalini experience in Oneness. Electrical energy moves up the seven chakras to impact the pineal gland, thus bringing forth spiritual enlightenment as an eight-step process. Examination of mystical literature and traditions shows that kundalini, called by various names, has been a universal phenomenon in esoteric teachings for at least three thousand years. Kundalini-type descriptions or experiences are found in esoteric teachings of the Egyptians, Tibetans, Chinese, Native Americans, and the Kung bushmen of Africa, among others.

Kundalini has been interpreted as "the solar principle in man," and is referenced in the Koran, the works of Plato and other Greek philosophers, alchemical tracts (the philosopher's stone), and in Hermetic, Kabbalistic, Rosicrucian, and Masonic writings. Typically, the yogi will meditate to arouse the kundalini, causing this electric-like energy to rise through the seven chakras which perform as resistors throughout the body. This energy then travels up the subtle pathways referred to as nadis, which exist parallel to the spinal column. The central axis is called the sushumna and is crisscrossed in a helix sequence by the ida and pingala. Traditionally personified as masculine and feminine principle within duality, it also represents logic and intuition. (Sadhguru, n.d., p. 01) As energy rises through kundalini exercise, the chakras are activated in succession. The objective is to raise the kundalini to the crown chakra, where it impacts the pineal to bring about spiritual illumination.

The human brain is an electrical circuit necessitating resistors, as with any electrical circuit. The neural plexus and endocrine glands, which relate to the specific chakras, provide this function as resistors. As the kundalini current is brought up from the base of the spine through meditation, the chakras act as resistors to provide a safeguard from any danger of triggering a wild-fire of kundalini heat, resulting in an overload of specific neural circuits. Higher consciousness gently guides electrical energy to engage the seven chakras via the stria pinealis to awaken humankind to their higher natures. The relevance of hearing devotional seekers chanting 'Ohm' is reflected in the contemporary and universal measurement of electrical resistance. As testimony from the Emerald Tablet reads: "Tis true without falsehood, and most real: that which is above is like that which is below, to perpetrate the miracles of One thing. And as all things have been derived from One, by the thought of One, so all things are born from One by adoption". ("Emerald tablets," n.d., p. 01) The phrase 'As above, so below', brings attention to the series of energies required to excite an electron in hydrogen from its lowest energy state to a higher energy state; this applies to meditation as well.

The case of interest for cosmology is when a hydrogen atom with its electron in the lowest energy configuration gets hit by a photon (light wave) and is boosted to the next closest energy level. Similarly, the universal mind (as above) represents the human mind (as below) in having many high-energy photons and hydrogen atoms working in both the absorption and emission of photons. In Lyman alpha systems, the hydrogen is found in regions in space, and the source for the photons are quasars, very high-energy light sources shining at us from behind these regions. In the human mind, the same source of high-energy light, reverentially referred to as God, is said to be a bright light that no one can approach, that no one has ever seen or can see.

Eta Carina fits that description well. The brightest light in the known universe pours out invisible ultraviolet light at one and a half million miles per hour. This great light from the space vacuum is a photon field. PhysOrg.com ("Scientists create light from vacuum," 2011, p. 01) writes about how scientists at Chalmers University of Technology succeeded in creating light from vacuum, observing an effect first predicted in 1970 by a physicist named Moore. He predicted that this should happen if virtual photons bounced off a mirror (aka SQUID, a superconducting quantum interference device) that is moving at a speed near speed of light. The phenomenon, known as the "dynamical Casimir effect," has been observed to transfer kinetic energy and materialize virtual photons. Speaking relatively, little energy is required in order to excite photons out of their virtual state to appear in pairs from the vacuum, validating the radiation properties based on Quantum Theory. Since the tetrahedron grid is the structure of vacuum, and the structure of vacuum is photon, we can look to mythological sources for resonance. The Emerald Tablets clearly elucidates the significance of the photon, as Thoth is often seen holding the Tetrahedron Photon or Great Light in his right hand. Similarly, in the Bible, scripture says that God is not a man, but light. Thus, in holding a photon, Thoth is holding God, and likewise, he is holding universal consciousness. Eta Carina is pouring out universal consciousness to transform life on Earth.

Physicists John Wheeler and Richard Feynman calculated the zero-point radiation of the quantum electrodynamic vacuum (QED) vacuum to be an order of magnitude greater than nuclear energy. (Ward, n.d., p. 01) In this context, it is no wonder that Nassim Haramein says, "May the Vacuum be with you". (Haramein, 2012, p. 01) The Emerald Tablets date back to time which historians conclude could be anywhere from 12,000 to 38,000 years or more and therefore, so does the symbol of the photon. The fundamental reality in the Emerald Tablet is expressed in what is called the eight-sided Octagenic Stone. The ancient Egyptian Octad inscribed the eight qualities of creation, which were kept in the temple of Hermopolis. Named from the Coptic 'Shmoun,' which is in turn derived from the Egyptian 'Khemenu' or City of the Eight, these eight qualities of creation refer to the four pairs of frog (the male element) and snake (the female element) who were worshiped there. Thoth was principal of this group of eight deities or eons symbolizing the state of the world prior to creation. (Verner, 2013, Chapter 04) Similarly, the Mayan calendar of Eight is synonymous with Pacal Votan, Thoth, the UFO commander and Jesus. The number eight is also highly significant to the human body. In the division of every human cell, a process known as mitosis takes place, which involves a sequence of seven transformation steps, resulting in an equal dividing of genetic material—and, in the eighth step, the creation of a new cell. The infinity figure 8 has held significance echoed throughout all cultures and all ages. Eight is the number of Pagan Sabbats celebrated each year to convey traditional teaching via a wheel like representation of perpetual cycle. Nostradamus believed that the great earth change would take place when the constellations Ophiuchus, Sagittarius, and Scorpio align, at which point the Sun will be at the center of their formation. That occurred on December 21, 2012 at 11:11am. Nostradamus presents this in drawings within his work, which features the wheel of eight. (Leoni, 2000, p. 01)

The drawing which Nostradamus used to show the constellation alignment on December 21, 2012, creates 8 points of the symbol of the Coptic key that legend says Jesus gave to the Coptic Gnostics of Egypt. ("Coptic key," n.d., p. 02) He allegedly said that this key would take one to the highest realm. The Coptic Key symbol from Jesus is the wheel of eight. The number 8 figures all pointed to Dec 21, 2012, as if to say that the sign has already taken place in the cosmos and is now awaiting only the human observer to activate the photon enabling them to perceive the Star Nations of the Emerald Tablets. The Hermetic goal of life is "gnosis" or an inner awakening in the light coming forth from God's Mind which is portrayed as an entrance in the supernatural strata of being, the Ogdoad, which borders the natural world and the Ennead. (the Ennead were the great Osirian gods)

The eight-pointed star is the Star of Redemption or regeneration and represents baptism. The figure eight is traditionally the symbol for infinity, the number of regeneration, and thus many baptismal fonts have an octagonal base. Providing added significance is the assumption that Jesus was circumcised and named when he was eight days old according to traditional Jewish practice. Baptism can be thought of as the New Testament equivalent of circumcision. Eight people were saved in Noah's ark, which is another Old Testament parallel of baptism: "When his son Isaac was eight days old, Abraham circumcised him, as God commanded him" (Genesis 21:4, NIV). Also, referenced by the KJV Holy Bible is this clause, "they formerly did not obey, when God's patience waited in the days of Noah while the ark was being prepared, in which eight persons were brought safely through water. Baptism, which corresponds to this, now saves you, not as a removal of dirt from the body but as an appeal to God for a good conscience, through the resurrection of Jesus Christ, who has gone into heaven and is at the right hand of God" (1 Peter 3:18-22, ESV).

Plato left little room to doubt that he subscribed wholeheartedly to the historical description of Atlantis and its repeated cataclysms. Nine thousand years before Plato's conversation was recorded as per Plato's Atlantis Dialogues; (c. 400 B.C.), a war took place between Athens and Atlantis. This was the source, says Plato, of the "impenetrable mud," which prevents passage beyond the Pillars of Heracles and across the Atlantic. Plato's description of Atlantis came shortly after the Jews were in exile in Babylon (c.600 B.C.) and were taking history lessons from Sumerian texts that contained the missing pre-history to the Hebrew Book of Genesis. These texts speak of a massive cataclysm that destroyed an advanced race. They tell how the Sumerian gods Enki and Ninharsag intervened in the evolution of humanity and created an advanced civilization that was destroyed and how they assisted in the long march to renewing civilization. These beings were the Shining Ones of Eden and early biblical times. In Plato's Atlantis story Enki became Poseidon, the ruler of the Atlantis, father of Pegasus and therefore the hope of mankind's return to full consciousness. In comparing text from the Holy Bible KJV and Emerald Tablets, many examples exist to suggest that messages from Thoth the Priest-King in the Emerald Tablets were also recorded in the Bible (Donahue, 2011, p. 01) For example, Emerald Tablet (E.T.) – "I began this incarnation from aeon to aeon where the river of life flows eternally". Jesus- "He that believes in me, out of his being shall flow rivers of living water. E.T.- "I descend but in a time yet unborn I will rise again for surely will I return". Jesus – "I go away and come again unto you. Tell no one until the Son of Man be risen again". E.T. – "I dwelt in the land of Khem doing great works- Jesus-" The father will show me greater works than these that you may marvel" ET- "Lift ever upwards your eyes toward the light" Jesus- "I am the light of the world; He that follows me shall have the light of the world". The Emerald Tablets description of being saved from the fountains and standing on the mountain again reflects the Bible story of Noah and the ark resting on the mountain after the flood. "Some who were living were standing on the mountain out of the water saved from the rush of the fountains where as in Genesis God remembered Noah and those living with him and the ark rested upon the mountains of Ararat". These many representations of the Solar Principle of the 8 unveil themselves as solar deities or sun gods forever preserving an open channel of communication throughout time. In the Hebrew Gematria, the Tetragrammaton along with all the sun gods, summed to 8 or the master number 888.

Mystic Bliss

Mystic knowledge can only be known by direct experience and cannot be gained through even the wisest of intellectual explanations. The journey of self-discovery that true mystics embark upon and that sincere philosophers aspire to, yields true knowledge. In truth, there is no enlightenment outside oneself. Confucius is reputed to have best illustrated this lesson with his saying: "When the wise man points at the Moon, the idiot looks at the finger." (Miller, n.d., p. 01) So too we must not be distracted by the pointing device called meditation, but rather let it be the guide which opens the door to personal experience with Oneness. Mystic knowledge is a coherent single-source of light produced in harmony with Oneness. The explanation, analysis and step-by-step instruction of meditation is but the finger pointing the way. It is only the direct personal experience garnered during meditation which can offer any knowledge of Oneness. Blissful experiences of enlightenment can only arise when ego and the mind are silent. The mystic's self-initiated path confronts an aspect of emergent psychedelic illumination to ultimately arrive at the final phase of stabilized integration by uniting the black and white facets of duality. Deep within stillness exists a vital anchor. It is a counter vibration equal and opposite to the frequency of stillness. When comprehended exclusively as frequency, these combined energies potently express zero-point energy. At the higher levels of pure consciousness alchemy, this dynamic potentization is universal dance of a catalyst. The dance conveys a charge through the catalyst to stimulate the vital force which in turn creates the material results. The zero-point however must be activated. Activation is the result of alchemical transformations which occur when various components of a frequency are separated out, refined, and put back together to form the wholly transformed version of what you started with. On any level of the equation, light remains key to understanding activation. Human consciousness interacts with light in the unlimited quantum field. The Bible explicitly defines God as Light in many passages such as 1 John 1:5 New International Version (NIV) where it reads "This is the message we have heard from him and declare to you: God is light; in him there is no darkness at all". ("1 John 1:5," n.d., p. 01) Further, the Bible also explicitly refers to mankind as light in Matthew 5:14 New International Version (NIV), "You are the light of the world…". It is in the power of distilling pure principle as the coherent state where our heart and mind are in true harmony and yield bliss that we experience ourselves as light or photon. The Photon eternally exists as our true selves and remains constant throughout all stages of physical life. Physicist John Cramer photon has found that photons navigate time unrestricted by soul and spirit (Tveter, 2001, p. 01) Everything is potential until the vital force receives that charge conveying the pure principle. Activating a sacred space catalyst to convey a higher state of love, compassion, gratitude or harmony, implosively compresses bliss. The late physicist Arthur Young says that the physicist's photon is the mystics divine light. (Miller, n.d., p. 01) That is because, the energy determined to be soul and spirit, is actually photon. In the world of light there is no time, space, or mass. Photons have complete freedom since they are independent of spacetime and are at the top of the causal chain. By meditatively traversing the primary chakras, represented in the cosmos 'as above' while the 'so below' element is represented by the human body, a fractal resonance impression literal imprints the energy body. University of Kyoto in Japan took pictures of people in a space with no light. Using a time lapse camera with open lens the researchers could photograph the body's photon. (Takumi Yamada, Yasuhiro Yamada, Yumi Nakaike, Atsushi Wakamiya, and Yoshihiko Kanemitsu, 2017, p. 01) The meditation elements delineate light photon as the bridge between observer and observed. Being and doing and "do be do be doing," as Amit Goswami would say. "It is not just do do do. It is not just be be be. It is do be do be do". – Amit Goswami. ("Amit Goswami Quotes," n.d., p. 01) The implication is that when we are doing, we are in ego. Conversely, when we are being, we are aligned with the Grand Designer of non-local consciousness and pure source energy. This illuminates' meditation and mindfulness as ways to be. The acknowledgement likewise affirms the assurance of affecting morphogenetic fields to produce a harmonious transformation and evolution of human experience. Overall, a system of analytical data provided as a workshop prior to meditation, provides and explains specific steps to not only initiate the interface frequency required to access one's sacred space, but also permit reproducible connectivity with ease. Friedrich Nietzsche described meditation as the "cave of inwardness." ("Nietzsche," n.d., p. 01) Imagine seeing the Universe as a giant brain to begin down the Mystic's path to this place. A zoom lens provides increasing magnifications taking you deeper until reaching the landscape perspective of the molecular level. From this perspective, the human body now appears equal in vastness to the cosmos as above. The molecular level, representing so below, is simply duplicated on a smaller scale. Following the Mystic path ever inward to deeper magnifications and inflowing perspectives permits an energetic inversion of awareness to take place.

Temple Arts suggest cognitive access to a black hole and the Holy Grail only remains elusive until meditation is recognized as the lost creative principle, or point-of-access. Expressed as the healing powers of love, the shape of the Holy Grail is a cup within a cup thus it has no inside, or outside which solves the problem of separation. The practice of meditation likewise creates an internal environment in perfect fractal self-reference to the whole or 'One' to expand human consciousness. In fact, meditation is one of the most essential exercises available for discovering the human environment, both inner and outer. Meditation gives access to the secret teachings of all ages. Meditation reveals the formula of non-judgmental observation of the vital force, which is the power that animates the whole organism. Meditation conveys the creative principle in communion with the center point of perfect embedding as the environment which controls biology. Epigenetics, as described by Dr. Bruce Lipton, (Lipton, n.d., p. 01) further validates meditation as signal transduction creating coherence. The workshop-meditation system, implements breathing techniques and awareness of breath to reinforce and amplify messages both to and from the human environments. The in-breath is the opportunity to interact with an extended external macro-quantum entangled Multiverse as the Void self-expressing as Eternity because it serves as the moment of surrender or "pause" where the vast expansion becomes so great that all is lost to the moment of crossing the threshold of the event horizon. The breath also facilitates the figure eight inducing the holy grail to arise in form. Likewise, the exhale continues the perfect embedding on every scale. Visualizing the breath as following a figure eight or lemniscate pattern reinforces the fractal message of phase conjugation embedding as a wormhole which becomes a vehicle for the expansion of awareness. In this way, the workshop-meditation system integrates breathing non-destructive charge to derive meaningful fellowship of sacred space accessing the universal Sacred Mind. Stepping across the threshold into some seeming great abyss is quite enough to overwhelm the intellect of the simply curious seeker. However, those who mindfully anchor the understanding that "everything is One" will engage feeling to transcend mental constructs, thus revealing all phenomena as manifestations of the same ultimate reality. The Cobra does not fear its own venom any more than the jaguar its roar; so too, the seeker mindful of their emersion in Oneness may freely journey through all worlds. The beloved God-Spark acts as a sacred interface to the All-That-Is, facilitating a connection between the eternal "one" you to the ever-changing "many" you(s) expressed through the Infinite Consciousness. The One and the Many cannot be mentally apprehended by desire alone, but only through awareness and the gnosis of intuition's guidance. The One is eternal, yet the Many (entities such as people, planets and stars) are temporal and experience time. Similarly, space is eternal and does not experience time. Time is motion. It is not possible to step into the same river twice, according to Heraclitus: here constancy and change are not opposed but inextricably connected. ("Heraclitus," n.d., p. 01) A human body could be understood in precisely the same way, as living and continuing by virtue of constant metabolism—as Aristotle for instance, later understood it. Heraclitus taught that flux is not destructive of constancy, but rather paradoxically, is a necessary condition of constancy. Similarly, to paraphrase Plutarch, we cannot come into contact with a mortal being twice in the same state. (Dolen, n.d., p. 01) A context richness occurs within the concept of simultaneously co-existing as a concrete unity of opposed determinations. The principle point of divine completeness is to behold absolute experience of opposites by transcending the interdependence. Empowerment is realized by the dynamic union of opposed elements.

Transcending intellectual concepts is analogous to the transitional state of 'becoming', as demonstrated in the exchange between two nerve cells, passing impulses by diffusion of a neurotransmitter. This action occurs within synapses. At the hub of a synapse lives eternal conscious potential, which house myriad intersecting pathways or opportunities.

Through electromagnetic induction, or voltage of opposite polarity, the induced magnetic field can be used to close circuits and can thereby enable lucid steering within the synapse to affect intentional objectives. Much like learning any language, these pathways are frequencies that can be sequenced as a map to access specific topics or regions within the great conscious One.

The language of shape is the language of magnetism which is the language of charge. Plasma domains describe waves converging as sacred letters at conjugate angles creating centripetal force accessing the collective unconsciousness. Each subtle nuance of infinite frequencies can be so similar as to create an overlapping precipitate known as the Mandala Effect. ("The Mandela Effect," 2017, p. 01) To deliberately invoke the Mandela Effect is to categorically access highly specific frequency sequencing. Parallel timelines can, in this way, intersect known junctions and interface with existing properties to result in super-imposed tones. Conversely, other frequencies, such as those derived through psychoactive drugs and neurotoxins, can change the properties of neurotransmitter release, neurotransmitter reuptake, and the availability of receptor binding sites. This too is a steering device clasping together alternative and sometimes opportunistic effects, such as the sense of alleged 'memories'. Counter memories observed as the Mandela Effect provide glimpses into parallel worlds previously enshrouded in veiled density. Mindful lucidity during the meditation encourages cognitive awareness in the current of that which lays behind the veil. With discernment and practice, this veil continues to dissipate, whereby the ever-present God-Spark becomes more accessible.

Meditation is but one example of a potential path to activate sacred space. Achieving resonance with your God-Spark by activating sacred space contains the essential tour de force to magnetize and align your highest good in coherence with pure energy. To capture your experience at these alternative levels of being requires an open channel permitting both Alpha and Beta brain frequency to translate vorticity congruous to longitudinal wave mechanics of lucid dreaming. Alchemical studies demonstrate the process of grounding or securing the subtle illuminations for convenient access any time, in or out of meditation. Referred to as holding open the channel of Distillation, (Osborn, n.d., p. 01) the frequency of your experience requires a carrier frequency, permitting the transportation of higher frequencies such as Alpha waves to be discerned in Beta. Lucid tracking of combinations such as the Alpha and Beta brainwave, cause charge to compress and implode resulting in Peak Experience or the euphoria of bliss. Peak Experience activates Phi harmonics of the brain and heart at these moments of self-reference as self-awareness and produces a perfect growth path seen as phyllotaxis to assure coherence while participating in the workshop-meditation system. (Winter, n.d., p. 01) As such, pure intention sustained through meditation is superconductive and commissions Scientists and Engineers to speak of spiritual traditions while providing Theosophists and Mystical Leaders the availability of mathematical solutions to visionary and spiritual experiences. Charge distribution efficiency is the definition of Sacred Space. Sacred Space is the frequency address of the sacred God-Spark interface. The resonance of this frequency enables conventional human attention to evolve from basic transverse EMF to consciously track the front of longitudinal waves accessing All-That-Is. As longitudinal waves are not restricted by matter or speed of light, yet do preserve the condition for self-embeddability or self-reference, a language of fractality as described by Dan Winter- in his paper on Phi mathematics provides a derivation of the Hebrew Alphabet and 'precipitation' or non-destructive charge compression. (Winter, 2012, p. 01) In other words, the knack for remembering information from the subtle worlds is developed much like any language is learned. Association, in and of itself, contains the trigger element through which the volatile or essence is withdrawn and grounded into Beta frequency. Keep in mind this occurs via kinesthetic feeling, as opposed to mental effort. "Electrical self-similarity fabricates information rich charge compression - that gives rise to the electrical phenomenon we call mind or awareness..." – Dan Winter (ISSUU [ISSUU], 2010, p. 01)

Accordingly, the transformative properties demonstrated by the alchemical process of distillation likewise explains the meditative experience as a translation of vorticity like lucid dreaming is to the volatile ascending. What Oriental alchemists called the Circulation of Light, (Morrell, 2003, p. 01) eventually becomes exalted as a crystallizing light full of power. Distillation is said to culminate in the Third Eye are of the forehead, at the Level of the pituitary and pineal glands, in the Brow or Ajna Silver Chakra. Containing the fixed solution of the greater good,

Fixing is like holding the awareness. Awareness of the subtler energies in one's mind, by distillation of lower everyday consciousness to higher subtler consciousness, requires a certain commitment to engaging the higher awareness, to ensure the journey beyond the synapse is more than just random wanderings. Distillation refers to the transformational stage of being spiritually and emotionally mature enough to merge with the collective conscious and unconscious despite coming face to face with the equal and opposite energies of our archetypal ideals. It heralds the influence of higher forces needed to bring balance to baser energies, thus 'grounding' wholeness into three-dimensional Earth experience. The ancient Egyptians personified this wisdom as the Neter, or force, known as Tehuti, or Thoth to the Greeks. A 'distilled' person is noted by the confidence of being guided by Soul rather than influenced by Ego. A person who has undergone psychological distillation gratefully surrenders to merge with forces of Light while yet acknowledging and honoring the existence of energies lower. The acclaimed symbol of this state of consciousness appearing in many spiritual and religious logos, is the double tetrahedron. Composed of two triangles, one pointing heavenward to imply humanity reaching toward the Great Creator and the other triangle pointing down to suggest the eternal grace of Light and Love offered to humanity symbolizing the descent of consciousness into physical matter. The tetrahedron is representative of the fundamental structure of the fabric of space time designating knowledge embedded into ancient texts. Nassim Haramein, Director of Research for The Resonance Science Foundation, relates the tetragrammaton as a double toroidal electromagnetic field which translates his vision of god. (Nasim Haramein CZ and SK FB page with the kind approval of Modern Knowledge and Resonance Project Foundation. [R.F.], 2015, p. o1) Knowledge passed down from ancients also describes the tetragrammaton to be the light body's MerKaBah or vehicle of inter-dimensional travel for body, mind and spirit to different planes or emanations. This state of consciousness which is synonymous with access to the MerKaBah arises after distillation has occurred annulling the ego. Revocation of the ego in this way permits the mysteries of the collective and personal shadow to then be illuminated. The shadow is expressed as that part of society's and personal consciousness that encompasses the dark, rejected and denied, but powerful aspects. Although often perceived as demonic, the 'shadow' surprisingly also serves as the inaccessible repository of gifts, skills and access to the Collective One's voice. Distillation brings the creative authority to comfortably merge these fields of energy.

This operation of light symbolizing the descent of consciousness into physical matter to reveal Light in all things is also called the Work of the Sun or The Great Work of Hermes. (Hayyan, n.d., p. 01) In striving to communicate in the language of light, identifying notes or frequency hold meaning to assist and guide meditative sojourns. The language of the Divine Spirit Self as encountered in meditation presents pure color to mean a single frequency. Light from a single source is always coherent, since incoherence requires two sources. In-phase light (produced from the same source) prevents it from scattering. Coherent light in perfect shapes like nested sphere waves or plane waves never cross each other, whether parallel or radial. Coherent light can also further elucidate the reference to the definition of phase conjugation as described by psycho-acoustic therapist, Vincent Bridges. "The universe can be described as a geometry of pressure. (Winter, n.d., p. 01) Geometry produces symmetry, which allows waves proceeding from opposite directions to meet each other and stand (to phase and phase lock.) Standing waves give the illusion of stability, segregation of momentum, and make possible the birth of matter. Pressure occurs where waves meet. For example, opposing lasers, such as those seen in 4-wave mixing of conventional optics, 'phase conjugate' when compressional waves are delivered precisely to center in geometry of dodeca-icosa. The compression waves come in at opposing angles and enter a material called the phase conjugate mirror which has the molecular geometry identical to the dodeca-icosa. Embedding in the cube of the dodeca going from the seven-spin of the tetracube to the five-spin of the dodeca creates the sacred space of phase conjugation. Just as the lines had to cross in opposing pairs to create 4-wave mixing so too The Great Work of alchemy, is an operation of Light. This light reaches beyond psychosomatic and archetypal nature, linking personal experience with the collective and spiritual experience of Oneness. Soul of the person refers to the Sun (Sol) of the collective as a fractal torus, the 'infinite spirit' whose center is everywhere but whose circumference is nowhere. Language as the symbolic representation of the universe also forms coherent light of symmetry and sacred waveform alphabets. Vincent Bridges, suggests that all sacred alphabets have geometric symbolism which underlies their sound/shape/symbol coherence.

"Reality cannot be found except in One single source, because of the interconnection of all things with one another". (Leibniz, 1670) Mystic bliss is found in the celebration of life beyond the boundaries of conditioned perception.

The Divine Code

In biblical and Kabbalistic teaching, the fabric of the human body resulted from utterances of the Divine Word. The Book of Knowledge: The Keys to Enoch (Hurtak, 1987, p. 01) makes the correlation that Divine Name was the key behind the transcription code of chemical letters encoded in the human body and responsible for its development. The Divine Code of 'letters' operates as firing mechanisms of coding and re-coding and claims that all human life is dependent on the initial conditions of vibratory language that exists on another plane of paraphysical reality. The Divine Code is the mechanism communicated through micro-signal ranges, where the vibratory link forms the "genetic matter" within the cells as a pattern of Divine energy flow. The body is seen as a bio-suit of light ware operating via a language of biochemical light that provides for billions of instructions per second, far exceeding even the DWave 2X supercomputer. The identity of each individual is housed in this inner labyrinth of chemical letters which equates the complete genome with the soul mechanism of life. The idea of an alphabet of symmetry to create resonant coherence across dimensions or realities has been well established. A phase angle alphabet, mapped from Phi-ratio torus by a Phi-based spiral, strongly imply the letter shapes of our sacred alphabets. In phase angle alphabets, the tilt of a photon is perceived as color. For example, the wave length of visible light is one octave. Dan Winter has demonstrated that the tilt angle of in-cube-ated torus, produces the perception of color in the cones of the eye. (Winter, 2015, p. 01) Echoing Sogyal Rinpoche who wrote the Tibetan Book of Living and Dying, (Rinpoche & Gaffney, 1994, p. 01) 'just what could a mystic with a scientific background tell us about reality, meditation derives levels of meaning arising through the context richness of mystical experience. "Meaning, internally, comes from the content of the experience balanced by the "gnosis" of its context'. -Vincent Bridges - Fifth Way Mystery School. (Bridges, n.d., p. 05)

Further correlations shape nested patterns of language throughout the many expressions of frequency, such as notes of language, notes of sound, notes of colour, and notes of fragrance. Through work with light and sound frequency entrainment of the brain, Vincent Bridges found that changes in neuro-chemistry can be taught as a sophisticated form of bio-feedback. (Bridges, n.d., p. 01) Open, calm and alert meditation triggers an interaction of electrical impulses and neurotransmitter activated buffers and filters in the personal brain/mind complex. Increased continuity of consciousness is a self-generating, self-regulating electro-magnetic field potential modulated by the action of conductivity sensitive chemicals in the spark gap of the synapses. The pause or the space between the notes of healing tones is synonymous with the flow of serotonin to the synapse where spiritual presence is heightened. The transformative interplay that occurs in this junction between the axon terminals of one neuron and the cell body or dendrites of another determine the waves of possibility based on the density of memory interconnections or the mind's temporal bandwidth. Like a hologram, memory is stored and retrieved by a process of broad-band neurotransmitter stimulation. Meditation triggers the impulse to attract and self-organize charge. This is the definition of life force and explains the mystery surrounding Hopi blue corn germination story passed down by the Hopi Elders through oral traditions from generation to generation. It was discovered that an ancient grain from the Hopi nation, had been in hibernation for a long-extended period of time. This sacred blue corn had been noted for its use in ceremony as well as basic sustenance as food for their people. After it was re-discovered in deep hibernation, attempts to germinate the corn failed until a surprising breakthrough was made. The Hopi blue corn responded with vigor only when it was exposed to song. The physics underlying the premise of singing to germinate post-hibernation blue Hopi corn is understood by phonon sonic wave effecting piezoelectric slinky like DNA. This bliss-related activity using coherent or implosive emotion such as singing, corresponds precisely in accord with results evident from the generalized holographic geometric relations of Planck entities. Fractal holographic braiding show that emotions program

DNA and identify how Earth's biomass is informed by Schumann resonance. The implication of this message that Hopi elders have passed on is that you only get soul into your DNA by knowing how to make bliss. The concept of utilizing meditation to activate bliss likewise demonstrates that meditation impacts the vitality of DNA. This is something tribal elders all knew and something humanities children should be taught. What makes electrical fields become self-aware is the very explanation for the germination of the post-hibernation blue Hopi corn mystery. Singing DNA implosively fires (phires) genes to provide, by heterodyne recursion, insertion of biological magnetism cascading through the speed of light into time for the purpose of inhabiting time. Gravity is created when waves meet non-destructive compression. The only geometry that permits this is the fractal geometry of self-embedding or self-similarity. Atoms have only as much gravity as self-similarity presents moderating electrons versus their nucleus. The premise continues to demonstrate frequency specific correlations exist to communicate symbolic representations of the universe. This language of frequency forms coherent light articulation cultivated within the practice of meditation. Examples of frequencies as a language correlating sound and light are found in the human body, essential oils, food, illness and therapies etc. Elemonics, the science of translating chemistry and molecules into audible music (Adams, 2016, p. 1) (Adams, 2017, p. 01) The spectrum of electromagnetic energy appears as red, orange, yellow, green, blue, indigo, and violet, in the visible spectrum are between 1014 & 1015 Hertz. Just as a colour reflects the absorption and projection of frequency, so too do your personal 'notes' illustrate an outside concept of the frequency spectrum inside. The wisdom of ordered polarity permits a tactile grasping of transitory diaphanous concepts, such as listening to the sound of your own note. The sound of your own note answers questions such as: who you are, where are you and how do you become aligned with your highest good in coherence with pure energy. Listening to the vibration of oneself not only locks in the love vibration specific to your very own well-being but is revelatory of your life purpose and meaning. It is often said that the meaning of life is to find your gift, and the purpose of life is to give it away. ("Quote investigator," n.d., p. 01)

The Sun sends ten million key notes on a "rainbow spectrum" to Earth. (Space.com staff, 2017, p. 01) We can measure this solar music to further understand how to communicate with Sol's heart. Not unlike listening to a song to understand the singer, the study of wave oscillations in the Sun is called helioseismology. The insight that results from listening to the Sun is derived from differences in temperature, composition and motion that influence oscillation periods. These data are expressed mathematically, metaphysically, and in terms of quantum entanglement. Properties determined by the vibrational state of the collective waves of this Helio-cosmic love energy can pervade the deep unconscious. How we absorb and respond to this sacred communication is determined by various parameters and correlations of influence. Research into the helio-cosmic effects on the natural environment validate Helio-physical imprinting as the adaptation and 'tuning in' of developing cells to Helio-cosmic conditions. Global Telepathic Experiment V.P. Kaznacheev-1985. (Korotkov, 2014, p. 01) The scientific study of Cosmism, originally derived from the research of V.I. Vernadsky, is the inquiry and analysis of Cosmic Consciousness of Humanity. This investigation of mind, thought, intellect and science in the cosmic realm functions as self-existing thinking layers dispersed throughout the universe. Earth adapted living matter integrates feeling perceptions and gnosis as part of the cosmoplanetary phenomenon understood as organization and motion of the Universe. As it was said by P. R. Masani in The Ecology of the Noosphere -1995 "noospheric pollution is the source of all pollution". (Masani, 1993, p. 01) The Noosphere refers to the human thinking layer within the planetary design. This design constitutes an evolving dynamic whereas biophotonics and coherent systems in biology track the influence of electromagnetic frequencies, geomagnetic storms, and helio-geomagnetic factors, all of which respond to the indwelling photon as Love. Sun gazing is one means by which the ancients and modern man alike have been infused with gnosis, as coherent light transduces itself into radio waves such as the holographic biophoton field. Sound is carried as information that decodes the 4-D form as a material object.

Quantum nonlocality is directly related to laser radiation from chromosomes (coherent light), which jitterbugs its polarization plane to radiate or occlude photons. Photons thus bridge the gap between physics, biology and philosophy. Our DNA expresses and directs matter through quantum bioholography, projected by coherent light and sound. Quantum bioholography shows that DNA literally produces coherent light, which transduces to sound to direct the formative processes of life. Although photons do not have mass, they do have momentum as radiation. Biophotons provide communication networks by radiating from the cells of all living things. A complex signaling system is thus formed, involving electric, magnetic, optical and acoustic effects. Quantum bioholography shows that DNA literally produces coherent light. The capacity to truly revere light can be called love. Love is the pure constant of the universe. Love encodes the coherent light of universal DNA with the infinite potential to command all fundamental particles to form infinite expressions of energy. Meditation observes and interacts in the behavior of subatomic particles that have been given the metaphysical name of Adamantine. "Vajrasattva" means "the Adamantine Being" who represents the Buddha of purification and healing. Vajrasattva is a force that can flow through the practice of meditation to touch all aspects of Being.

The development of a holistic understanding of the Universe, guided by Love on the waves of Light, conveys a magnetic radiance. Meditation evokes and modulates magnetic radiance through pineal activity, which coordinates chemicals and electromagnetism. While it has been found that Universal life is electric, its control takes place magnetically, thus we function electromagnetically. Plasmas, which can be efficient sources of radiation, are conductive and respond to electric and magnetic fields. Meditative techniques that catalyze sacred space cause a pulsing vibration to resonate at certain frequencies that match the related "antimatter continuum." This continuum is charge distribution efficiency, the definition of Sacred Space.

The distribution of the character frequency in genes is fractal, so nucleotides of DNA molecules can form holographic pre-images of biostructures. This process of reading and writing the very matter of our being is based on the genome's associative holographic memory, in conjunction with its quantum nonlocality.

Phonons restoring DNA

The bases of human genes, which come in four types—A, T, C and G—are called nucleotides. We must understand the code to understand the context. The braiding action of the longwave phonon (sound in liquid) is a soundwave created by compression of the heart muscle causing emotion which illustrates why it is said to be stokio or structure related. (Kamiya, 2015, p. 01)

The symmetry of tetragrammaton actuated in the 7 tilt angles of heart muscle throw a vortex casting a sound shadow like fire letters to the dragnet of the thymus. Responsible for emotion and coherence of sound waves, the emotion induced sounds of the heart mechanically braid the DNA. This magnetic field effect is known as compassion of mastery and creates the shape mirroring the inside to the outside which creates the self- similarity needed to compress and embed recursively. This is perfect embedding as demonstrated by the holy grail of DNA, the feminine reproductive organ and symbolically expressed as the Sufi heart with wings and cup within a cup, heart within heart, perfect fractal nesting and the cascade of harmonics. Literally braiding a magnetic X superluminal self- reference manifestation into time with the ability to steer itself, creates a soul and is identified by the ability to lucid dream.

Compassion and bliss create the charge density or implosion shape to make perfect compression or implosion and the existence of gravity, the centering force as fire (phi re) in the heart 'in phi knit ly' (infinitely) possible. The hectagonal in cube ation 444 into 555 perfect implosion lights the inner fire to illuminate Bliss (pent, from hex 7 spin to pent 5 spin, 'repent and be saved') as the purpose of DNA.

Illumined by the ancient code of The I Ching, Nassim Haramein among many others before him, noticed that the 64 hexagrams fit together to form a three-dimensional Star Tetrahedron Grid. (Haramein, 2014, p. 01) The 64 hexagrams of the I Ching fit together to form a three-dimensional Star Tetrahedron Grid. From this arrangement, Metatron's Cube of sacred geometry appears. Revealed in the 3-dimensional form of Metatron's Cube is the ancient and sacred symbol known as the Flower of Life. A system of relevant analytical information delivered prior to meditation opens dynamic vital experiences to engage with pure principles such as the Flower of Life to facilitate in-depth gnosis gained only by experience. Intellectual study of, for example, the Flower of Life, may provide factoids and data, however, it is not until the Flower of Life speaks to you holographically, via DNA that genuine knowing can be apprehended authentic and personal.

The four Hebrew letters Yod, He, Waw and He correspond to YHWH. These are referred to as "Tetragrammaton". Yahweh is commonly interpreted as "The LORD" or "God". The origins of language are now being attributed to DNA. It is now demonstrated that the context richness of DNA grammar has served as the blueprint for the development of human speech. Garjajev's group discovered that the text of the DNA abstract can be altered. ("Language of DNA," 2011, p. 1) The codons of the DNA string can be rearranged in different sequences to reprogram DNA molecules. Research has revealed that the triplets in the DNA string can exchange places, neatly solving the codon mystery. The workshop-meditation system delivers specific frequency to influence the heart of these DNA molecules. As well, intellectual constructs such as for example, understanding the sacred geometry of the Flower of Life and the 64 Tetrahedron grid provide freedom meditating upon this pattern underlying universal structure. Many of today's most influential scientists share this observation highlighting attention to this missing link to DNA reclamation, including Nassim Haramein. (Haramein, 2014, p. 01)

"64 tetrahedrons are needed in the structure of the fabric of space-time to begin to create the first two of infinite scalar octaves of the vector equilibrium: the seed geometry of the holofractographic structure of the entire universe...

As well:

- 64 codons in human DNA.
- 64 hexagrams in the I Ching.
- 64 sexual positions in the Kama Sutra.
- 64 classical arts listed in many Indian scriptures.
- 64 is the number of cells we have before our cells start to bifurcate (differentiate) shortly after conception.
- 64 "tantras" (books) of the "Tantrism", which is a form of Hinduism.

- 64 is fundamental in computer memory bits and coding.
- 64 is the maximum number of strokes in any Chinese character.
- 64 things are needed to be able to approach the Ark of the Covenant of the Lord according to the 2 copper scrolls that were found among the Dead Sea Scrolls.
- 64 is encoded in the description of the Tetragrammaton in the Hebrew Bible, in the 4-letter theonym YHWH which means God in Hebrew.
- 64 is the number of generations from Adam until Jesus according to the Gospel of Luke.
- 64 forms or manifestations of the Lord Shiva in Hinduism.
- 64 squares on chess and checker boards.
- 64 Braille characters in the old 6-dot system.
- 64 demons in the Dictionnaire Infernal.
- 64 is the smallest number with exactly seven divisors.
- 64 reduces to 1: $6 + 4 = 10$ and $1 + 0 = 1$"

(Abzu, n.d., p. 01)

Phonons restoring DNA follow the rules of basic syntax to communicate human genetics in a completely new light.

Circumnavigating the spiral

Knowledge of oneself is ultimately knowledge of the world. Hence, the Oracle of Delphi's proclamation to 'know thyself' has withstood the test of time. Although ages have passed, and the Oracle's voice fell silent as our solar system journeyed far into the darkened realms of chaos and separation, our solar system has returned once more into the light of Oneness. The Delphic Oracle speaks again (Rev. Dr. Evans, 2015, p. 1) from the Oracle's deltoid home in the Fornix/Fornax constellation, translocating as an angled gradient of light to strategically disentangle linear perceptions of limitation and separation. The Oracle stands ready to reveal intimate details of empirical phenomena ritually concealed. This Oracle has long held the secret key, the lost word, the holy grail.

The Oracle speaks of using the dark meditative space to reveal the inner light, understanding that the Pineal secretes melatonin, the hormone of darkness. Placing puzzle pieces where they can be neatly solved, the sacred interface stands ready to empower all who dare reach for this destiny. The Delphic Oracle is the event horizon; you are the event horizon... I Am; Thou Art! (Evans, 2015, p. 01)

Legend records the Python as a feminine serpentine or dragon/plasma earth spirit, who was conquered by the arrows of Apollo. The arrows of Apollo are allegory to the rays of the sun which implies information from an era of time. This story details an example of the cycle of completion seen as an old goddess falling to the younger new sun god. The elder goddess/ era, once passed, was buried under the Omphalos. Yet the Omphalos which implies center or umbilicus, remains always connected to the Great Mother. This myth references the new god setting up his temple on the grave of his predecessor, to continue in time as the new ruler. This myth has further been described as an allegory for the dispersal of the fogs and clouds of vapor which arise from ponds and marshes represented as the 'Python spirit', due to the rays of the sun which refers to the passing of time, represented as the 'arrows of Apollo'. The Python was the serpent worshipped at Delphi, as the symbol of wisdom, from whom the Pythian priestesses took their name, and from whom Apollo, as succeeding to the oracular power of the serpent, took the same adjective. The name Pythia derives from Pytho, the original name of Delphi. Etymologically, 'pythein' to rot, referred to the sickly-sweet fragrance of the decomposing Python slain by Apollo. Apollo went to Crete to be purified from murdering the Gaia goddess and then upon his return, imaged sailors from Crete into dolphins to become his priests at the newly named shrine temple Delphi. The blacksmith known as Hephaestus is said to have gifted Apollo with a silver bow which represented the moon and with golden arrows, which represented the sun. ("Hephaestus," n.d., p. 01)

Apollo was believed to be the god of reason. He was associated with many forms of rational thought such as music, law, science, and prophecy. To many Greeks of that age, his slaying of Python was seen as a triumph and a new beginning. In their eyes, they saw Apollo, god of prophesy, defeating old ways. No longer did Greeks sow their seeds as simplistic generations of habit. Apollo taught when to plant, when to water, and when to fertilize. They no longer relied on faith and prayers to Gaia for fertile crops. Through Apollo's tutorage, farming practices developed from an intellectual knowledge base. Apollo was thus crowned with laurel to consummate the appropriation of the Oracle at Delphi. To honour the former precedent, the priestess of Delphi was called Pythia, in honor of Python who lost her life. Eventually however, the hunters become the hunted, as we walk the great medicine wheel of life. Experiencing every nuance contained in the Four Directions becomes our objective. Exploring life both subjectively and objectively until all fear drops away and we return to the living light of full consciousness.

Heretofore meditation extends the opportunity for the serpent of DNA to once again arise as kundalini energy and complete the circumnavigation of nature's spiral. The serpent of DNA calls once again as spirit, inner light or photon, in the furnace of enlightenment to transcend the limitations of an old paradigm and dwell in the new Temple of Oneness.

Admission to Triumph

Within each of us everything is contained: God, Christ, the angels, celestial and terrestrial kingdoms, and the powers of hell. Outside of us is nothing of which we can conceive, and we can know nothing except that which exists in our minds. No god or devil, no spirit or any power whatsoever can act upon us unless it centers into our constitution. Only that which exists in us has existence for God or The All-That-Is. The secret of meditation lies in non-desire; you must take no desire, on any level for anything, as the very act of desire nullifies the thing itself. Desire (will, wanting) is an act of the ego, which must completely dissolve before one's lower self can merge with the higher self. While in meditation, just be there, fully present, have no desire for an outcome, and in an instant, it will happen.

What was once referred to as a spiritual context is now acknowledged to coincide with the realm of sub-atomic science. But just like a radio emitting static interference, the frequency must be specifically tuned to hear it. When vibrations from the Crystal Palace become resonant with cosmic design, conscious awareness will arise in the human mind to be reflected and observed in the experience of three-dimensional living. (Chia & Thom, 2017, p. 01) The world of the invisible becomes familiar and palpable through meditation. As mentioned above, the inner oracle speaks of using darkness to reveal the inner light, as the Pineal secretes melatonin, "the hormone of darkness." The word melatonin comes from the Greek Melos which means black, and tosos which means labor. Melatonin therefore presents the "night worker." Meditation in the dark stimulates the pineal gland and reception of the electromagnetic impulses from Eta Carina to change one's DNA via the Pineal Gland. Scientists believe that the pineal body is a magnetoreceptor, capable of monitoring magnetic fields and helping to align the body in space. There is a pathway from the retinas to the hypothalamus, called the retina tract. It brings information about light and dark cycles to a region of the hypothalamus. From the suprachiasmatic nucleus (SCN), nerve impulses travel via the pineal nerve to the pineal gland. These impulses inhibit the production of melatonin. When there is no light to stimulate the hypothalamus, pineal inhibition ceases, and melatonin is released.

The pineal gland is a photosensitive organ and an important time keeper for the human body. Science News Digest for Physicians and Scientists, by John Gibbon, chief of biopsychology at New York State Psychiatric Institute in New York reports that the amount of melatonin in the blood increases after dusk and declines near dawn. ("Stopwatch of the brain," n.d., p. 01) Shielding the eyes of premature infants nearly doubles the amount of the urinary metabolite of the melatonin. In humans Mel1a is encoded by a gene on chromosome 4 and Mel1b by a gene on chromosome 11. By engaging meditation in total darkness, this same increase in melatonin effects the DNA to make extra-sensory information available for conscious processing. By focusing in meditation on the Pineal, direct engagement with Source Energy photon, is the macrocosmic equivalent to reuniting with the microcosmic family, whose inheritance is in light as electro magnetism that flows to the Earth.

Communication with the 'supreme light' via spirit, where spirit is the inner light or photon, can occur through the activation of the Pineal Gland. The sacred interface, or god spark, is seeking to make contact in the quantum realm within humanity, but first must find a receptive electron. Meditating in darkness greatly stabilizes the physical activation process. Shutting down the flow of thought quiets the left hemisphere, which enables an engagement with the right hemisphere to activate the flow of melatonin from the pineal. Holding a space void of thought and desire amplifies and hastens the firing of the pineal to 'sit at the right hand of God' in meditation. By letting go of desire, the ego more easily relinquishes control and can be led into a dormant state. This further encourages kundalini energy to rise and merge with or permit conscious integration of the higher self. Entraining the mind to specific frequencies found in classical music assists in diverting left-brained thought processes into right-brain feeling mode, thus supporting the role of the observer. Photons can only be absorbed when electrons in the pineal begin to vibrate. These are the messenger particles, perceived as angels or messengers of God when received at the specific angle of bliss-inducing phase conjugation.

In mythological narratives, the famous Golden Fleece represents the activated Pineal gland. Determined to reclaim his throne, Jason agrees to retrieve the Golden Fleece and must go beyond the known world to do so. ("Jason and the Argonauts," n.d., p. 01) The golden bough is likewise a reference to the Pineal gland on fire, as its golden color is associated with the sun. Before you can get past the darkness, to the place of the next world where wisdom will be given, you must find a 'golden bough' growing in the forest on a tree. Only with this in hand will you be admitted to the next world. The tree represents the physical body. Going into the great wilderness of trees figuratively means literally going into the mind. This is the real location of the tree of life and the tree of knowledge referred to in Genesis. The tree of knowledge signifies the left hemisphere and the tree of life signifies the right hemisphere. But chaotic or random thoughts distract and deter one from obtaining the golden bough. The word mystic used to mean one who saw through a veil. Vision was clouded but the promise was that the veil could be torn away in the higher realm of consciousness attained through silencing the mind in meditation.

On the cosmic scale, Pluto has opened the gate to the other realms. On the human scale, a rising energy is firing the memories of Christ consciousness found inside the hippocampus, along with: Supernova 1987a as Pineal, Fornax as the Fornix, the temple as the Dura Mater, Pia Mater, and Arachnoid of the brain. Pluto is accompanied by the gray satellite Charon, which in Greek lore is the gray boatman who directs the ferry to cross the Styx on the way to Elysium. (Donahue, n.d., p. 01) The symbolic revelation is thinly disguised as language. The orbit of the great light Charon, ferries those who have activated their pineal glands, across the river to the House of Darkness being Hades or Pluto the distant dark planet. The messianic bride speaks through Song-of-Solomon 2:1 ("Song-of-Solomon 2:1," n.d., p. 01) I am the rose of Sharon, and the lily of the valley to herald the coming of cosmic consciousness. This is referencing Charon, the rose shaped fractal orbit of light. The Elusian Mysteries of ancient Greece further elucidate these mysteries focused on interpretations of Nature's most precious secrets. The Elusian mysteries were dramatized during distinct parts of the year. They were split into two groups, the Lesser and Greater Mysteries. To understand the mysteries, one had to be familiar with Greek mythology, which the Eleusinians interpreted esoterically. (Hall, 1928, p. 01) Although once consigned to the world of spirituality, these principles are now known to belong to the realm of sub- atomic science. All atoms have gravity or implosive collapse only because their nuclear geometry is golden ratio fractal to their electrons and are self-referring to the Pineal to realign with mother light of the Bliss body. The torus- like flow, forms the Anu and the atom, providing the precise navigational formula to project, or steer, your Ka self as a toroidal plasma body during dreaming and death. Egyptian hieroglyphs defined the Plasmasphere as the Electric Field that Collects Plasma' named Shu.

As the electric field of the Plasmasphere, Shu formed the torus shaped region of charged particles believed to protect Earth's gravitational orbit. ("Shu the Plasmasphere," n.d., p. 01) "The amount of coherence in your aura's charge field or plasma- is called your KA", as Dan Winter states is the essence of the real science behind spirituality. "Those with a Ka, are those who have learned to attract the kind of aura/ plasma charge field which is projective…" Precisely linked to learning the skill to become centripetal or phase conjugate, literally defining the quality of grace. (Winter, n.d., p. 01)

The Seal of Solomon is a symbol of the unity of man's lower mind with his higher self; it is also known as the Star of David and consists of two interlaced triangles. Human consciousness the upward-pointing triangle merged with Universal Consciousness, the downward pointing triangle, to complete the Unity of mind. The close associations between this seal and the Philosopher's Stone was demonstrated by the 'fiery water' combination of the two triangle symbols: The upward-pointing Fire and downward pointing Water of the Materia Prima. The treatise Esh M'Saref states the old midrashic interpretation of the Hebrew word for heaven, 'Shamayin' is a combination of esh, meaning fire and mayim, meaning water. Midrashic idea of prophecy was a recognition of pattern rather than the Western concept of prediction and fulfillment as explained by Leonora Leet PhD in her book The Universal Kabbalah (Leet, 2004, p. 1) The fifteenth-century alchemist Basilius Valentinus wrote, "Come to the center of the earth, and there you shall find the Philosopher's Stone." ("Basilius Valentinus," 2014, p. 1) Metaphorically, we can view the center of the earth as the human skull, and the philosophers stone as the Pineal gland of the brain. The true secret of the Philosopher's Stone is that we are all connected as a unified mind called Consciousness. This description of the nature of consciousness suggests either useless lead, or priceless gold, which will be derived by focused, attention driven, centripetal and golden ratio 'sharing' within the donut-shaped phase conjugate plasma or charge field.

DNA History

As Socrates wrote, "The only good is knowledge and the only evil ignorance." (Tsarion, 2015, p. 01) This knowledge comes from many spiritual texts, which describe a similar concept: the fractal demonstration of overcoming the lower mind rooted in the first three chakras of the body, otherwise referred to as 'the beast'. Annunaki of Sumeria also references the Pineal which, as mentioned above, secretes melatonin. As the Hormone of Darkness, melatonin implies the night worker, much like Charon, who ferries us across the river to the House of Darkness, or Hades. In the ancient Sumerian language, Sharon signifies the orbiting or circling light. ("Rose shape formed by galactic tsunami," 2017, p. 01) Rose of Sharon, and Charon, both correlate to the fractal rose orbiting light, entailing the mechanics or means to cross the river, pass Hades to Elysium, the kingdom of paradise. Here the charge lines converge to implode forming a rose symmetry. This is the sacred interface where ancient tribal shaman and participants in meditation can call upon and communicate with their ancestors. This is where the air is measurably fractal and the charge is distributable, thus presenting a sacred space in the configuration of a rose. Nature uses slip knot geometry of 5 spin inside, golden ratio pent (i.e. protein) phase conjugation for perfect charge distribution and 7 spins outside for perfect charge containment. The journey to Fornax describes the path and potential of entering the furnace of transmutation.

Syncretism, as determined by the Latin expression interpretatio graeca, implores mindful respect and graceful interpretation of all religions to recognize one's own deity in the pantheon of other nations. E.g. the Greeks identified the Akkadian supreme god Anu with the Greek supreme god Zeus. Ancient Sumerian texts reveal the god Anu was considered the supreme Lord of the Sky. ("the Divine world," n.d., p. 01) By appointment of the Sumerian family tree, Anu is presented as having two sons: Enki (Ea), Lord of the Earth and Waters, and Enlil (Ilu), Lord of the Atmosphere and Lord of the Command. Anu emerges as the Ophanim sigil of truth and informs the shape of sacred space. Anu is the knot of perfect fusion found in the heart of the sun, the heart of hydrogen, and the human heart.

The sounds of the heart mechanically braid DNA, and the presence of enzymes indicate how tightly the DNA is braided into nests, otherwise referred to as "donuts." Bliss creates the attraction forming long-wave donuts into a sonic ponytail self-referring, self-organizing because of the centering force of perfect implosion. Creating a phase conjugate echo of the perfectly shareable wave enables negentropic implicate order and explicate order. Implicate order moves like a cloud of ether as charge compression. Explicate order is tonal and is converged into mass or wave nodes. El conveys the place of phase shift and translation of vorticity. Mathematically defined as the curl of velocity, vorticity is how you learn to lucid dream and become ELohim. Sustaining the resulting tornado by successful compression through light speed inhabiting time creates Tron. El ec Tron. 'Because of the Tron's ability to steer a magnetic vector (simply a wave) from a circle (matter) into a line (energy), they were said to be able to steer in time'. The French word that means whirlwind, 'Tourbillion', is a scrollwork made of light, and is produced by tying the knot successfully (aka, making the turns necessary to re-enter a donut) and are the burning Heart of ANu. The Anu was named after Enki's father AN, who was called the Sun God. A system of relevant analytical information and meditation that teaches this spin angle will produce self-re-entry through the Sun.

Focused human awareness such as group or global meditations, measurably reduce radioactivity of solar metabolism. DNA is a biological magnetic compressor. "Compression due to recursion is identical to acceleration. Wave heterodynes in Phi recursion accelerate by adding and multiplying wave velocities- therefore recursive compression is identical to making gravity. Negotiating the turns (of 'mind') necessary to hang in there while swinging around a donut, became the origin of alphabet - as on EA's EArth.". -Dan Winter (D. Winter, & S. Evans, personal communication, July 17, 2016) (Evans & Winter, 2016, p. 1)

The story of Enki reconciles many of the paradoxes of historical religion. Enki was the guardian of the Tree of Knowledge, otherwise viewed as wisdom or the serpent. The Hebrew word for serpent is nachash, which comes from the root word NHSH, meaning to decipher, to divine, to learn by experience and to diligently observe. (Deschesne, 2009, p. 01) Therefore, Enki is often referred to as the God of Wisdom. He knew that men who ate the fruit from the Tree of Knowledge could become like Gods. The tree is understood to be the human body, and fruit of this tree refers to the Pineal.

As written in Genesis 3:22: "And the Lord God said, Behold, the man is become as one of us, to know good and evil: and now, lest he put forth his hand, and take also of the tree of life, and eat, and live forever…". ("Genesis 3:22," n.d., p. 01) The word Paradise implies a state of purity and innocence and happiness yet omits any connotation of knowledge. By virtue of eating from the fruit which then allowed for learning the ways of good and evil, it was impossible to remain in Paradise where obtaining said knowledge of good and evil was optional. Learning about evil to comprehend good was acknowledged as the primal will of the Divine Order, whereby eating from the Tree of Knowledge leads to enlightenment. This is structurally like the movement of electrical energy up the spine to merge with the magnetism that comes down from above. Enki, guardian of the Tree of Knowledge, was also called Sa'am or Samael. Depending upon your knowledge of the code of IEOU and the ability to name the symbol of 8, Azozeo, and 4555, you will be directed either to the left or right along Charon's ferry transport to the after-life.

Recorded from ancient Sumeria are Samael's words: "Nothing is obtained by wanting. And nothing is achieved by relinquishing responsibility to a higher authority. (Gardner, n.d., p. 01) Belief is the act of believing, for to be alive is to believe, and will is the ultimate medium of the self." This is Samael saying that you must be true to yourself. As consistent with all aspects of life, Samael has a female counterpart, Samothea, the death goddess, queen of the mysterious land of the Hyperboreans. She tutored in the arts, astronomy, and science, and two of her more notable student in the mystical place beyond the veil was Pythagoras and Apollo. All the discipline and culture that Pythagoras advocated was cultivated because of his studies with the enigmatic Samothea.

The key to Enki's story is the manner in which he learned from his winged dragon Mag Queen mother, Aide, how to tie the slip knot of Anu to create life. Within this symmetry is the secret of making the relationship between awareness and gravity clear, and the instructions for ensouling DNA. Annunaki is the Star Fire of the Pineal gland or Tree of Knowledge. On a cosmic scale Annunaki is also Supernova 1987a. The Annunaki star fire was the flower conveyance or cup bearer disseminating the rich food of the matrix. The angles of this slip knot are more than alphabet, they are the blueprint for starting the phi re (fire) of life.

The star phire cup or flower, is the womb from which flows the 'nectar of supreme excellence' or that which is the anointing oil. Annunaki in this capacity was also called the Rose of Sharon. The ancient Sumerian language translated Sha to mean orbit, while Ra and On relate to light. The city of On was also known as Heliopolis, the City of Light, and Ra is the Sun God. The Eleusinian Mysteries disclosed the nature of the human problem and agony of the soul. (Mission, 2014, p. 01) Perception is subject to mental and environmental constructs and once entrapped by limitations and illusions of the human environment, the sacred photon identity cannot be expressed. The Eleusinian mysteries disclose the blatant reality and responsibility for becoming actualized centers in contact with mother. The outermost layer of the human brain is called dura mater, which means "hard mother." The innermost layer of the human brain is called pia mater, which means "tender mother." Between the outer and the inner lies a reticulated layer of tissue called the arachnoid. Overcome the desire to be a part of this profane system to instead belong to the sacred order of light. The Eleusinian Mysteries state that you will carry with you into the invisible world those same desires that you cannot gratify here.

The Kingdom of God is thus a matter of consciousness. As Psalm 19:4 states, "Their line is gone out through all the earth and their words to the end of the world. In them has he set a tabernacle for the sun. Truly the kingdom of God is within us." ("Psalm 19:4," n.d., p. 01)

The Meditative Power of Ohm

Once experienced, returning to an awareness of the kingdom of God within is achieved as resonant vibration through deep meditation, centering prayer, or utilizing differential auditory patterns such as the sacred sound Ohm. This sound is a vibration of the universal consciousness and can be harnessed in transcending expansive subtle worlds and spiritual realms. Chanting Ohm as a meditative practice initiates a vibration that offers entrainment with a greater universal awareness. The momentary silence between each chant becomes a world unto itself. Mind moves between the opposites of sound and silence until the cessation of all sound becomes a doorway. In the silence, the single remaining impulse is a vibratory impression of Ohm, until even that thought is gone. The doorway opens into a trance state. Here mind and intellect transcend the individual self, to merge with the Infinite Self. Within the context richness of the infinite self's vast potential of universal opportunity, worldly affairs are reduced to petty trivia. Sacred in significance and found in temples and shrines around the world, Ohm is a common daily practice in long-standing cultural expressions. Symbolizing profound concepts expressed in Hindu belief, Om is of great utility throughout even the most mundane of daily demands. In the Hindu tradition, you may begin the day or any journey by uttering Om, writing the sacred symbol at the beginning of letters or important documents, exams, and so on. A newly born Hindu child is ceremoniously welcomed into the world with this holy sign. After birth, the child is ritually cleansed, and the sacred syllable Om is written on her or his tongue with honey. (Shroff, n.d., p. 01) Many within the global community adorn themselves with the symbol Om on pedant or jewelry or tattooed body art, expressing a greater spiritual awareness. This use of this symbol has thus permeated the collective consciousness.

According to the Mandukya Upanishad, "Om is the one eternal

syllable of which the great 'All-That-Is exists in the past, the present, and the future. All that exists beyond the three forms of time is also implied in it. Om is made of three Sanskrit letters, aa, au and ma." (Sharvananda, 1920, p. 01) Correct intonation will penetrate to the center or atman/soul. This is an expression of perfect spin of the torus producing music of the soul which is said to harmonically contain all sounds. Through the Om, peace and bliss thus produced gives rise to the 'stateless eternity' referred to in the Bhagavad Gita. ("Bhagavad Gita," n.d., p. 01) Encompassing all potentialities, it remains omnipotent yet undefined. Om thus stimulates electrons in the Pineal, causing the supreme universal photon—aka God— to respond. ("1 John 1:5," n.d., p. 01) The meditative practise has been deeply honored within many cultures. The tribe called 'meditators' within the esoteric Hebrew tradition are referred to as the tribe of Judah. The word Judah, is derived from the Christian gnostic word Jeu, from the book of IEOU. Jeu, in the Coptic book, says that those who were Jeus (Jews) are those that receive light in meditation. Thus, those that meditate are to be called the tribe of Judah. (Scott-Moncrieff, 1913)

Gates in both computers and the human brain are logic circuits. They open and close to change understanding. By engaging in meditation, the electrons in the pineal gland are stimulated to absorb the photons, which are equated with spirit or God. To activate the sacred interface God-Spark, the receiving electrons in the Pineal must vibrate in response to the appropriate current. Electrical resistance is the essential key to raising Kundalini energy up the spine to engage and activate the Pineal. The law of electrical resistance is the Ohm, whereby each chakra represents one of the body's resistors, also referred to as the seals. Ohm's Law, (Voltage = Current X Resistance) is demonstrated by light energy in photons being converted into electric current when the photons strike a suitable semiconductor device. ("Ohm biography," n.d., p. 01) These photons are messenger particles that can be described as angels of light, or even the messengers of God. The appropriate angle of light needed to fulfil the messenger particle criteria in the body, forms in response to the flow of melatonin from the Pineal. Stimulating the right hemisphere of the brain activates the flow of melatonin from the pineal gland. This occurs by shutting down the left hemisphere of the brain in meditation by letting go of all thoughts. The logic circuits engaged in meditation are gates through which an increased understanding is offered.

NASA released a paper referring to the ability to change logic circuits in computers by using light and living tissue. (NASA science beta [N.A.S.A.], 2000, p. 1) New, optical quantum computers would be able to produce more data in one hour then a current computer can produce in eleven years. The D-Wave computer far surpasses even this, and is now cubing its production every three months, including fourth-dimensional data. The sorting mechanism for the hyper-cube of fourth-dimensional data requires a point of reference. This is the equivalent of back engineering matter. Like the logic circuits in both computers and the human brain, these open and close to affect a desired change in understanding. The act of meditation is an experiential science that can truly liberate the human soul from the bondage of the matrix currently ensnaring humanity. The secret key, the lost word, the holy grail, the valuable pearl of discovery is found through freedom from restriction of belief systems and the parameters of established formulas.

The Ouroboros, Death and Resurrection

The name originates from the Greek oura meaning tail and boros meaning eating, thus 'he who eats the tail'. (Omohundro, 2014, p. 01) The ouroboros has been important in religious and mythological symbolism, but has also been frequently used in alchemical illustrations, where it symbolizes the circular nature of the alchemist's opus. It is also often associated with Gnosticism and Hermeticism. (Gnostic Warrior, 2015, p. 01) The Ouroboros, or 'tail devourer,' is one of the oldest mystical symbols in the world. It can be perceived as enveloping itself, where the past (the tail) appears to disappear but rather, moves into an inner domain or reality, vanishing from view but still existing. The ouroboros has several meanings interwoven into it. Foremost is the symbolism of the serpent eating its own tail. This symbolizes the cyclic nature of the Universe creating by renewal as assimilation of its opposite or shadow which sustains its life. Sometimes depicted in a lemniscate shape (figure eight), it represents cyclical nature as a fusion of opposites. Just as the doctrines of Heraclitus characterized all existing entities by pairs of contrary properties, whereby no entity may ever occupy a single state at a single time, the frequency of synapse and threshold invite the 'one and the many' of our collective into a solitary gnosis through the ouroboros. (Quantum Future Group, n.d., p. 01)

Found in Gnosticism and alchemy symbolizing the transcendence of duality and was related to the solar God Abraxas, the Ouroboros signifies eternity and the soul of the world. In alchemy, it represents the spirit of Mercury (the substance that permeates all matter), in continuous renewal (a snake is often a symbol of resurrection, as it appears to be continually reborn as it sheds its skin). As a symbol of the eternal unity of all things, including the cycle of birth and death, it signifies release and liberation by uniting opposites such as the conscious and unconscious mind. (Chwalkowski, 2016, p. 01)

The alchemical textbook Chrysopoeia (gold making) of Cleopatra contains a drawing of the Ouroboros representing the serpent as equally light and dark, echoing symbols such as the Yin Yang, which illustrates the dual nature of all things. But importantly, these opposites are not in conflict. The book is mainly centered around the idea of "one is all," a concept that is related to hermetic wisdom. The famous Ouroboros drawing from the early alchemical text The Chrysopoeia of Cleopatra dating to second-century Alexandria features the words hen to pan, or 'one is the all.' ("Chrysopoeia," 2011, p. 01)

Ouroboros symbolism has also been used to describe Kundalini energy. According to the second-century Yoga Kundalini Upanishad, "The divine power, Kundalini, shines like the stem of a young lotus; like a snake, coiled round upon herself she holds her tail in her mouth and lies resting half asleep as the base of the body" ("Ouroboros," n.d., p. 011.82). Kundalini equates to the entwined serpents of the caduceus of the Greek god Hermes, the entwined serpents representing divine balance or, esoterically, DNA. The Ouroboros appears in many other cultures. The Serpent Jormungand of Norse legend, one of the three children of Loki and Angrboda, grew so large that it could encircle the world and grasp its tail in its teeth. It guarded the Tree of Life and is often depicted as an ouroboros. ("Jormungand, Midgard serpent," n.d., p. 01) The Aztec serpent God Queztacoatl was depicted similarly, and Chinese alchemical dragons have both similar shapes and meaning. In Hindu, you have the dragon circling the tortoise which supports the four elephants that carry the world. ("Ouroboros – The Tail Devourer," 2013, p. 01) The subtle yet boundless element between the layers of matter and antimatter yields simply to our beckoning as the sacred interface. Here the Ouroboros is born. This ancient symbol depicting a serpent or dragon eating its own tail is a frequency one enters between the vibrational synapse of one's matter and anti-matter self. The timeless worlds of fractal dimensions and parallel existence yield to man-made constructs and parallel timelines through observation.

The Cosmic Mind

"Reality is neither structure nor chaos, but a process in which structure and chaos dance between form and formlessness. This is the eternal cycle of death and renewal". -Iona Miller (Miller, 2009, p. 01) Matter is composed of and utterly dependent on organic light that fills the universe and our bodies. This light has an earthly and spiritual aspect, as well as a psychosomatic and archetypal nature. Contained in this light, self-knowledge describes the science of Creation. While neurotransmitters are the key to understanding the chemical and electrical nature of the central nervous system and its influence in human behavior, understanding the role of our subtle bodies is key to engaging the restorative adamantine particles role in our return to full consciousness understanding and self-knowledge. Leading to unity and integration, the experiential component of exploration during meditation provides the necessary balance expressed as the Vayu. (Perm, n.d., p. 01) Vayu, in popular interpretations of the five elements theory, governs universal movement from subatomic particles to galaxies. Measurable by the Veda Pulse feedback system as movement including nerve impulse, blood flow, muscle contraction, secretion of glands, the governing principle of Vayu leads to separation and disintegration. ("VedaPulse," n.d., p. 01) The equal and opposite or integration and unification provided by relevant analytical learning lab/ workshops, activate through meditation, an expanding awareness into the subtlest aspects of DNA. Insightful and qualitatively positive dissolution of the ego to merge with the Pure Source Energy of Oneness avails the experience of bliss. Science may now include spirit with heads held high in dignity while the Mystic may forever be freed of woo-woo negating an expanded awareness. The Vedas call Maha Siddhi a form of super power, which is part of the cosmic mind of the natural universe and include such phenomenon as telepathy, teleportation, levitation, bilocation, dematerialisation. ("Aetherforce," n.d., p. 01)

Movement and stillness, or the particle and wave of Mahat or the Cosmic Mind, is illustrated by and often translated as water. Just as one may experience passage through a vast ocean by moving from the southern shore to northern shore as a droplet of water, so too the experience of being the entire ocean touching both shores simultaneously precludes the need for movement. Yet both experiences describe fractal expressions of the superior mind that connects all minds, or Mahat. It is this self-referring principle of synthesis whereby individual mind and reason are transcended in the state of Mahat or the universal Buddhi. Here individual faculties are included as an expression of the cosmic mind. Consciousness moves through the individual mind but is not the individual mind. Using characters from a Shakespeare play as an example, the character is an effect caused by Shakespeare however Shakespeare is not the effect of his characters. Atoms can likewise be seen as an effect of electrical thinking but are not the thinking itself. Much like a wave is not the ocean but a characteristic of the ocean's effect, or heat from a fire is not the fire but an effect caused by the fire. Vibrations therefore are effects. We can experience the vibration and resonance of aspects and expressions of the universe moving through our physical senses. Our five+ senses function like filters through which a percentage of the vibration's spectrum may be perceived. Therefore, the awareness of the environment in the subtle fields is a merging or compounding of the memory of five+ narrow ranges of vibratory phenomena perceived through these physical senses added to vibrations perceived only during experiences not restricted by the denser physical body. According to Ayurveda, one's basic constitution, determined at the time of conception, is called Prakriti. The term Prakriti is a Sanskrit word describing an individual's permanent constitution type, whereas Vikruti is highly variable and influenced by a workshop–meditation system to return homeostasis of Prakriti to the state of perfect health. (Mubārak, 1894, p. 01) Although Prakriti mirrors the unique qualities such as a fingerprint or DNA, the energetic restraint acknowledged as essential to maintain homeostasis is a universal principle emerging from Cosmic Mind (Mahat). This restraint is referred to as Ohm, a unit of measure describing resistance to a flow of electricity. Likewise, the meditation chant of OM also provides essential resistance of electrical energy flowing through nerve centers in the spine called chakras. These chakras provide appropriate resistance to permit specific energetic impact within the brain.

All aspects of meditation when combined with a learning lab workshop depict a summation of one unifying principle reflected in the Sanskrit word Hatha. Ha means sun and Tha means moon, so literally Hatha means sun-moon, striving to balance opposing parts of the micro- and macro-cosmic expression of life. Just as Apollo represented a swing of the proverbial pendulum attempting to achieve balance, the opposing parts of the human-universe are ready for the still point of evanescent radiation instead of perpetually swinging amidst polarities. The radiation of pure Source energy is available through the recoding of DNA activated by the God-Spark within sacred space. Meditation unifies blissful stillness with joyful movement throughout an expanding familiarity of the fractal Oneness, via activation of the sacred interface God-Spark.

Meditation can be a tactile, kinesthetic, and a feeling-based heart journey. This can be done in co-operation with the mind but not by the intellect. Although enhanced results are obtained consistently by providing a seminar prior to the meditation component to discuss the concepts, only the literal meditative experience can garner the bridge into subtle worlds. No amount of talking about going on a journey can ever equal the gnosis gained by doing it. Pineal Activation is not an extension of, nor does it rely upon your faculty of comprehension; it does however require discernment. Heart-directed discernment maintains your intention without becoming distracted by thought. Although thoughts can derail or detain your successful activation, they are not bad or wrong. Certainly, when permitted to flow along in the background of your awareness, they can in fact keep that pesky ego out of your way. The ego—that measuring, judgmental device on autopilot—cannot infiltrate or otherwise besiege your heart, for the ego's frequency is viable only via the brain. In fact, the ego might not even notice that you have 'left the building'. But don't worry, it will still be there, rambling away when you return, as surely you will. The autonomic system of these third-dimensional bodies nurtures and preserves an alliance within the field of Oneness of All That Is. In other words, don't worry about what will happen during your meditative journey because the frequency of worry precludes activating the resonance of your god-spark. Achieving resonance with your god-spark contains the essential tour de force to magnetize and align your highest good in coherence with the pure Source energy. Holding open the channel of Distillation permits higher frequencies to be discerned in an evanescent wave or field where the energy is spatially concentrated near source. It will not be the dream-like sensation running away with your mind as the continuous circulation of the meditative experience cause charge to compress and implode as a peak experience of Bliss. Becoming aware of the subtler energies accessible to mind, facilitates 'distilling' the lower everyday consciousness. The nexus point of peak experience reflects the point of reference from which access to other dimensions becomes familiar territory. As a central link or connection to these access points, the meditation is easily repeatable at any time. Alchemically speaking, all the operations necessary to activate the god-spark can be reduced to the term digestion. Digestion implies transformation from one substance to another to obtain something more useful. Thus, the energies encountered in our inner world are expressed via digestion. Time, defined as charge rotation, and focused energy, are transmutable in this way and assist the uptake of photon spirit self collapsing the divine blueprint to potentize the channel of reciprocating communication within consciousness.

From the cryptic Emerald Tablets, we find written, "The connecting link between the material man and the spiritual man is the intellectual man, for the mind partakes of both the material and immaterial qualities. The aspirant for higher knowledge must develop the intellectual side of his nature and so strengthen his will that is able to concentrate all powers of his being on and in the plane, he desires. The great search for light, life and love only begins on the material plane. Carried to its ultimate, its final goal is complete oneness with the universal consciousness. ("Emerald tablets," n.d., p. 01)

Chapter Thirteen

Protocol, Description and Guidelines

To participate in the AcuLomi Temple Learning Lab, students first receive a description of the etymology of the name AcuLomi Temple.

Acu- Patterns of energy

Lomi- Flow/Qi, effectively tilting the angle of phonon wave to cast sound shadows, most noticeably initiated in the

Temple - Area within the human cranium. The Temple overlies the temporal and sphenoid bone. Here in the crystal palace, brain waves converging at Planck's distance, length and time implement the onus to take responsibility for and deliberately choose, the pressure that emotion creates (likewise affecting the thymus).

The Learning Lab workshop further aroused curiosity and interest to desire remembering Oneness. The discussion centered on the mechanics of an interface and what it means to be lucid or lucidly discern between Ego and Observer while retaining full self-awareness. Participants receive insights on the process required to merge with any frequency such as, an element, a remedy, or an archetype. The discussion provides research data, anecdotal perceptions and insights to convey how 'merging' occurs most easily by closing one's eyes to mute the outside world. The instruction suggests 'observing yourself'. This third-party-perspective of being the 'Observer', causes a collapse of the magnetism (light) wave to a microdot, which can enter via the Pineal gland and influence one's DNA. Also offered was the suggestion to hold the breath for three or four seconds to shut down the mind and allow the new activity to take place unhindered.

After a short half hour Learning Lab experience, the meditation was made immediately available although not mandatory.

AcuLomi Temple Mediation Technique

To participate in the AcuLomi Temple meditation, students receive further instruction on the process required to merge with any frequency such as, an element, a remedy, or an archetype. Initiate "merging" by closing your eyes to help minimize any external stimulation. Tell yourself that you are observing yourself. This third-party-perspective causes a collapse of the magnetism (light) wave to a microdot, which can enter via the Pineal gland and influence your DNA. Hold your breath for three or four seconds to shut down the mind and allow the new activity to take place unhindered.

Step One – Enlightened and blissful experiences occur when the ego and mind dissolve through frictionless spin. Visualize and feel the movement of your body/mind flowing in a hula-like figure-eight radiation and contraction of the Golden Ratio pattern that expands into counter-rotating fields. This is the vehicle of entry into the space in which creation happens. For example, purple is the space between red and blue, an A sharp exists in the space between the notes A and B. The God-Spark interface exists between physicality as matter and physicality as anti-matter yet encompasses them both. Call upon and set an intention to merge in both matter and anti-matter with your divine God-spark of creation, the sacred interface.

Feel the energy pathways where the kundalini will rise

Step Two – Opening to the higher expression of your Archetype/Ascended Master occurs by first acknowledging the limitations of the three-dimensional intellect. Feeling is the necessary vehicle to leave third dimensional limitations. Dan Tien (Taoist), Hara (Japanese), and Kanda (Vedic) are energy points in the subtle body where the 72,000 nadis, or energy pathways will pass through as the kundalini rises. The three primary channels include the central Sushumna over which the left (Ida) and right (Pingala) crisscross in an upward trajectory. Ida is feminine, cool, soft, reflective and moon-like, whereas Pingala is associated with strong masculine activity and heat like the sun. These two spiral up the Sushumna crisscrossing at each chakra.

Visualize your body via your third eye

Step Three – As you see and identify with your body, expand your awareness 360 degrees around you, becoming all that is in that space. Continue expanding your outward awareness of yourself as all that is.

Delta Fornicis, magnitude +5: brain, Fornix and celestial star, Fornax, are referred to as "Delta." Constellation Fornax is located just below the constellation Orion. Take your own trip of expansion, allowing your attention to fully perceive your community, country, planet and solar system. Become the Sun.

Now a Simultaneous Journey Inward

Step Four- This is a little bit like patting your head and rubbing your tummy at the same time, but while maintaining consciousness of merging with the sun, begin the visualization again from your original starting position. This time, however, you will contract infinitely smaller instead of infinitely expanding. See and feel all of that space as you. Kanda (the cave) is a center of the astral body beneath the base chakra, where the vital energy or Sukshma Prana will pass along the united energies of Ida and Pingala. Peak perception begins to embed in the space of awareness, and inertia or stability is gained by feeling compassion. As compassion grows stronger, more spin symmetry implodes the hearts perfect compression in harmonic ascension. As you see and identify with your subtle bodies, again allow your perceptions to experience all aspects of space.

Ride the expanding wave of your awareness. Allow all experience to flow through and around you without stopping the flow to analyze any one point. See and feel all of that atomic space. The energy of this space is continuously responding to a magnetic flow which causes a self-organizing expression in shape and form. The all-pervading fluid and magnetic flow of Universal Life Force we know as Love constantly influences, ignites and directs adamantine particles into manifestation. The adamantine particle, as both matter and anti-matter, is the divine spark of creation.

Rest here a moment at the pure and infinite point of potential to command the adamantine particles by feeling the loving intention simultaneously accepted as already realized. Love is the ultimate force in the Universe. Through the power of Love, every galaxy, star and planet, and every cell, atom and molecule, is held in place. In the presence of Love, patterns of beauty (Acu), perfection, harmony and efficiency manifest spontaneously (Lomi) within the crystal palace of your own Temple. Taoists refer to the AcuLomi Temple area between the two brain hemispheres amidst the pineal and pituitary as the Crystal Palace, which appears as "a thousand suns" when activated. During the height of this illumination, an intense opiate-like production of dimethyltryptamine (DMT), called the "White Drop," Amrita or "nectar of the gods" is released and descends to the heart center.

Step Five – As your perception comes to rest at the infinitely balanced zero-point, call upon your personal higher awareness which may appear as your Higher Self, Archetype or Ascended Master.

Continue expanding your awareness to travel through the zero-point of the synapse. This crossing over transcends intellectual concepts and is analogous to the transitional state of "becoming." As seen in the exchange between two nerve cells passing impulses through the diffusion of neurotransmitters, this same action occurs within the synapse interfacing the sacred space of the God-Spark. At the hub of the synapse live eternal conscious potential. Conceive again your loving, shareable intention and release. Letting go is the essential component for the crossing of the synapse to be actualized; however, be ready to pick up the frequency imprint on the other side.

As your perception becomes infinitely diminished fractals like a Mandelbrot set, your body, by contrast, seemingly appears ever larger. You have entered inner Earth/Agartha and may now once again feel the wholeness of your physical body, albeit on this altered plane.

Encounter Inner Earth as an exact replica

As above, so below

Step Six – Continue the process of expanding your inner awareness and find that a duplicate solar system exists at this dimension as well. As above, so below. Here, your infinitely contracted and infinitely expanded selves become one. See and feel all as you. Eventually encompassing the entire solar system at this level, become the sun.

Earth Sol, Agartha Sun

Step Seven – Here you identify with the infinitely contracted Sun, as seen from Agartha and yet find the overlay of the expanded self/Sun, as seen from Earth. Observe your conscious awareness encompassing both simultaneously. By so doing, you hold the conscious awareness of both your matter and anti-matter self. You cannot simply desire something, i.e.. some restoration from your Divine Blueprint; you must follow the light and phenomena within you, for this IS you, and this is your path to that Divine Blueprint.

Harmony of Apollo

Step Eight – Play and explore with the frequency of the sacred Trinity known as the "Harmony of Apollo." It is composed of:

1. You physically as third density Matter
2. You as anti-matter
3. You as the consciousness that encompasses both, the all and nothing.
4. Call upon higher Divine guidance

Step Nine – Unified as three [contracted self, expanded self and God/ Goddess/All That Is] begin your journey home towards bliss.

Step Ten – Journey from Supernova 1987a in the constellation Dorado to delta Fornax

Transcending

Step Eleven – Here you are joined by a fourth- your Divine Spirit Self

Onward to Galaxy NGC 4555

Step Twelve – The galaxy, located in the Constellation Coma, which means "Mother and Child or Virgo. Arrive in an explosion of white light. Explore. Be. Observe.

Maintain conscious awareness with your Divine Spirit Self

Step Thirteen – Repeat meditation in reverse, back to step one. Call upon and merge with your sacred interface God-Spark to journey back as your Divine Spirit Self, and call upon your Archetype/Ascended Master.

Observe yourself as a merged expression with your Higher Self

Step Fourteen – Become your Archetype/Ascended Master/Higher Self to assist in collapsing the Divine Spirit/Blueprint into physical 3-D.

Visualize your body via your third eye

Step Fifteen – As you see and identify with your body, expand your awareness 360 degrees around you. Remembering all that is in that space. See and feel all of that space as you.

Observe Self as All-That-Is

Step Sixteen – Continue expanding your awareness of yourself as all that is until you have collapsed your cellular god-spark sun, our solar sun, and the Bliss body/Sun back into 3-D physicality. With your eyes still closed, again hold your breath for three or four seconds, and acknowledge the action of watching yourself. Close by releasing the experience. Do it as often as you are comfortable. Observe the utility of the AcuLomi Temple meditation resulting as positive shareable exchanges in your life. As the frequency of your DNA (word of God) becomes more shareable, the old defective patterns are resolved to a more inclusive, harmoniously fractal resonance.

AcuLomi Temple "Ask Yourself" Questionnaire Survey

When we meditate, we drop below the dualistic ego. We temporarily disconnect from the superficial layers of mind and connect to our shared awakened nature—our collective buddha-nature.

1. Do you believe there is a Higher Power that exists beyond human perception?

    O Yes
    O No
    O Maybe

2. Imagine making a request of someone (by phone or text) who has never met you; Now also Imagine that same request made of someone whom you know is on the same page as you, completely relates and understands where you are coming from. Three words that best describe each scenario.

    Never Met

    O vague, indistinct, hazy
    O hopeful, uncertain, dubious
    O feel judged
    O I prefer to answer in my own words

    Know Well

    O plain, open, clear
    O hopeful, translucent, positive
    O feel heard
    O I prefer to answer in my own words

3. When you pray or meditate, do you feel/know with certainty that you have communicated directly with a Higher Power?

❍ Yes
❍ No

According to N.A.S.A, the ideal observer is one who causes no unnecessary perturbations to the system being observed. An observation made by such an observer is called an objective observation. ("The Observer in Modern Physics," n.d., p. 01)

4. Answers come from connecting with the Observer: Are you able to view personal circumstances through a 'third party-perspective' maintaining a channel to the Observer?

❍ Yes, and I lucidly discern between Ego and Observer
❍ No, I just get a feeling
❍ Both because at times I doubt myself
❍ I prefer to answer in my own words ⌐

Bonus- Please describe bliss and compassion

A. Bliss

❍ enlightenment
❍ Aha! moments
❍ unconditional, altruistic love, compassion and joy for All
❍ Other (Please describe) ⌐

B. Compassion

❍ caring but detached emotion
❍ understanding the impermanence of temporal relations
❍ mindful equanimity
❍ Other (Please describe) ⌐

The AcuLomi Temple Meditation and Workshop System, act as the bridge between science and religion by demonstrably engaging the biophysics of compassion and bliss. The analytical workshop or Learning Lab component, defines pure principle while the meditation protocol ignites the fractal attractor of sacred space to catalyze the expansion experience resulting in bliss and compassion. Golden-ratio phase conjugation produces the wave geometry of this "Holy Grail of fusion." The geometry of the Holy Grail has no inside or outside, thereby resolving the problem of perceived duality or separateness. This is identified as a simultaneous shift throughout all parameters, enabling coherent reorganization.

Attaining compassion and bliss releases the miasma permeating the current paradigm of fear-induced separation. Compassion and bliss are coherent emotions naturally expressed due to a realigning with the sacred geometry of golden-ratio phase conjugation achieved by meditatively focusing on pure principle, such as compassion. AcuLomi Temple's concluding questionnaire reveals that thoughts of compassion and bliss are shareable with all DNA because they are aware of themselves as Consciousness lucidly discerning between ego and the Observer. This supports the intended frequency of the charge symmetry of coherent emotions to qualify the newly acknowledged dynamic. The Learning Lab provides foresight anticipating projected intentions which result in an internal initiative willing to experience the unknown with novel and unique awareness. This leads to validation of the experiencer's understanding of the contextual meaning despite the exotic and recondite process. Registered as definitive statements in AcuLomi Temple's concluding questionnaire, acknowledging the new-found ability to lucidly discern Consciousness engaging the Observer, 100 percent success occurs in phase conjugate (golden ratio) negentropic charge collapse results from activating the sacred God-Spark interface through AcuLomi Temple meditation and training.

The participants realize a 40 percent increase in affirming certainty that they are in fact communicating directly with a 'Higher power'. 100% of the participants who believe there is a Higher Power that exists beyond human perception, also fully acknowledge the simultaneous sense of being infused with the sensation of hope which served to sharpen their awareness of being conscious of themselves as the Self, the Observer Self and part of the field expressing itself as Consciousness.

These research results affirm the human experience is reflected in both known and unknown, seen and unseen, environments. AcuLomi Temple meditation permits the catalyzation of the sacred interface to allow conscious interaction with those subtle and previously unseen environments captured and accessed within DNA. Measured by qualitative questionnaires, the meditation demonstrates a viable model of third-dimensional human access with the infinite worlds of anti-matter and subtle fields of energy. It turns out that both matter and anti-matter are required to make sense of our existence and the E at Delphi could well indicate the quantum foam E -volving via hyper-cubing the particle and wave. In this way, the share-ability as a symmetrical fractal structure converges to phase and phase-lock with like waves travelling hypercubed, thus resulting in 4 waves of bliss mixing to validate Plato's solution for the citizens of Delos. (Plato's work addressed several levels of meaning and was directed to those he thought capable of understanding.) The meditative experience relates symbolically and often to the Oracle at Delphi's consultation. One further example is the means to determine how to defeat a plague sent by Apollo. The Oracle had responded that they must double the size of the altar to Apollo, which was a regular cube and founded the belief that all life's answers lay in geometry and mathematics. Bliss however is the warp-drive lane for quantum acceleration to wellness and available to everyone through AcuLomi Temple meditation. Not knowing what we didn't know offered freedom otherwise not available within the parameters of mathematical calculations and belief systems. Through lucid and conscious mapping of a new language within those mathematical calculations and belief systems, a new means of garnering data has emerged which proves congruent with science and mystical imperatives. Previous tracking perceptions of the third dimensional mind did not offer awareness of the All-That-Is. Our DNA has contained the fractal wholeness of the All-That-Is Oneness all along. AcuLomi Temple meditation permits access to exploring the subtle worlds of Oneness in the All-That-Is contained within DNA and has opened the door for DNA to speak back, clearly concisely in all languages. The organic natural production of the messenger molecule Dimethyltryptamine (DMT) self-induced by the focus of pure principle in the AcuLomi Temple meditative state supports the means of accessing the subtle worlds through bliss that has been referred to as within the domain of 90 % junk DNA. Through the continued practise of meditation our return to full consciousness has made rigorous progress.

The greater truth of who we humans are, has always been with us, both within our DNA and all around us, as the heavenly cosmos. These truths, preserved in mythologies, and sacred but obscure texts are revealed to humanity from time to time at the nexus points of evolution. When humanity as a collective resonates at a frequency conducive to becoming One with the greater truth, then calibration takes place on the evolutionary scale. If humanity is not a match for this jump in frequency, the nexus points pass, and the cycle continues, giving rise to half-baked truths designed to enslave and conquer instead of resolving sovereignty and freedom. Humanity is once again at a nexus point of opportunity. AcuLomi Temple stands ready to share that frequency adjustment by enabling activation within DNA via phase conjugation. The reason AcuLomi Temple meditation causes phase conjugation is because the meditation process induces a compressional wave (derived from focus on pure principle) to align directly in the dodeca-icosa formation that completes the circuit to reawaken our connection to the All-That-Is. AcuLomi Temple Meditation triggers an initial reaction in the space between points of frequency covering three perspectives simultaneously, where the distance of expansion is equal to the distance of contraction, or depth. For example, - 9 density inward contraction equals + 9 density dimension outward expansion, whereby the mid-point is the 4 ½ dimensional expression of our present third-density Earth known to some as Nibiru (not to be confused with the alleged Planet X or Wormwood). The AcuLomi Temple meditation has demonstrated holistic gain exponentially for all participants that experience Oneness. Empowered by knowing freedom as a self-reliant/ self-referring alternative to the pseudo-authority of ego-based separation, all expressions of personal wellness are amplified. The sense of certainty derived from AcuLomi meditation on pure principle reinforces self-referral and self-reliance frequencies as the outcome of bliss imploding charge distribution efficiency. In this way, conventional human attention evolves with the ability to track faster than light longitudinal EMF emission of photons. Science has long held that the movement of electrons, or charge, creates a magnetic field. Because the electric field is established, an electromagnetic field is generated. Changes in an electric field, such as a group of meditators, can generate magnetic activity which generate the observed outcome as a change in electrical activity. The observed outcome experienced as bliss, certainty, self-reliance or peak experience is the big 'E', the 'Effect' of the electromagnetic field re-penting called phase conjugation. Pent means staying true to yourself in a universal sense by taking responsibility for psych-navigation through the subtle worlds. Guided through the seven-spin tetracube to the five-spin dodeca initiates the implosive compression resulting in the ability to lucid dream. Consistent with 4-Wave Mixing of conventional optics, AcuLomi Temple meditation affects a similar crossing of opposing pairs of magnetic lines to catalyze charge distribution efficiency of sacred space. Achieving and maintaining the frequency of loving kindness or bliss creates the attraction to become the magnetic lens of perfect embedding where the point of reference can be aware of the entire whole. Confirming both straight and exotic trajectories of the particle and wave concept from the principle of quantum superposition, AcuLomi Temple advances the observer effect by using the sum or superposition of two wave functions to ride the hypercube into other dimensions. (Zyga, 2017, p. 1) The act of conscious observation during pure principle meditation creates a ripple effect throughout the path participants viewed from their initial conditions. Where speculation is noise as opposed to legitimate signal, the familiar terrain of consistent and repeated participation in AcuLomi Temple meditation provides certainty as the measure of success. No longer fluctuating between polarities that eons of sun-gods will attest to, humanity stands at the brink of evolutionary opportunity marked as the full circle return to the original mother of the universe, held always in trust within our DNA until the appropriate photon /light could be once again activated. Joyfully relinquishing enslavement to ego is brought about by the components within AcuLomi Temple meditation. Sound, symbolized by the conch shell indicating the mystical 'Ohm', certainty symbolized by the lightning bolt, mastery over physical, mental and spiritual energy during meditation is symbolized by the trident and surrender as symbolized by the golden sun/lion demonstrates freedom from fear.

While all research data reflect unique individual results, the consistent demonstration of an improved sense of well-being and joyful curiosity about life brought renewed vigor inclusively experienced at the Supramental, Mental, Vital, and Physical levels, to open new dimensions of healing and metaphysical gnosis. AcuLomi Temple meditation findings fully supports the approach of Dr. Paul Drouin, who writes: "As we refine our observation of the individual from a broader and deeper point of view, applying the elements of quantum physics to the field of Integrative Medicine, also provides the ability to integrate multi-dimensional approaches of healing." (International Quantum University of Integrative Medicine [IQUIM], n.d.,

p. 1) The bridge established between scientific and mystical imperatives resolves the paradox in the field of physics by providing access to the sacred interface between physicality and the subtle worlds of consciousness.

The sacred interface, or God-Spark, as the perfect echo of charge distribution, makes a wave sustainable, which is the very frequency that defines the term "sacred." The interface aspect of self-referring fractality in space conducts value greater than the sum of its parts experientially by integrating the knower, the known and the field of knowledge. Examining the sacred interface, or God-Spark, refers to the perfect echo of charge distribution because this nature which makes a wave sustainable is the very frequency which defines the term sacred. The interface aspect is a self-referring fractality in space which conducts value greater than the sum of its parts by integrating the knower, the known and the field of knowledge, knowingly! Whether drawing harmonics from the well of bliss, exploring morphogenetic fields or developing paranormal abilities, the conclusions attained by catalyzing the Sovereign God-Spark free you from suppression by the pseudo-authority of separation and ego by interfacing Buddhi Self-Actualization and Oneness. An immediate physiologically shift accompanies the heightened integration of gnosis, as the experience of Oneness tangibly communicates the Divine Order through the AcuLomi Temple meditation. Consciousness is unitive, thereby counteracting the illusion of separateness. First-hand experience as a result of the repeatable technique to interface through DNA a shareable harmonic frequency opens access to the well of bliss, exploration of morphogenetic fields, and the development of paranormal abilities. Through the catalyzing of the Sovereign God-Spark, freedom from separation and the ego by interfacing Buddhi Self-Actualization and Oneness enabled the repeatable encounter of Oneness as your sovereign Quantum Self.

As Jesus said, "wisdom is justified by her children". In other words, what is the result of your creation.

> **'Compassion and love are not mere luxuries.As the source, both of inner and external peace, they are fundamental to the continued survival of our species.'**
> *His Holiness the XIV Dalai Lama* ("Quote; His Holiness the XIV Dalai Lama," n.d., p. 01)

Conclusion

The experience of compassion and bliss results in a quantum collapse due to coherent self-awareness called Consciousness lucidly discerning between ego and the Observer. This leads to validation of the experiencer's understanding of the contextual psychophysical parallelism. Consciousness provided new meaning as 'aha' moments gleaning the possibilities manifest in the mind, vital body, and the bliss body creatively surpassing conditioned response. Eureka moments acknowledge the new-found ability to lucidly discern Consciousness engaging the Observer. Phase conjugate (golden ratio) negentropic charge collapse results from activating the sacred God-Spark interface through AcuLomi Temple meditation and training.

"The real voyage of discovery consists not in seeking new lands but seeing with new eyes".

—Marcel Proust

"Freeing yourself was one thing, claiming ownership of that freed self was another."

—Toni Morrison,

Take Quiz 1 Now

IS SOMETHING IN OUTER SPACE
EFFECTING YOUR INNER SPACE

Or ...Is something in inner space effecting your outer space?

1. When you find yourself on autopilot, is there often a common theme to your thoughts?
   Habitual thoughts are a frequency which trap you into recreating the same experience over and over and over. Is this what you want?

   Don't cry because it's over, smile because it happened...and move on!

2. Do you often daydream or imagine yourself rescuing someone?
   To be appreciated, appreciate your self and THEN you will be appreciated in the eyes of others.
   "Be yourself; everyone else is already taken." - Oscar Wilde

3. How often do you catch yourself editing your dialogue depending on the audience?
   Have you thought it through, have you felt it through? Is it your truth in this moment?
   Then- "Be who you are and say what you feel, because those who mind don't matter, and those who matter don't mind." — Bernard M. Baruch

4. What secret dream is still clinging to life inside you?
   Your values are the greatest navigator imaginable, do you know what they are?

"You only live once, but if you do it right, once is enough." — Mae West

5. What do you do in your spare time; Why? What do you enjoy talking about; Why? How do you decorate your space; Why?
    These are your values!
    "You've gotta dance like there's nobody watching,
    Love like you'll never be hurt,
    Sing like there's nobody listening,
    And live like it's heaven on earth." — William W. Purkey

6. Who do you surround yourself with?
    Increase your potential and raise your energy by hanging out with people you admire.
    "Friendship ... is born at the moment when one man says to another "What! You too? I thought that no one but myself . . ."" — C.S. Lewis, The Four Loves

𝒥ake 𝒬uiz 2 𝒩ow

IS SOMETHING IN OUTER SPACE
EFFECTING YOUR INNER SPACE

Or …Is something in inner space effecting your outer space?

Try doing something you haven't ever done before. Then do it twice again. The first time is to get over the fear of doing it. The second time is to learn how to do it. And a third time, to figure out whether you like it or not. - Virgil Garnett Thomson

Expanding your awareness

What addictive behavior are you most sensitive about?

Regardless if the behavior is yours or another's, the act of resistance only blocks a gift you have refused to accept. "What', you say, "Gift"? The gift is to reveal where you have not loved yourself, where you have withheld love because of a judgment. Judgment not only blocks a ray of light from being transposed into love, but it creates a shadow which inevitably threatens you like a scary monster which is quickly shut away in a closet. How much of your energy is invested in keeping the closet door slammed shut so that monster isn't noticed by others around you? How much of your energy is being syphoned off in pushing against that closet door so you don't have to deal with whatever message that monster holds?

What if we just let that monster out for a minute? Can we get a good long look at it? That monster has an important message for you. It only takes 5 seconds of courage to let the message in… listen… Courage is not the absence of fear, but rather the judgement that something else is more important than fear.

There most certainly is a benefit to the addictive behavior. For every addiction there is a Sub -diction to be gained. What are you hiding from? This is your subdiction, replacement or gain.

I.e. adding alcohol to subtract loneliness, or, adding money [workaholic or miser] to subtract fear of poverty

Once you have determined the gift, you can then choose better options to provide you with the desired subdiction/objective.

Maybe you could choose to make yourself your best friend instead of choosing alcohol to numb you from the feeling of loneliness. From the very moment you engage in friendly thoughts and actions toward yourself, a non-local validation from the outside world will appear. This is a quantifiably proven Scientific fact!

What means, other than the path of a workaholic or miser, might allay the anguish culminating in poverty mentality? Perhaps finding that there is equal proof to substantiate your wellbeing? Challenge yourself to find at least ten ways to demonstrate your security so you can celebrate your life!

When your only tool is a hammer, all problems start looking like nails.

1. Do you know where you are blissfully unaware or simply ignorant?

Don't get me wrong, I know you are also shining brilliantly in many other areas …but…if we could take a moment to explore the unknown, we will find an abundance of treasure has been there, silently waiting to be claimed.

"It is the mark of an educated mind to be able to entertain a thought without accepting it". - -Aristotle

2. Do you wish there was just some 'rule' to follow"? …just somebody tell me the rule and I will follow it…there is so much chaos and confusion and pain. Every which way you turn you find out you are doing it all wrong, nothing is working and…uhh!... just someone tell me how to do life!

You would think connecting your heart intelligence to your brain intelligence would be a natural process, however physiological, cognitive, and emotional systems, modify complex signaling pathways by lifestyle.

Your body, brain, heart and gut play a direct and important role in determining perceptions, thought processes, and emotional experiences.
Sing with your heart and listen to your gut.
"The heart has reasons that reason cannot know." - Blaise Pascal

3. Have you ever wondered how to pray, to actually trigger reliable 'action/reaction' type of results?

You know praying is talking to a higher Source, right? And if you are talking to Pure Creative Source Energy your authentic sincerity should probably render you completely vulnerable and fully open in your supplication. So open in fact as to allow your Great Creator to merge with you and effectively lift your frequency to match your desire, right? I mean isn't that the purpose of prayer...to get something? Be it understanding, relief or even just communication, prayer is you reaching out. Satisfaction is to know that you have hit your mark, delivered your message and been heard.
"Perfection is achieved, not when there is nothing more to add, but when there is nothing left to take away". —Antoine de Saint-Exupéry

4. Have you ever wondered how to meditate?

You know meditating means to listen right? Listen to the wind, the water or better yet, listen to the silence. It is golden...and so are the results. But maybe you want to listen to wisdom...so how do you do that? Thinking of your question is like lifting the string of a guitar... to hear the resulting tone you have to let the string go! Get it? Lifting the string establishes potential, but Letting it Go sets the wave pattern into motion... Results!
"When I let go of what I am, I become what I might be". -Lao Tzu

5. Do you communicate your feelings and thoughts with precision?

Communication is really an extension of the same process you have already mastered.
When you were an infant it required more than just a few awkward days learning how to extend your awareness out into each of your limbs

until eventually you mastered control on a variety of levels. You learned many a lesson on sensation, both energetically and physically eventually expanding this gnosis throughout the body. But Hey! It's in the bag so then you repeated that same process learning how to ride a bike and drive a car.

Driving a car requires that you send those sensate feelers out through the tires onto the road and into every little sound your engine makes. All of this information flows in easily and expands your awareness far beyond your car. Once you become really present to these conditions you can continue to expand your awareness until next you have developed Extra-Sensory Gnosis. Send your feelers out and discover we are all part of the Great One.

"Though free to think and act, we are held together, like the stars in the firmament, with ties inseparable. These ties cannot be seen, but we can feel them." – Nikola Tesla

Take Quiz 3 Now

-IS SOMETHING IN OUTER SPACE
EFFECTING YOUR INNER SPACE

Or …Is something in inner space effecting your outer space?
"I've learned that people will forget what you said,
people will forget what you did,
but people will never forget how you made them feel." — Maya Angelou

1. Have you ever wondered how to communicate with Pure Source Energy in order to maintain your spirit and mind in harmony with God?

Communication is really an extension of the same process you have already mastered as an infant, remember?

It works the same for communicating with Pure Source Energy.

Your inner infant can teach you to gradually extended your sensation of awareness into the subtle bodies of your physical vessel and beyond. In this way you have access to merge on the subtlest level with any element, condition or frequency you desire to love or learn more about.

"Who looks outside, dreams; who looks inside, awakes". - Carl Gustav Jung

2. Love thy neighbor as thyself…but … do you love thyself?

Maybe the better question is where are you withholding love from yourself? To reveal this answer, consider where you have any judgement… on yourself or any other person, situation or experience. Judgement casts a shadow. Judgement is a huge pointer showing you exactly where you are not loving yourself. Let's start with Self-Acceptance. This requires the action male energy and the intuitive female energy be mutually supporting each other enabling your Spirit and Mind to exist in harmony with God. As one reaches the state of willful surrender by separation from thought in meditation, instructions come through as inner knowing, inner balance and inner composure; now what's not to love about that!

Most of the shadows of this life are caused by standing in one's own sunshine. ~Ralph Waldo Emerson

3. How do you relate Oneness to the fabric of consciousness?

Oneness IS the fabric of consciousness. Matter and Energy are two poles of the same unity. Shamans and Mystics call this Oneness or Interconnectedness. Consciousness may be the agency that focuses the waves, so we can observe them as particle at one place. This is a tangled hierarchy within the immanent self-reference of a system observing itself. The trick is to distinguish between consciousness and awareness.

"Through our eyes, the universe is perceiving itself. Through our ears, the universe is listening to its harmonies. We are the witnesses through which the universe becomes conscious of its glory, of its magnificence." — Alan W. Watts

4. How do you relate to time?,... consider when technology is fully implemented?

Time doesn't exist. Clocks exist. "Everything connected with life on the planet earth moves through the same rhythm, whether it is in the cosmos amongst planets, constellations and nebula, or in the human body amongst flesh, blood and atoms. The story of Jesus is the story that governs the universe and all life on this planet. If you understand this, you will understand the great mystery that has eluded the worlds minds since creation

"Time and tide wait for no man". -Geoffrey Chaucer

Time doesn't exist. Clocks exist. +Mass is only a name for the inertia stored by charge rotation, +Time is only a name for measuring charge rotation, +Space-time is a name for the array of rotating charge, +Dimensions are only a name for how many axes of rotating charge can be superposed in one nest (harmonic inclusiveness in the frequency signature, ...

"This way of turning compression into (charge) acceleration is hypothesized to be the core wave mechanism of phase conjugation (apparent self-organization) and the centripetal forces of gravity, life force, color, and perception." – Dan Winter

"Observations are to be regarded as discrete, discontinuous events. In between are gaps which we cannot fill in when we consciously see, consciousness collapses the quantum state of the brain-mind. Unconscious processing does not affect collapse of the quantum wave-function, pinning down quantum entities to one reality. Thus, unconscious processing permits the expression of non-local phenomena.

Matter and Energy are two poles of the same unity. Shamans and Mystics call this Oneness or Interconnectedness. Consciousness is the agency that holds the waves, so we can observe them at one place. The trick is to distinguish between consciousness and awareness.

"Through our eyes, the universe is perceiving itself. Through our ears, the universe is listening to its harmonies. We are the witnesses through which the universe becomes conscious of its glory, of its magnificence." — Alan W. Watts

"T 'ain't what they call you, it's what you answer to". -W.C. Fields

5. Have you ever wondered what the rising of Kundalini is all about.? (aka, the opening of the 7 seals)

Kundalini is a Hindu term however all spiritual or religious teachings describe this phenomenon using other names, for example, Baptism of the Holy Spirit. This psycho-spiritual impulse can be aroused through meditation as electrical energy to rise up the Sushumna nadi channel, passing through 7 chakras to ignite the pineal gland bringing forth spiritual enlightenment. In the Law of Correspondence, we see the cosmic kundalini likewise move through 7 constellations- Mensa, Dorado, Hydrus, Reticulum, Horologium, Eridanus, Fornax, just as the Stria Pinealis runs from the Pineal Gland of the brain into the fornix. In so doing, Kundalini passes through 5 levels of consciousness represented by these natural elements;

1ˢᵗ stage - EARTH

2ⁿᵈ stage - WATER (also a symbol of truth)

3ʳᵈ stage – AIR (separation from thoughts)

4ᵗʰ stage – (Fire higher realms of spirit)

5ᵗʰ stage – (the RENEWED MIND)

Once the Kundalini Shakti has ascended to the highest psychic center at the crown of the head, it compels a new state of consciousness.

"Life is a flow of love, only your participation is requested. Blessed are the ones who serve others. They are the ones who find heaven on earth". - Yogi Bhajan

Kundalini in all Cultures

Let's look at the definition revealing a bit more about Kundalini After all, a Rose by any other name is still a rose.

Mystical texts and shamanic traditions show that kundalini has been a universal phenomenon and thus is found in esoteric teachings for at least three thousand years. Kundalini-type descriptions and experiences are found in the esoteric teachings of the Orient, Asia, South and North America, Egypt, and the Kung bushmen of Africa. In the Bible, Kundalini has been interpreted as "the solar principle in man". In the Koran, the works of Plato and other Greek philosophers, alchemical tracts and in Hermetic, Kabbalistic, Rosicrucian, and Masonic writings, Kundalini is an effect of the energy directed by consciousness. This coiled serpent of yoga was said to reside within the sleeping body yet could be aroused through spiritual discipline or spontaneous mystical illumination. It was called the coiled serpent of yoga because it behaves like a serpent in the root chakra at the base of the spine. Described as liquid fire or liquid light in Tantra Yoga, kundalini is revered as an aspect of Shakti, the divine female energy and consort of Shiva.

Having influenced the teachings of people throughout the world for many countless ages, kundalini holds a notorious presence.

Meditation can arouse the kundalini to raise it energetically up a subtle pathway parallel to the spinal column, activating the chakras in succession as it climbs. The objective is to raise the kundalini along the sushumna or central axis, where it is crisscrossed in a helix by the ida and pingala, ultimately reaching the crown chakra, where it unites with the Shiva, or the male polarity, and brings illumination. This male energy is the action, supportive energy responding and protecting one's female intuitive guidance.

Nadis

According to the Ancient Teachings of Tantra and Kundalini Yoga at Tantra-Kundalini.com, there are a network of subtle channels known as nadis through which the life force (prana) circulate, in addition to the basic seven chakras of the subtle body. These Tantras have described fourteen principal Nadis. Of these streams, Ida, Pingala and Sushumna are considered the most important.

Ida is the left channel. Ida is white, feminine, cold, represents the moon and is associated with the river Ganga (Ganges). Originating in Muladhara, Ida ends up in the left nostril.

Pingala is the right channel. Pingala is red, masculine, hot, represents the sun and is associated with the river Yamuna. Originating in Muladhara, Pingala ends up in the right nostril.

Sushumna is the central channel and is associated with the river Saraswati. Within the Sushumna nadi there are three more subtle channels: Vajra, Chitrini and Brahma nadi through which Kundalini moves upwards running up the body from just below Muladhara chakra to Sahasrara chakra at the crown of the head.

The kanda in Muladhara chakra is the meeting place of the three main nadis and is known as Yukta Triveni (Yukta: "combined", tri: "three", veni: "streams"). In Muladhara, Shakti, the static unmanifested Kundalini, is symbolized by a serpent coiled into three and a half circles around the central axis Svayambhu-linga at the base of the spine. The serpent lies blocking the entrance to Sushumna, the central channel with his mouth. Sushumna remains closed at its lower end as long as Kundalini is not awakened.

The technique of Kundalini Yoga consists in using Prana (the vital air), guiding its circulatory movement through Ida and Pingala down to the base of the spine into the space where Kundalini lies coiled. The vital energies of the opposite forces circulating in Ida and Pingala will be unified and Shakti Kundalini will then awaken and rise up Sushumna, energizing the seven chakras.

From Muladhara chakra, Ida and Pingala alternate from the right to left sides at each chakra until they reach Ajna chakra where they meet again with Sushumna.

In Ajna chakra the meeting of the three main nadis is called Mukta Triveni (Mukta: "liberated"). Continuing beyond Ajna chakra, Ida and Pingala end in the left and right nostrils respectively.

Once the Kundalini Shakti has ascended through Sushumna to Sahasrara, the highest psychic center at the crown of the head, it is made to reverse its course and return to rest in the base center again.

The Five Levels of Consciousness

Five levels of consciousness can be represented by various natural elements.

1st or lowest stage is represented by EARTH
2nd stage, the next step up is represented by WATER and is also a symbol of truth
3rd stage which can be reached only by separation from thoughts is represented by AIR
4th stage, encountering the higher realms of spirit, is represented by Fire
5th stage is the RENEWED MIND

Just as a child gradually develops an ability over time to broaden awareness and coordinate control over the basic five senses of the physical body's sight, taste, touch, smell and hearing, so too must we all mature, and in this same way gain control of our higher senses through meditation. These higher senses reveal the sanctum of your holy temple.

The temple is the symbol of the human mind. Your temple must be constructed spiritually in the silence of meditation. To achieve total silence, means, to empty the mind or achieve the absence of thought. Thus, biblical scripture will allude to this secret by revealing that no tools were heard in its construction. It was built in silence because it represents the temple of the mind, which can only be reached when one is totally free of thought.

Epilogue Chapter

"You are not a drop in the ocean. You are the entire ocean in a drop." -Rumi

ello, I am Dr. Shelley Evans. I use my PhD education in Quantum Medicine to train people how to induce a Blissful Peak experience naturally, so they feel complete and fulfilled, no longer needing access to depleting habits.

Have you or someone you know, ever just needed a lift, either physically, emotionally or spiritually, to manage a situation that would otherwise continue to escalate? ...well, I have a variety of means to help people access natural bliss, so their wellness fast-tracks the lifestyle they want. Bliss is the fastest way to wellness. Until now, our society has lacked the natural modality to recalibrate joy, happiness and freedom when life experiences present fear, pain or trauma. Instead, when overloaded by the demands of today's world, people have escaped into behaviors of restriction at best but often even find a wide range of addictions as substitutes for their freedom, paying the price of deep stress, shock, loneliness, financial debt-loads or Poverty!

There are many paths to achieve bliss, ... What path do you find interesting or easy? For example, do you know how to breathe? So, appropriate breathing rhythm and technique could be an easy, natural way for you to access bliss .... have you thought about your diaphragm today? Or, would you prefer state of the art technology that does it all for you? We can do that, however for today, right now, would you like me give you a technique, once learned, you could create bliss?

Everyone who has room in their day to be happier is provided the means to develop foolproof intuition and well-being through self-compassion. YogAha rejuvenation system simply repairs, relaxes, regenerates and recharges, emotionally, mentally, spiritually etc., to manage those situations that otherwise could continue to intensify, thus produce fear, trauma and pain. Through meditation on pure principle, communication with this field is not only possible but it will become your portal to higher learning. Have you noticed that when our lives are consumed with minor distractions, misaligned demands, fears, guilt, prestige or pride, we become restricted, tense and feel trapped?

Trauma and stress, produce acidic heat and inflammation which is recorded as shock in the subconscious mind. The mind stacks every such experience creating endocrine fight or flight hormonal response, chemical, and other neurological effects in our cellular memory. Remember I told you that Bliss is the fastest path to healing? Well, it is also the portal to freedom, to shut off the fear and connect to Your internal soul compass.

This moment holds your purpose. you are alive: what are you going to do about it?

If you ever need a boost…. Align to your internal soul compass to that which is wholly shareable. As a bonus, you will find that you have developed a foolproof intuition. You will feel more joy and more powerful certainty as you train your neurological process for gratitude, happiness, relaxation and inspiration to find and live your purpose, guided by dreams and desires!

Dan Winter has provided the source material for much of the physics contained within YogAha. Likewise, his work inspires and sustains the spiritual purpose defined throughout these pages.

Authentic living fast tracked the opportunity for exponentially increasing the frequency of aha and bliss moments. What vibration are you a match for? What vibration do you want to be a match for?

Through the Yogaha's we come to know our oneness with the Infinite Intelligence, Pure Source Energy and Joy which gives life to all and which is the essence of our own Self.

Signed- nonlocally you, Shelley

Part Two

Yogahas

Yogaha's are the aha moments produced by tuning in to sacred space. Sacred space is created through the union or yoking of the Observer's awareness with Consciousness conveying pure principle. Sort of like a zygote, or a translator interface which would allow two different operating systems to talk with each other, YogAha is your ally. The resulting bliss moment is suspended as stillness, to attain liberation. If only for the moment, liberation provides the cosmic area code (which is a specific frequency) for conscious union with the blissful Spirit. This is freedom. Yogahahas, the companion workbook, on the other hand, are the aha moments produced when pursuit of pure principle demonstrates the fractal waves of charge to create centripetal compression or duplication as the reflection within your own personal experience revealing Oneness. 'If you spot it; you got it' kind of idea. When we can laugh at ourselves and enjoy the simple, sometimes even petty qualities that Earth humans evolve through, we can embrace the journey, celebrate all life and ground heaven here on Earth. There is nothing new under the sun. We do not have consciousness; rather Consciousness has us!

Statement- AcuLomi Temple Meditation is defined as the bridge between science and religion by demonstrably engaging the biophysics of compassion and bliss.

Meditation induced aha -Refinement of scientific concepts provide a more rigorous description of spiritual experience and further encourage new neurological pathways to exponentially proliferate the pattern of diversifying expansion. This literal 'out-branching is the physical expression of the infinite mind and spirit metamorphosing into something biological and practical.

The economy of nature embeds pure thoughts, morals, and principals, to be discovered, adapted and then initiated into practical useful models as our revered Guides for everyday life. The repeatable meditation protocol ignites the fractal waves of charge to create centripetal compression as an attractor of sacred space to catalyze the expansion experience resulting in bliss and compassion.

Statement- As the frequency of your DNA (word of God) becomes more shareable, the old defective patterns are resolved to a more inclusive, harmoniously fractal resonance.

Meditation induced aha- Peace is precipitated through vivid conviction of core and fundamental Celebration of all Life. It is a simple matter to celebrate myriad life forms that serve ones values, however, do you 'celebrate' all the life forms regarded as destructive or producing negative impact such as germs, virus and bacteria, ET's tinkering with our DNA, or that comet racing toward Earth? Within the certainty of Being, infinite and eternal sparks of Oneness elicit joyful CELEBRATION of ALL life from the perspective of Divine Order.

The celebration of all life demonstrates that ego has relinquished control of interpretive designations regarding the 'meaning' of experience to permit the absolute celebration of all life forms inclusively.

Statement- AcuLomi Temple meditation utilizes universal language of light as the carrier to ensure the process is reproducible.

Meditation induced aha – Pure principle induces the frequency required to enter the sacred space in wholeness and balance which is mandatory in order to be able to emerge with the memory of the meditative experience intact. This replicates the ego death of the Hero's Journey having discovered the living universal language of light very much igniting all DNA. Having passed through the refiner's fire to return home to center, humbled and true, the outside now is perceived self-similar to the inside. All illusion of separation has been burned away to reveal the Holy Grail has indeed preserved and eternalized the living universal language of light.

Statement - Golden-ratio phase conjugation produces the wave geometry of this Holy Grail of Oneness.

Meditation induced aha-The geometry of the Holy Grail has no inside or outside, thereby resolving the problem of perceived duality or separateness. From the event horizon of this fractal feedback dynamic, the All-That-Is becomes accessible via the medium of a vacuum structure of infinite potential. Inducing a manifestation meditation requires the frequency of what you want to manifest must first be found inside you it will be mirrored in the external perception we call reality.

Proof does not arrive through grasping onto measurements such as the Heisenberg Uncertainty Principle would demonstrate but rather arrives, just as the ancients knew, by submitting your will to the alleged will of God thereby becoming self-similar and through the Hero's Journey to become the all-that-is of the singularity/wholeness, Sufi, Sophia/ain soph etc.

Pure Principle can be demonstrated as any spiral, such as the wind up and pitch architype that Freemasons turned into the game of Baseball or the shadow of sacred letters as the gestures & perspectives of DNA. To 'think' morally, lovingly and generously is circular; to 'act' morally, lovingly and generously is square – and Masonic. The circle with a square within depicts the union of heaven and earth, by analogy, the goal to 'ground' or secure Heaven on Earth. This is consistent with Kabbalistic philosophy that the goal of all humans is to transcend the lower emotional and intellectual planes, being reborn into the divine and commune with the full consciousness of

To square the circle and allow spin is where Hydrogen and pi meet. Our DNA has contained the fractal wholeness of Oneness all along. AcuLomi Temple meditation permits access to exploring the subtle worlds of Oneness in the All-That-Is contained within DNA and has opened the door for DNA to speak back, clearly concisely in all languages.

Statement- Understanding Pure Principles such as 'squaring the circle' have been relegated to esoteric mystery schools.

Meditation induced aha - Pure Principle can be tracked via loving thoughts that are shareable with all DNA as the sacred spiral found in the flame letters of original language. Pure principle can also be tracked via something as mundane as the wind up and pitch architype that Freemasons turned into the game of Baseball. According to Masonic tradition, holding thoughts that are moral, loving and generous relates to the "circle" but to act morally, lovingly and generously relates to the "square". The circle holding a square within depicts the one and the many as a union of heaven and earth and by analogy, is consistent with philosophy that the collective goal of humanity is to transcend the lower planes of the emotional and intellectual bodies, to be reborn into the higher...aka 'divine' full consciousness of light.

Statement- Meaningful breakthroughs, such as experiencing the return to full consciousness, occurs through the activation of what is termed 'junk' DNA.

Meditation nduced aha - Stories store information and catalogue relationship/relationshape in linguistic, mathematical, and biological forms. Form is information fractally conserved and perpetuated. From the mudras of India, to Hawaiian Hula, and the hand gestures revealing Hebrew flame letters, manual gestures of speech are inherent to conscious expression. All letters are the gestures /perspectives of DNA connected to the creative force of the All-That-Is and express the point in movement and coding symmetry like a strip wound around a column. The activation of alleged 'junk' DNA has produced profound holographic-like experiences where Ancestral Beings become present to communicate and interact physically. I have been engaged in this way with -Samothea (Apollo visited her in the north during the Greek winter season), Tiamat (Goddess of primordial ocean appeared to me October 2016 in Hawaii, wearing a red dress), Ganesha has an ongoing relationship with me which I am grateful for (Ganesha phenomena), Hopi flower of Death, Lakshmi, Kuan Yin, Thoth. As well this DNA activation has enabled sight of the subtle worlds such as visitors from Star nations, off-worlders, various plant beings such as Tobacco, Ayahuasca, homeopathic proving, mineral kingdom and animals. Through the activation of alleged junk DNA, I was visited by an earth Being and told to expect conception of my daughter. Similarly, I knew about the conception of my granddaughter sometime before her mother even knew she was pregnant. All of these experiences are fully received while in the normal day-to-day Beta awake frequency. There are far too many experiences to convey individually, however collectively, they have provided certainty which has expanded my own perception of what life is. Recognizable patterns emerge everywhere. For example, in AcuLomi Temple meditation the awareness travels to the heart of Dawa our Sun. Here the sun vortex appears as a Rose. The shape of the rose is a fractally repeated pattern throughout all life. Just as passion and compassion are like the fruit which contains its own seed, will ripen and fall to the ground to reseed the next tree which is the event horizon between singularity and wholeness. The recursive tree of life pattern not only branches in Fibonacci or golden spiral pattern and factor of phi, the golden ratio also produces the fruit which has the seed to grow the tree which produces the fruit which has the seed to grow the tree...

AcuLomi Temple meditation connects sustainability and integration of insights. **Statement Q**-Ease of repeatable access to sacred space; Can prayer induce scientific and meaningful access to sacred space?

Meditation induced aha A- Engaging the science of Prayer requires an observer-determined attention that underlies space and time itself. The spiritual values of mind and God arise from experience inside the perception of consciousness. Acknowledging a power beyond or outside of our self might be perceived as an external event to stimulate the far richer internal gnosis interpreting a meaningful life. But in fact, within our own DNA is access to that power we call God/Goddess/All-That-Is. I personally have experienced this Source within my DNA as Lakshmi, Lord Ganesha, Tiamat, Saamothea, Hopi Flower of Death, Quan Yin, Thoth/Tehuti and others. These beings live and can express through all DNA. The ancient Egyptians personified this wisdom or force as the Neter. This is the sacred force which conquers everything subtle and penetrates everything solid.

We are student and teacher to self until full consciousness is restored, but then gnosis, that flash of intuition, arrives in the 'flash of an eye. One scintillating twinkle is all it takes. Prayers meaning is generated internally and comes from the content of the experience balanced by the "gnosis" of its context. Our DNA comes prepackaged to convey that syntax, share the resulting meaning and deliver a coherent being, awake and effective, adding value to the Universe. Embedded within our DNA is the ancient wisdom awaiting activation to restore awareness fully conscious as the Family of One.

Focus on pure principle as prayer, seeks out the solution by finding a seed for the perfect (fractal) in the DNA. Thus, the micro cosmos is created according to the prototype of the macro cosmos. Focus on pure principle such as prayerful compassion, creates self-symmetrical frequency recorded as hertz, number of waves, oscillations, and vibration. Frequency is like the zip code address for every particle/wave in the All-That-Is.

Think of it from the perspective of charge: positron plus electron = light.

Through prayer we are trying to birth new light. Light causes an extra axis of spin, which superimposes a harmonic of frequencies leading to an envelope of pressure we call in-form-ation.

Form is the only thing the universe conserves by maintaining the ratio of length, area and volume of the golden mean (Phi). The 'aha moment' in prayerful (focused) ecstasy and bliss achieved as a harmonic cascade called holography, establishes a connecting field of resonation with all frequencies.

Dawa, the sun vortex as a Rose

Acu- Patterns of energy

Lomi- Flow/Qi, effectively tilting the angle of phonon wave to cast sound shadows, most noticeably initiated in the

Temple - Area within the human cranium. The Temple overlies the temporal and sphenoid bone. Here in the crystal palace, brain waves converging at Planck's distance, length and time implement the onus to take responsibility for and deliberately choose, the pressure that emotion creates (likewise affecting the thymus).

Registered as scales of measurement, phase conjugate (golden ratio) negentropic charge collapse results from activating the sacred God-Spark interface through AcuLomi Temple meditation and training.

Wise Questions

"The quality of your life is based partly upon the quality of the questions you ask yourself daily". -John Demartini

Q and A follows;

The sample questions and answers provided below, are provided here with permission, to share a modest example of Aha revelations that await those who can ask meaningful questions. Your question is more important than the answer. Whomever asks high quality questions will likewise live a high-quality life.

Q-

I got struck between these two extremes:

"The more we oblige, the more we self-censor, the more we appease, the bolder the enemy gets." & "I'm pleased to oblige", Please give me some wisdom

A-

This is a wise observation, first- Know Thyself, in so doing you recognize that there is no 'characteristic or human quality' that is not shared by all. In other words, Freedom comes to the person who knows himself as the All-That-Is. Your very own preponderance or inclination toward qualities/characteristics that are comfortable to you or 'flavor favorites' can be honored without being derailed by someone who needs to make different choices. It boils down to the adage," live and let live"; the person who recognizes the Oneness or All-That-Is as self, finds no judgement that leads to separation but rather makes choices about who and what defines acceptable/comfortable energy to be around. I think you have a natural inclination toward harmony which might appear initially to be 'appeasing others'. Harmony is soul path to know yourself. This however requires that You have enough respect for Your current awareness that you love and honor boundaries that protect and honor the space and time you deserve to develop. When you do not respect your own space and time, appeasing others will serve only to push you into deferring to some other person's choices/needs/understanding. Appeasing others to maintain an illusion of harmony might have provided some experiential insight (Divine Order remember) to refine and define what is acceptable and what is Not acceptable which is essential knowledge if you are to in fact 'Know Thyself'. You have not made any mistakes, you needed to understand the subtle nuances of this conundrum in order to become your own authority! Self-Acceptance of who you are and where you are along the path of development will encourage the self-respect needed to uphold safe boundaries without compromising harmony. 'to thine own self be true' is liberty instead of disregard for others. Think of it from a parent's perspective honey; imagine you have a wee toddler child just taking his first steps in learning to walk; are you going to be excited to support and celebrate his progress, even though his balance may have lasted only a few seconds before toppling over...or... would you be upset that the child couldn't run first try? Naturally you are going to create safe boundaries (like a soft flat surface to practice on instead of sticking the kid on stairs or gravel road in the middle of traffic etc.) and happily encourage your wee toddler to give it another try, allowing time to slowly developing muscle strength, balance and connect the dots of what action equals what reaction; cause and effect etc. Honey, only you can be the internal 'loving parent/caregiver/champion' that is required provide safe boundaries aka self-respect to live and let live while you get to 'know yourself'. You obviously recognize that while Giving in to others may be appropriate in some conditions or circumstances, putting them on a pedestal and disregarding yourself will not ever lead to success, therefore you are halfway there; all that needs tweaking is Potentize your self-caring internal parent' and the rest will flow along into your awareness naturally

Q-

Does having contact with Gods give one natural confidence and success mindset?

A-

Good morning...Contact with the Gods is even WAY better than that...it comes with a Solid Certain Knowing of your trajectory in life because you are aligned and in coherent resonance with the expression of consciousness through you as the vehicle and beingness of the God/Goddess. your confidence is a result of allowing that God/Goddess consciousness as light and love flow through you...that also implies rising to resonance in your behaviors, thoughts and actions etc., not to imply that you suddenly have superior insight or develop any self-righteous behavior-it is more like a commitment to be the vehicle pleasing to the God/Goddess so that you are an appropriate vessel for them to communicate through. We as humans are not some superior specie that Has consciousness, rather Consciousness has us! Consciousness is all-that-is and expresses through us and all life be it a virus, ameba blade of grass, worm, tree, horse, star, planet, bird...we have free will to filter that consciousness through our own perceptions and beliefs etc. however the more refined we become the clearer pure consciousness of the Gods/Goddess can be expressed through us

Q-
Do you think I can come above normal humanly qualities? Like selfish desires for survival, sexual gratification, gratification of senses, power seeking, fear, slavery to emotions?

By having Dharshan of Lord Ganesha, by traveling between worlds, have you gained anything?

They say we shouldn't have such low intentions like praying god to get things, but I don't understand how one can be unconditional and self-less just like that

A-
IMAGINE IF YOU COULD HAVE EVERYTHING AND ANYTHING MY

...what would you value after living with every desire you could ask for. Also practice this imagination...as if you had every EVERY freedom and security and opulence and material comfort; what would you most desire to experience? For me it is two things...guarding and preserving what is pure and honing and sharing the purest expression of love. This requires understanding light, which is just part of the journey that I am able to see from where I am currently at. When I have mastered this, my vista and viewpoint will be embracing the next goal or mountain top. Perhaps self-judgement of wrongdoing, etc., is a spotlight on some place that we have not loved ourselves yet. Perhaps this negativity has been able to grow so monumentally daunting because of our resistance which is fear. Perhaps if we did not fear we would have never felt separated from love. By never feeling separate from Love, perhaps we did not recognize the great blessing love is

Perhaps by grounding the meaningful concept that 'love is a great blessing' into the dense material called 'three dimensions' we ourselves can be/have been, a blessing to life.

You are very much a blessing!

Q- why do some religions have protocols that insist you need a middle-man such as a priest to speak to Creator on our behalf. I want darshan with the goddesses too, is this wrongful thinking?

Q-

Why do some religions have protocols that insist you need a middle-man such as a priest to speak to Creator on our behalf? I want darshan with the goddesses too, is this wrongful thinking?

A-

I think you have sovereign freedom to pray to God or Lakshmi or Lord Ganesha or anyone although, like anything 'Use it or lose it'. Exercise your freedom. How can you ever find your truth if you are not permitted the freedom to open your heart? How can you open your heart if you follow made up rules instead of your own heart? How can you Know your own heart if you are not permitted to expose your true questions/ Unconditional love welcomes the wholeness of a person, not just that which is deemed by society as desire able?

Society always changes what is considered good and bad and right and wrong.

The Master does not live in a perfect world, rather the Master is able to see Pure Source Energy perfection of Divine Order in what is.

The belief you hold on the inside is reflected by what you perceive on the outside. this is demonstrated by the story of ten blind men all standing around an elephant. Each describes only the part of the elephant immediately in front of him that he can touch but do not have the full 360 degrees access to get the complete picture therefore what they perceive their outside world to represent is limited by their own experience. Same holds true in the bigger metaphor... what we see outside of us is a direct reflection of our inner beliefs. Asking the question is a crack where the light can come inside and illuminate more of truth. Many religions do not want that crack to let light in because then you will not be so easily controlled therefore, you are told 'Do not question'

Your fantasy of order is because you have recognized your own truth

Now follow that truth to the great creator and you will meet our ancestors and have Dharshan of Lord Ganesha and many others along the way.

We are infinite eternal Beings and can open to All-That-Is where we are one with All. The All exists in us and we exist in the All. Think of drinking water while floating in a lake or pool or seaside lagoon...you are in water and water is in you. Now imagine if your consciousness can merge with the water you could be conscious of everything that has water in it. This is all life...you can do same exercise with fire, air, plasma, colours, etc. This is one way to begin to experience Oneness intellectually and then helps to enable feeling the subtler worlds. When you consider the limitations of three dimensional senses but know we have senses unexplainable by 3-D such as intuition, gnosis, psychic foresight and premonitions and many more examples, we KNOW there is more to life and then can begin to become free of dark limitations and trust our questions as

Great Creator's gift to find our way 'home'. We have emergent skills becoming conscious. Emergent skills such as psychic abilities, lucid dreaming, navigation through the subtle fields etc. It is like the magnetic field itself is awakening. This returns us to our full consciousness aka knowing Oneness. Your breath awareness will strengthen this 'ability'. Freedom is one component of Bliss but, it must be claimed. What is freedom? Where is freedom? What happens when you feel like you have truly connected with someone? On some subtle level, you can truly let go because that connection was made. Are we all just trying to reconnect with one another?

Needing revenue restricts and can even completely freeze conceptual freedom. Revenue becomes the underlying miasma or foundation, causing every thought and action instead of our attention coming from our natural resonance with love. Gratitude can weave a pathway back to freedom. Take one moment to find What you feel grateful for, take 2 or 3 if your mind wanders on this subject...it is well worth beginning in the frequency which supports love and light. Build an appropriate foundation for the resonance you wish to attract.

Yogahas are the aha moments produced by being the perfect charge distribution of sacred space. This means you are sharing in pure principle. Sacred space is perfect shareable charge distribution created through the union or 'yoking' of the Observer's awareness with Consciousness conveying pure principle. The resulting bliss moment is suspended as stillness to attain liberation. If only for the moment, liberation provides the cosmic area code (which is a specific frequency) for conscious union with the blissful Spirit. This is freedom.

Our subtle bodies, such as supramental, etheric, astral, emotional etc., are in the conscious field. Bliss enables communication with this field. Freedom

Living lucid; choose which thoughts to allow. Those thoughts which are not a match to your desired life expression can be released. I.e. "This thought did not originate with me and is not a match with who I want to be". Whatever you don't forgive is what you cannot release. Therefore, whatever you cannot forgive impedes your freedom.

Hope is the light that shows you the area ready for improvement… and there is always room for improvement.

Trajectory to truth will not dance around material trappings preferring the natural path out of illusion to authentic abundance…if you choose to play along the way, with ego objectives, such as 'getting stuff', that's ok but be wary not to lose sight of your real goal and value or you may find yourself so lost that a lot of backtracking will necessary to reach your destiny's reward.

Authentic living fast tracks the number of aha's and bliss moments which further amplifies the opportunity for exponentially increasing your aha and bliss moments.

What vibration are you a match for?

What vibration do you want to be a match for?

We come into this world as receptive uncensored recipients to the frequencies of our environment. Unmitigated sponges we are, absorbing patterns and programming without inhibition or reserve. Sometimes, oftentimes, these patterns did not serve our wellbeing. Limited in consciousness, our perceptions are unable to contain 360 degrees of focus simultaneously and therefor we bounce back and forth from good to bad, from happy to sad, and from right to wrong. Now if we were able to expand our awareness to a fully conscious state we would see the divine order rippling out all around us. However, …

Until we can at least achieve a third-party perspective as 'observers' of nature while simultaneously maintaining our unique perception of 'what is'…each of us is defined by our relative, historical and empirical ecology (the branch of biology that deals with the relations of organisms to one another and to their physical surroundings.) Because this is a very limited perception, we strive to understand Creation through science and Philosophies or religion and theosophies. AcuLomi meditation develops Critical thinking; because we don't have to be right or wrong... Sort of like a translator interface which would allow different operating systems to talk with each other, Success is strategically aligned action with spirit guidance.

There is something about a campfire that opens the soul to sharing.

Shareable pure intention through the heart of an atom is the point in AcuLomi meditation where contraction pops through to expand on the 'other side' as the Holy Grail...follow the spinning knot. Antimatter, matter; particle, wave turning inside out like birthing. In seeking pure principle, let the emotions be like still water to see what is below the surface.

An idea worth sharing is that Divinity/Pure Source Energy exists in you and is expressed through you.

References

Abzu (2012). The Adamantine particles. Retrieved from https://abzu2.wordpress.com/2012/10/13/the-adamantine-particles/

Adams, M. (2016). Now you can hear chemistry: Health Ranger translates molecules into music in stunning video demonstration that will blow your mind. Retrieved from http://www.naturalnews.com/2017-01-04-elemonics-hear-chemistry-molecules-music-harmonics-elements-mike-adams-health-ranger-demonstration.html

Aquiliana (2014). Greek Mythology: The Horae. Retrieved from https://aquileana.wordpress.com/2014/10/30/greek-mythology-the-horae/

Bhagavad-Gita. (n.d.). Retrieved from http://www.bhagavad-gita.org/index-english.html

Book of IEOU. (n.d.). Retrieved from http://gnosis.org/library/1ieo.htm

Bridges, V. (1997). Neurochemistry of death and transcendence. Retrieved from http://vincentbridges.com/post/139667739809/on-the-neuro-chemistry-of-death-transcendence-my

Clarke, A. C. (2010, December 24). Fractals the colour of infinity [Video file]. Retrieved from https://www.youtube.com/watch?v=Lk6QU94xAb8

Collective Coherent Oscillation Plasma Modes in Surrounding Media of Black Holes and Vacuum Structure – Quantum Processes with Considerations of Spacetime Torque and Coriolis Forces. (2005). Retrieved from http://haramein.resonance.is/research/

Demonstration of VedaPulse meditation group. [Video file]. (2015, April 29, 2015). Retrieved from https://www.youtube.com/watch?v=eRbaem46Pos

Donahue, B. (1998). Supernova 1987a. Retrieved from http://www.hiddenmeanings.com/cosmos.html

Donahue, B. (n.d.). 293B Five To One [Video file]. Retrieved from https://www.youtube.com/watch?v=7aAsThxvhOY

Donahue, B. (n.d.). It is not a sin to question tradition. It is a sin to be afraid to. Retrieved from http://www.hiddenmeanings.com/storiesjuly02.html

Dr. Rife's true original frequencies. (2016). Retrieved from http://rifevideos.com/dr_rifes_true_original_frequencies.html

Dr. Strauss, B. (n.d.). The global consciousness experiment. Retrieved from http://drstrauss.weebly.com/informative-facts.html

Dunn, J. E. (2011). DNA molecules can 'teleport', Nobel Prize winner claims. Retrieved from http://www.techworld.com/news/personal-tech/dna-molecules-can-teleport-nobel-prize-winner-claims-3256631/

Evans, S. J. (2015, April 26-May 17). Meditation 1 engaging beloved God-Spark [Video file]. Retrieved from https://www.youtube.com/watch?v=eRbaem46Pos&t=754s

Evans, S., & Winter, D. (2016). Mystic View Bioactive technology with Dan Winter. Retrieved from http://shelleyaloha.com/videos/

Fideler, D. (1939). Ancient cosmology and early Christian symbolism. Adyar, Chennai, India and USA: Quest.

Winter, D. (2016). Path out of chaos. Retrieved from http://theraphi.net/the-path-out-of-chaos/

Besant, A. (1911). *The Ancient wisdom* (reprint ed.). [pdf].

https://doi.org/http://realitychange.net/wpcontent/uploads/2017/07/TheAncientWisdom_AnnieBesant.pdf

Burns, T., & Moore, J. (2007). The Hieroglyphic Monad of John DeeTheorems I-XVII: A guide to the outer mysteries. Retrieved from http://www.jwmt.org/v2n13/sign.html

Change the World. (Mar 16, 2011). Retrieved from

https://www.youtube.com/watch?v=jE8ojvJJ8ew

Donahue, B. (n.d.). Is God a photon. Retrieved from

http://www.hiddenmeanings.com/Sermon9sacrifice.htm

Evans, S. (n.d.). AcuLomi Temple Meditation. Retrieved from http://shelleyaloha.com/

Henry, W. (2017). Chintamani, the wish fulfilling jewel of Tibetan Buddhism. Retrieved from http://www.williamhenry.net/2017/04/there-is-a-light-being-within/

John 1:1. (n.d.). Retrieved from https://www.biblegateway.com/passage/?search=John+1%3A1-

14&version=KJV

Secrets in plain sight;the cosmic sequence. (2013). Retrieved from

http://www.stillnessinthestorm.com/2013/12/secrets-in-plain-sight-cosmic-sequence.html

Winter, D. (2014). *Fractal conjugate space and time* (1st ed.). Mullumbimby, Australia: Implosion

Group.

Winter, D. (2016). Phase conjugate fractality. Retrieved from

http://www.fractalfield.com/conjugategravity/

Winter, D., & Botte, P. (2017). Flamenmind. Retrieved from www.flameinmind.com

Winter, D., & Harris, P. (n.d.). TheraPhi. Retrieved from www.theraphi.net

Winter, D. (n.d.). 7 Arrows: Shamanic control / Embedding in the cube of space. Retrieved from http://www.sevenarrows.net/

Winter, D. (n.d.). Phase Conjugation. Retrieved from

https://www.learnitlive.com/content/1498/Phase-Conjugation-Science-Powerpoint-from-

Dan-Winter/download/true http://www.antonparks.com/main.php

Martin, Yolanda Zigarmi, http://www.spiritualresources.info

Gold Chloride. (2014). Retrieved from https://dublinsmick.wordpress.com/2014/03/31/gold-chloride/

Goswami, A. (1995). The self-aware universe. London, United Kingdom: Penguin.

Hall, M. P. (1928). The secret teachings of all ages. London, United Kingdom: Penguin.

International Quantum University of Integrative Medicine. (2016). Dr. Amit Goswami, PhD. Retrieved from https://iquim.org/dr-amit-goswami/

International Quantum University of Integrative Medicine (Producer). (n.d.). Dr. Paul Drouin's Course on Creative Integrative Healthcare [Audio podcast]. Retrieved from https://iquim.org/courses/creative-integrative-healthcare/

International Quantum University of Integrative Medicine (Producer). (n.d.). Dr. Paul Drouin's Course on Creative Integrative Healthcare [Video podcast]. Retrieved from https://iquim.org/courses/creative-integrative-healthcare/

King, C. W. (1908). Plutarch's morals theosophical essays. Retrieved from http://www.sacred-texts.com/cla/plu/pte/pte07.htm

King James Bible. (n.d.). Retrieved from http://www.kingjamesbibleonline.org/

Korotkov (2016). Art and science technologies. Retrieved from http://korotkov.info/index.php?/topic/145-institute-of-cosmic-anthropoecology/

Leet, L. (2004). The Universal Kabbalah. Retrieved from https://www.amazon.ca/Universal-Kabbalah-Leonora-Leet-Ph-D/dp/0892811897

Mura, R. (2014). Location of the Large Magellanic Cloud. Retrieved from http://www.constellation-guide.com/large-magellanic-cloud/

NASA science beta. (2000). Now just a blinkin' picosecond. Retrieved from https://science.nasa.gov/science-news/science-at-nasa/2000/ast28apr_1m

Nelson, R. (2014). Coherent consciousness creates order in the world. Retrieved from http://noosphere.princeton.edu/

Anomalous teleportation has been scientifically investigated and separately documented by the Department of Defense among many other notable sources.

Rev. Dr. Evans, S. (2015). Modern day Delphic oracle serving the emerging consciousness of One. Retrieved from www.shelleyaloha.com

Russel, P. (1999). Opening speech given at first international conference on science and consciousness, Albuquerque, April 1999 Opening speech given at first international conference on science and consciousness,

Albuquerque, April 1999 . Retrieved from http://www.peterrussell.com/Speaker/Talks/SoC99.php

Sacred texts archive. (n.d.). Retrieved from http://www.sacred-texts.com/

Science news digest for physicians and scientists. (n.d.). Retrieved from http://bio-mirror.im.ac.cn/mirrors/bioscience/news/scientis/biolcloc.htm

(Stedman's Concise Medical Dictionary, 1997)

Sun god's zodiac biblical allegory meditation Emerald Tablets. (n.d.). Retrieved from http://thehiddenlighthouse.blogspot.ca/

Supernova 1987A. (2006). Retrieved from http://hyperphysics.phy-astr.gsu.edu/hbase/Astro/sn87a.html

The first book of IEOU. (n.d.). Retrieved from http://gnosis.org/library/1ieo.htm

The language of DNA Can language be reprogrammed by words and frequencies. (2011). Retrieved from https://noeticdigest.wordpress.com/2011/10/11/the-language-of-dna-can-dna-be-reprogrammed-by-words-and-frequencies/

The Twelfth Planet by Z. Stichin PDF proofread and corrected from OCR TXT version by.: ZT|TS:.407 - 460 [PDF]. (2016). Retrieved from http://www.tikaboo.com/library/12thPlanet.pdf

Trismegistus, H. (n.d.). Hermetica : the Greek Corpus Hermeticum and the Latin Asclepius in a new English translation, with notes and introduction. Retrieved from Cambridge University Press 1992

Untimely meditations [PDF]. (1874). Retrieved from http://la.utexas.edu/users/hcleaver/330T/350kPEENietzscheSchopenTable.pdf

VedaPulse hardware and software kit for performing pulse analysis. (2016). Retrieved from http://vedapulse.com

VedaPulse is a hardware and software kit for performing pulse analysis. (n.d.). Retrieved from http://vedapulse.com/

West, B. (2014). Black whole dynamics: The foundation of our fractal-holographic universe. Retrieved from http://www.wakingtimes.com/2014/05/09/black-whole-dynamics-foundation-fractal-holographic-universe/

Winey, T. (2007). U.S. Patent No. US 11/518,614. Washington, DC: U.S. Patent and Trademark Office.

Winter, D. (2014). Origin of alphabets. Retrieved from http://www.goldenmean.info/dnaring/

Winter, D. (2017, January 13). Dan Winter-Real Heart Coherence and Stress Measure with itHRVe.com [Video file]. Retrieved from https://www.youtube.com/watch?v=D8l-sRJsy5E

Winter, D. (2017, January 13). Dan Winter-Real Heart Coherence and Stress Measure with itHRVe.com [Video file]. Retrieved from https://www.youtube.com/watch?v=D8l-sRJsy5E

Winter, D. (n.d.). Seven arrows. Retrieved from http://goldenmean.info/7arrows/

Winter, D. (Producer). (n.d.). animation of Holy Grail, fractal charge of bliss entering DNA [Video podcast]. Retrieved from http://goldenmean.info/grail/

Yoga and Quantum Mechanics II. (2015). Retrieved from https://dondeg.wordpress.com/2015/06/17/the-yogic-view-of-consciousness-17-yoga-and-quantum-mechanics-ii/

Zyga, L. (2017). Physicists detect exotic looped trajectories of light in three-slit experiment. Retrieved from http://phys.org/news/2017-01-physicists-exotic-looped-trajectories-three-slit.html

Masaru Emoto's Hado World http://www.masaru-emoto.net

Abzu (2012). The Adamantine particles. Retrieved from https://abzu2.
wordpress.com/2012/10/13/the-adamantine-particles/

Adams, M. (2016). Now you can hear chemistry: Health Ranger translates
molecules into music in stunning video demonstration that will blow
your mind. Retrieved from http://www.naturalnews.com/2017-01-04-
elemonics-hear-chemistry-molecules-music-harmonics-elements-mike-
adams-health-ranger-demonstration.html

Aquiliana (2014). Greek Mythology: The Horae. Retrieved from https://
aquileana.wordpress.com/2014/10/30/greek-mythology-the-horae/

Bhagavad-Gita. (n.d.). Retrieved from http://www.bhagavad-gita.org/
index-english.html

Book of IEOU. (n.d.). Retrieved from http://gnosis.org/library/1ieo.htm

Bridges, V. (1997). Neurochemistry of death and transcendence.
Retrieved from http://vincentbridges.com/post/139667739809/
on-the-neuro-chemistry-of-death-transcendence-my

Clarke, A. C. (2010, December 24). Fractals the colour of infinity [Video
file]. Retrieved from https://www.youtube.com/watch?v=Lk6QU94xAb8

Collective Coherent Oscillation Plasma Modes in Surrounding Media
of Black Holes and Vacuum Structure – Quantum Processes with
Considerations of Spacetime Torque and Coriolis Forces. (2005). Retrieved
from http://haramein.resonance.is/research/

Demonstration of VedaPulse meditation group. [Video file]. (2015, April 29,
2015). Retrieved from https://www.youtube.com/watch?v=eRbaem46Pos

Donahue, B. (1998). Supernova 1987a. Retrieved from http://www.
hiddenmeanings.com/cosmos.html

Donahue, B. (n.d.). 293B Five To One [Video file]. Retrieved from https://
www.youtube.com/watch?v=7aAsThxvhOY

Donahue, B. (n.d.). It is not a sin to question tradition. It is a sin to be afraid to. Retrieved from http://www.hiddenmeanings.com/storiesjuly02.html

Dr. Rife's true original frequencies. (2016). Retrieved from http://rifevideos.com/dr_rifes_true_original_frequencies.html

Dr. Strauss, B. (n.d.). The global consciousness experiment. Retrieved from http://drstrauss.weebly.com/informative-facts.html

Dunn, J. E. (2011). DNA molecules can 'teleport', Nobel Prize winner claims. Retrieved from http://www.techworld.com/news/personal-tech/dna-molecules-can-teleport-nobel-prize-winner-claims-3256631/

Evans, S. J. (2015, April 26-May 17). Meditation 1 engaging beloved God-Spark [Video file]. Retrieved from https://www.youtube.com/watch?v=eRbaem46Pos&t=754s

Evans, S., & Winter, D. (2016). Mystic View Bioactive technology with Dan Winter. Retrieved from http://shelleyaloha.com/videos/

Fideler, D. (1939). Ancient cosmology and early Christian symbolism. Adyar, Chennai, India and USA: Quest.

Gold Chloride. (2014). Retrieved from https://dublinsmick.wordpress.com/2014/03/31/gold-chloride/

Goswami, A. (1995). The self-aware universe. London, United Kingdom: Penguin.

Hall, M. P. (1928). The secret teachings of all ages. London, United Kingdom: Penguin.

International Quantum University of Integrative Medicine. (2016). Dr. Amit Goswami, PhD. Retrieved from https://iquim.org/dr-amit-goswami/

International Quantum University of Integrative Medicine (Producer). (n.d.). Dr. Paul Drouin's Course on Creative Integrative Healthcare [Audio podcast]. Retrieved from https://iquim.org/courses/creative-integrative-healthcare/

International Quantum University of Integrative Medicine (Producer). (n.d.). Dr. Paul Drouin's Course on Creative Integrative Healthcare [Video podcast]. Retrieved from https://iquim.org/courses/creative-integrative-healthcare/

King, C. W. (1908). Plutarch's morals theosophical essays. Retrieved from http://www.sacred-texts.com/cla/plu/pte/pte07.htm

King James Bible. (n.d.). Retrieved from http://www.kingjamesbibleonline.org/

Korotkov (2016). Art and science technologies. Retrieved from http://korotkov.info/index.php?/topic/145-institute-of-cosmic-anthropoecology/

Leet, L. (2004). The Universal Kabbalah. Retrieved from https://www.amazon.ca/Universal-Kabbalah-Leonora-Leet-Ph-D/dp/0892811897

Mura, R. (2014). Location of the Large Magellanic Cloud. Retrieved from http://www.constellation-guide.com/large-magellanic-cloud/

NASA science beta. (2000). Now just a blinkin' picosecond. Retrieved from https://science.nasa.gov/science-news/science-at-nasa/2000/ast28apr_1m

Nelson, R. (2014). Coherent consciousness creates order in the world. Retrieved from http://noosphere.princeton.edu/

Anomalous teleportation has been scientifically investigated and separately documented by the Department of Defense among many other notable sources.

Rev. Dr. Evans, S. (2015). Modern day Delphic oracle serving the emerging consciousness of One. Retrieved from www.shelleyaloha.com

Russel, P. (1999). Opening speech given at first international conference on science and consciousness, Albuquerque, April 1999 Opening speech given at first international conference on science and consciousness, Albuquerque, April 1999. Retrieved from http://www.peterrussell.com/Speaker/Talks/SoC99.php

Sacred texts archive. (n.d.). Retrieved from http://www.sacred-texts.com/

Science news digest for physicians and scientists. (n.d.). Retrieved from http://bio-mirror.im.ac.cn/mirrors/bioscience/news/scientis/biolcloc.htm

Sun god's zodiac biblical allegory meditation Emerald Tablets. (n.d.). Retrieved from http://thehiddenlighthouse.blogspot.ca/

Supernova 1987A. (2006). Retrieved from http://hyperphysics.phy-astr.gsu.edu/hbase/Astro/sn87a.html

The first book of IEOU. (n.d.). Retrieved from http://gnosis.org/library/1ieo.htm

The language of DNA Can language be reprogrammed by words and frequencies. (2011). Retrieved from https://noeticdigest.wordpress.com/2011/10/11/the-language-of-dna-can-dna-be-reprogrammed-by-words-and-frequencies/

The Twelfth Planet by Z. Stichin PDF proofread and corrected from OCR TXT version by.: ZT|TS:.407 - 460 [PDF]. (2016). Retrieved from http://www.tikaboo.com/library/12thPlanet.pdf

Trismegistus, H. (n.d.). Hermetica : the Greek Corpus Hermeticum and the Latin Asclepius in a new English translation, with notes and introduction. Retrieved from Cambridge University Press 1992

Untimely meditations [PDF]. (1874). Retrieved from http://la.utexas.edu/users/hcleaver/330T/350kPEENietzscheSchopenTable.pdf

VedaPulse hardware and software kit for performing pulse analysis. (2016). Retrieved from http://vedapulse.com

VedaPulse is a hardware and software kit for performing pulse analysis. (n.d.). Retrieved from http://vedapulse.com/

West, B. (2014). Black whole dynamics: The foundation of our fractal-holographic universe. Retrieved from http://www.wakingtimes.com/2014/05/09/black-whole-dynamics-foundation-fractal-holographic-universe/

Winey, T. (2007). U.S. Patent No. US 11/518,614. Washington, DC: U.S. Patent and Trademark Office.

Winter, D. (2014). Origin of alphabets. Retrieved from http://www.goldenmean.info/dnaring/

Winter, D. (2017, January 13). Dan Winter-Real Heart Coherence and Stress Measure with itHRVe.com [Video file]. Retrieved from https://www.youtube.com/watch?v=D8l-sRJsy5E

Winter, D. (2017, January 13). Dan Winter-Real Heart Coherence and Stress Measure with itHRVe.com [Video file]. Retrieved from https://www.youtube.com/watch?v=D8l-sRJsy5E

Winter, D. (n.d.). Seven arrows. Retrieved from http://goldenmean.info/7arrows/

Winter, D. (Producer). (n.d.). animation of Holy Grail, fractal charge of bliss entering DNA [Video podcast]. Retrieved from http://goldenmean.info/grail/

Yoga and Quantum Mechanics II. (2015). Retrieved from https://dondeg. wordpress.com/2015/06/17/the-yogic-view-of-consciousness-17-yoga-and-quantum-mechanics-ii/

Zyga, L. (2017). Physicists detect exotic looped trajectories of light in three-slit experiment. Retrieved from http://phys.org/news/2017-01-physicists-exotic-looped-trajectories-three-slit.html

The Observer in Modern Physics Some Personal Speculations. (n.d.). Retrieved from https://www.grc.nasa.gov/www/k-12/Numbers/Math/ Mathematical_Thinking/observer.htm

Book of the Prophet Daniel. (n.d.). Retrieved from http://biblescripture. net/Daniel.html

Editors of Encyclopædia Britannica. (1999). Proclus. Retrieved from https://www.britannica.com/biography/Proclus

1 Corinthians 3:16. (n.d.). Retrieved from https://www. kingjamesbibleonline.org/1-Corinthians-3-16/

1 John 1:5. (n.d.). Retrieved from http://biblehub.com/1_john/1-5.htm

1 John 1:5 New International Version (NIV). (n.d.). Retrieved from https:// www.biblegateway.com/passage/?search=1%20John%201:5

1 Thessalonians 4:17. (). Retrieved, from

25 Mind-boggling Examples Of The Mandela Effect. (2017). Retrieved from http://list25.com/25-ming-boggling-examples-of-the-mandela-effect/

Abzu (n.d.). The Flower of Life and the 64 Tetrahedron grid: the mother and father of the geometry of the fabric space. Retrieved from http:// www.abzu2.com/2014/01/29/the-flower-of-life-and-the-64-tetrahedron-grid-the-mother-and-father-of-the-geometry-of-the-fabric-space/

Adams, M. (2017, January 03,). *Scientist translates chemistry into MUSIC! (ELEMONICS)* [Video file]. Retrieved from https://www.youtube.com/ watch?v=TghTECI5MJo

AETHERFORCE. (n.d.). Retrieved from http://aetherforce.com/ the-aohm-materia/

Albert Einstein Quotations. (1879-1955). Retrieved from http://oaks.nvg. org/einstein-quotes.html

Allan Watts quotes. (n.d.). Retrieved from https://www.goodreads.com/author/quotes/1501668.Alan_W_Watts

Amit Goswami Quotes . (n.d.). Retrieved from http://www.goodreads.com/quotes/535404-it-is-not-just-do-do-do-it-is-not

Baerbel (2005). Russian DNA Discoveries Explain Human 'Paranormal' Events . Retrieved from http://www.rense.com/general62/expl.htm

Beta waves (12 TO 38 HZ). (n.d.). Retrieved from http://www.brainworksneurotherapy.com/what-are-brainwaves

Beyer, C. (2017). The Sigillum Dei Aemeth, or Seal of the Truth of God. Retrieved from https://www.thoughtco.com/sigillum-dei-aemeth-96044

Bhagavad Gita. (n.d.). Retrieved from http://www.bhagavad-gita.org/

Biography of Georg Simon Ohm. (n.d.). Retrieved from http://theor.jinr.ru/~kuzemsky/gohmbio.html

Biontology Arizona Dr-Fritz-Albert-Popp. (n.d.). Retrieved from http://www.biontologyarizona.com/dr-fritz-albert-popp/

Book of Ezekiel 1:1-2. (n.d.). Retrieved from https://biblia.com/bible/esv/Ezekiel%201.1%E2%80%9328

Bridges, V. (n.d.). On the Neuro-Chemistry of Death & Transcendence. Retrieved from http://vincentbridges.com/post/139667739809/on-the-neuro-chemistry-of-death-transcendence-my

Bullinger, E. (2007). The witness of the stars . Retrieved from https://philologos.org/__eb-tws/chap11.htm

Cain, F. (2013). Dark matter halo puzzles astronomers. Retrieved from https://www.universetoday.com/9993/dark-matter-halo-puzzles-astronomers/

Chandra's Find of Lonely Halo Raises Questions About Dark Matter. (2004). Retrieved from http://chandra.harvard.edu/press/04_releases/press_102604.html

Chia, M., & Thom, J. (2017, May 04). Opening the Third Eye: Powerful Ancient Practices for Activating the Pineal Gland and Expanding Consciousness. *Conscious Lifestyle Magazine.* Retrieved from http://www.consciouslifestylemag.com/pineal-gland-activation-third-eye/

CHIA, M., & THOM, J. (2017). Opening the Third Eye: Powerful Ancient Practices for Activating the Pineal Gland and Expanding Consciousness. Retrieved from http://www.consciouslifestylemag.com/pineal-gland-activation-third-eye/

Chrysopoeia. (2011). Retrieved from http://absentofi.org/2011/01/chrysopoeia/

Chwalkowski, F. (2016). *Symbols in Arts, Religion and Culture: The Soul of Nature.* Newcastle upon Tyne: Cambridge Scholars Publishing.

Cicero, M. (1560). *Cicero's De officiis.* Retrieved from By Marcus Tullius Cicero - site http://www.godotedizioni.it/images/Cicerone.jpg, Public Domain, https://commons.wikimedia.org/w/index.php?curid=3378255

Constellation guide Fornax constellation. (n.d.). Retrieved from http://www.constellation-guide.com/constellation-list/fornax-constellation/

Coptic Gnostics of Egypt. (n.d.). Retrieved from https://www.metahistory.org/READING/NHL/ReadingPlan3A.php

Daniel 5:24, New American Standard Bible: 1995. (1995). Retrieved from https://biblia.com/bible/nasb95/Dan%205.24-28

Delphic E Faustina the elder, coin. (138-161). Retrieved from https://finds.org.uk/romancoins/emperors/emperor/id/18

Deschesne, D. (2009). נחשnachashnaw-khash. Retrieved from http://www.
fortfairfieldjournal.com/mpl_nachash.htm

Divine   Pymander   Theosophical   PDF.   (n.d.).
Retrieved   from   http://www.theosophical.ca/books/
DivinePymanderOfHermesMercuriusTrismegistus,The.pdf

Dolen, W. (n.d.). Law Of Contradiction. Retrieved from http://
becomingone.org/law-contradiction.html

Donahue, B. (2011). *UFO Commander and Jesus Christ* [Video file].
Retrieved from https://www.youtube.com/watch?v=LM9yezr4rBM

Donahue, B. (2011). *UFO Commander and Jesus Christ* [Video file].
Retrieved from Some who were living were standing on the mountain out
of the water saved from the rush of the fountains where as in Genesis God
remembered Noah and those living with him and the ark rested upon the
mountains of Ararat"

Donahue, B. (2012). *588 Computer Ram in the human brain* [Video file].
Retrieved from https://www.youtube.com/watch?v=EZCR4wEbkeI

Donahue, B. (2012, May 8). *359 Meditation* [Video file]. Retrieved from
https://www.youtube.com/watch?v=c22ygxxfYVk

Donahue, B. (n.d.). Hidden Meanings. Retrieved from http://www.
hiddenmeanings.com/

Donahue, B. (n.d.). Hubble Space Telescope News. Retrieved from http://
www.hiddenmeanings.com/Supernova1987a2004.htm

Donahue, B. (n.d.). Pluto and Charon. Retrieved from http://www.
hiddenmeanings.com/pluto.html

Donahue, B. (n.d.). The Bible Identifies the Emerald Tablet. Retrieved
from http://www.hiddenmeanings.com/Sermon690100209.htm

Emerald Tablets. (n.d.). Retrieved from http://linkedtheory.blogspot.ca/2011/02/emerald-tablets.html

Eriksen, K. (2012). Die before you die. Retrieved from http://www.wakingtimes.com/2012/12/19/die-before-you-die/

Evans, S. (2015, August 24). Health Innovators at the World Summit of Integrative Medicine [Online Forum comment]. Retrieved from http://www.starseeds.net/profile/ShelleyJoyEvans

Franckena, E. (2017). DNA the gene code. Retrieved from http://www.chintamania.com/single-post/2017/01/07/DNA---The-Gene-Code

Friedrich Nietzsche on the need to be alone. (n.d.). Retrieved from http://philosophicalsociety.com/Archives/Nietzsche%20On%20The%20Need%20To%20Be%20Alone.htm

Gardner, L. (n.d.). Genesis of the Grail Kings full lecture transcript. Retrieved from http://www.graal.co.uk/genesis_lecture_full_2.php

Genesis 3:22. (n.d.). Retrieved from http://biblehub.com/genesis/3-22.htm

Gnostic Warrior. (2015). Godlike men who were born of the serpent. Retrieved from http://gnosticwarrior.com/godlike-men-who-were-born-of-the-serpent.html

Goswami, A. (1995). Consciousness, not matter, is the ground of all existence, declares University of Oregon physicist Goswami, echoing the mystic sages of his native India. He holds that the universe is self-aware, and that consciousness creates the physical world. In *The Self-Aware Universe: How Consciousness Creates the Material World*. PenguinPutnam Inc. New York,NY: Penguin Putnam.

Goswami, A. (2014). . United States: Hay House.

.Gov, N. (1994, May 19). *HUBBLE FINDS MYSTERIOUS RING STRUCTURE AROUND SUPERNOVA 1987A*. Paper presented at the

Release 94-77, Washington. Abstract retrieved from https://www.nasa.gov/home/hqnews/1994/94-077.txt

Griffith, R. (1896). The Rig-Veda. Retrieved from http://www.hinduwebsite.com/sacredscripts/rigintro.asp

Hall, M. (2015). *The Pineal Gland the eye of god* (reprint 1934 ed.). Montana, United States: Kessinger Publishing.

Hall, M. P. (1928). *The Secret Teachings of All Ages* (1 ed.). Retrieved from Simon and Schuster

Haramein, N. (2014, March 19). 64 tetrahedrons [FaceBook comment]. Retrieved from https://www.facebook.com/Nassim.Haramein.official/photos/a.112729698918297.1073741828.106168786241055/232563813601551/?type=1&theater

Haramein, N. [Nassim]. (2012, May 05,). Nassim Haramein delegate program Joshua Tree Retreat Center, Joshua Tree,Ca [Facebook page]. Retrieved https://www.facebook.com/events/714287015366708/

Haramein, N. [WizardSkyth]. (2015, June 24,). *Nassim Haramein Holofractographic Universe Theory* [Video file]. Retrieved from https://www.youtube.com/watch?v=S0Ck707K6CA

Hayyan, J. (n.d.). The Emerald Tablet of Hermes. Retrieved from http://www.sacred-texts.com/alc/emerald.htm

Hephaestus Greek God of Fire and Metalworking. (n.d.). Retrieved from https://greekgodsandgoddesses.net/gods/hephaestus/

Heraclitus. (n.d.). Retrieved from https://plato.stanford.edu/entries/heraclitus/

Hermetics Kybalion. (1908). Retrieved from http://www.hermetics.org/pdf/kybalion.pdf

Hurtak, J. (1987). *The Book of Knowledge: The Keys to Enoch*. Hekpoort, Gauteng, SOUTH AFRICA: The Academy For Future Science.

IEOU GEMATRIA A Preliminary Investigation of The Cabala contained in the Coptic Gnostic Books . (2005). Retrieved from https://archive.org/stream/Gematria-APreliminaryInvestigation/Gematria-APreliminaryInvestigation_djvu.txt

Isaiah 7:14King James Version (KJV). (n.d.). Retrieved from https://www.biblegateway.com/passage/?search=Isaiah+7%3A14&version=KJV

Isenberg, W. (n.d.). he Nag Hammadi Library The Gospel of Philip. Retrieved from http://gnosis.org/naghamm/gop.html

ISSUU. (2010). Sacred Geometry coherent emotion . Retrieved from https://issuu.com/earthcat/docs/sacred-geometry-coherent-emotion

Jason and the Argonauts. (n.d.). Retrieved from http://www.pbs.org/mythsandheroes/myths_four_jason.html

John 1:1-5 KJV. (n.d.). Retrieved from https://www.biblegateway.com/passage/?search=John+1%3A1-5&version=KJV

John 14:20. (n.d.). Retrieved from https://www.biblegateway.com/passage/?search=John+14:20

John 14:6 . (n.d.). Retrieved from https://www.biblegateway.com/passage/?search=John+14:6

Jormungand. (n.d.). Retrieved from http://norse-mythology.org/gods-and-creatures/giants/jormungand/

Kamiya (2015). *Induction of action-at-a-distancemutagenesis by 8-oxo-7,8-dihydroguaninein DNA pol λ-knockdown cells* (DOI 10.1186/s41021-015-0015-7). Retrieved from http://download.springer.com/static/pdf/531/art%253A10.1186%252Fs41021-015-0015-7.pdf?originUrl=http%3A%2F%2Fgenesenvironment.biomedcentral.

com%2Farticle%2F10.1186%2Fs41021-015-0015-7&token2=exp=
1493868240~acl=%2Fstatic%2Fpdf%2F531%2Fart%25253A
10.1186%25252Fs41021-015-0015-7.pdf*~hmac=489c02f5a8
7ce21120765a773f3658653dee36fe34111bbf42c257d0d93a33c4

King, C. (1882). *Plutarch's Morals: Theosophical Essays*. London, England:
George Bell and Sons.

King James Bible, in the book of Acts, chapter 7:48 "The most high dwells
not in temples made with hands". . (n.d.). Retrieved from http://biblehub.
com/acts/7-48.htm

Korotkov (2014). Dr.Korotkov. Retrieved from http://korotkov.info/index.
php?/topic/145-institute-of-cosmic-anthropoecology/

Leoni, E. (2000). *Nostradamus and His Prophecies* (2nd ed.). Mineola, New
York: Dover.

Lipton, B. (2012). Wisdom of your cells. Retrieved from https://www.
brucelipton.com/resource/article/the-wisdom-your-cells

Lipton, B. (n.d.). Epigenetics. Retrieved from https://www.brucelipton.
com/what-epigenetics

Luc Montagnier - Facts. (2008). Retrieved from https://www.nobelprize.
org/nobel_prizes/medicine/laureates/2008/montagnier-facts.html

Luke 23:46, "Father, into thy hands I commit my spirit. (n.d.). Retrieved
from http://studybible.info/KJV/Luke%2023:46

Masani, P. (1993). The unscientific side of the ecological movement [65
JOURNAL ARTICLE]. *Current Science Association, volume 65, number
8*. Retrieved from http://www.jstor.org/stable/24096018

Matthew 3:11. (n.d.). Retrieved from https://www.biblegateway.com/
passage/?search=Matthew+3:11

Matthew 5:14 . (n.d.). Retrieved from https://www.kingjamesbibleonline.org/Matthew-5-14/

Meade, G. (n.d.). Orphic Pantheon. Retrieved from http://www.piney.com/Orphic.html

Meyl, K. (2011). *"DNA and Cell Resonance"* (2 ed.). Villengen-Schwenningen, Germany: Indel GmbH.

Miller, I. (1993). Monistic idealism. Retrieved from http://www.bibliotecapleyades.net/ciencia/ciencia_psycho08.htm

Miller, I. (2009). CHAOS NATURAE: Chaos, Complexity & Alchemical Process. Retrieved from http://ionamillersubjects.weebly.com/transmodern-alchemy.html

Miller, J. (n.d.). Quotations - Confucius. Retrieved from http://www.solitaryroad.com/q15%20Confucius.html

Miller, R. (n.d.). *Pantheon*. Retrieved from http://www.nwbotanicals.org/books/pantheon/pantheon_chap_10.htm

Mission, P. (2014). Ascending and descending dialectics implied in myths. Retrieved from http://www.advaita-vedanta.co.uk/index.php/component/content/article/11

Morrell, P. (2003). *Hahnemann & Homoeopathy* (1 ed.). New Delhi, India: B. Jain Publishers.

Mubārak, A. (1894). *The Ain I Akbari, Volume 3*. Retrieved from https://books.google.ca/books?id=ZKQoAAAAYAAJ&dq=Prakruti,+Vikruti,mahat&source=gbs_navlinks_s

NASA. (). . Retrieved, from

Nasim Haramein CZ and SK FB page with the kind approval of Modern Knowledge and Resonance Project Foundation. . (2015, December 05,).

Nassim Haramein 2015 - The Connected Universe [Video file]. Retrieved from https://www.youtube.com/watch?v=tbE5bVl8r2g

Omohundro, J. (2014). *Think like an Anthropologist* (ed.). : . []. http://dx.doi.org/. Retrieved from

Oroboros [Mythical creatures and gods comment]. (n.d., n.d.). Retrieved from https://www.wattpad.com/368875339-mythical-creatures-gods-ouroboros

Osborn, L. (n.d.). Three Gems of Alchemical Initiation. *Powers of Transformation*. Retrieved from http://www.rexresearch.com/alchemy4/osborn.htm

Ouroboros – The Tail Devourer. (2013). Retrieved from http://www.rejects.com.mt/?p=796

Paracelsus (1493-1541). (Paracelsus). Retrieved from http://www.sciencemuseum.org.uk/broughttolife/people/paracelsus

Perdue, T. (2011). *Passover & Sukkot*. Indiana, USA: AuthorHouse.

Plait, P. (2012). Anniversary of a Cosmic Blast. Retrieved from http://www.slate.com/blogs/bad_astronomy/2012/12/27/cosmic_blast_magnetar_explosion_rocked_earth_on_december_27_2004.html

Prem, Y. (n.d.). Vayu: an introduction to the divine wind. Retrieved from http://www.vedicpath.com/Articles/Vayu.html

Psalm 11KJV. (n.d.). Retrieved from https://www.biblegateway.com/passage/?search=Psalm+11&version=KJV

Psalm 19:4 . (n.d.). Retrieved from https://www.biblegateway.com/passage/?search=Psalm+19%3A4&version=KJV

Qazi, V. (n.d.). Kashmir Shaivism. Retrieved from http://www.hindupedia.com/en/Kashmir_Shaivism

QUANTUM ENTANGLEMENT1935. (1935). Retrieved from http://erenow.com/biographies/einsteinhislifeanduniverse/21.html

Quantum Future Group. (n.d.). Heraclitus early Stoicism. Retrieved from http://cof.quantumfuturegroup.org/events/66

Quantum gravity and the holographic mass. (2014). Retrieved from https://www.cosmosdawn.net/forum/threads/haramein-physics.159/

Quote from XIV Dalai Lama. (n.d.). Retrieved from http://www.viewonbuddhism.org/immeasurables_love_compassion_equanimity_rejoicing.html

Quote investigator. (n.d.). Retrieved from http://quoteinvestigator.com/2014/06/16/purpose-gift/

Rinpoche, S., & Gaffney, P. (1994). *Tibetan Book of Living and Dying*. New york, New York: HarperCollins.

Sadhguru (n.d.). The Three Fundamental Nadis – Ida, Pingala and Sushumna. Retrieved from http://isha.sadhguru.org/blog/yoga-meditation/demystifying-yoga/the-three-fundamental-nadis/

Scientists create light from vacuum. (2011). Retrieved from https://phys.org/news/2011-11-scientists-vacuum.html

Scott-Moncrieff, P. (1913). *Paganism and Christianity in Egypt*. [PDF]. http://dx.doi.org/31761 02781298 1

Sharvananda, S. (1920). *Mandukya Upanishad* (5 & 6 ed.). [Mandukya Upanishad with Sanskrit text]. Retrieved from http://estudantedavedanta.net/Mundaka_and_Mandukya_Upanishads%20-%20Swami%20Sarvanand%20[Sanskrit-English].pdf

Shedrach, Mesach, and Abednigo from the book of Daniel KJV. (n.d.). Retrieved from https://www.biblegateway.com/passage/?search=Daniel+3%3A16-18&version=KJV

Shroff, D. (n.d.). "OM" -the symbol of the absolute. Retrieved from http://www.indiancentury.com/om.htm

Shu. (n.d.). Retrieved from http://www.godelectric.org/shu

Song-of-Solomon 2:1 . (n.d.). Retrieved from http://biblehub.com/kjv/songs/2.htm

Space.com staff. (2017). Black hole blues and other songs from space. Retrieved from http://www.space.com/17933-nasa-television-webcasts-live-space-tv.html?utm_source=facebook&utm_medium=social

Stedman, T. (2000). *Stedman's Medical Dictionary* (27 ed.). Pennsylvania, United States: Lippincott Williams & Wilkins.

Taittireeya Upanishad. (n.d.). Retrieved from https://ocoy.org/

Takumi Yamada, Yasuhiro Yamada, Yumi Nakaike, Atsushi Wakamiya, and Yoshihiko Kanemitsu. (2017). Photon Emission and Reabsorption Processes in CH3NH3PbBr3Single Crystals Revealed by Time-Resolved Two-Photon-Excitation Photoluminescence Microscopy. Retrieved from https://journals.aps.org/prapplied/abstract/10.1103/PhysRevApplied.7.014001

The Divine world. (n.d.). Retrieved from http://www.balaams-ass.com/alhaj/sumergod.htm

The Gospel of the Holy Twelve: 82:26: . (n.d.). Retrieved from https://www.bibliotecapleyades.net/biblianazar/esp_biblianazar_28.htm

The stopwatch of brain; the internal timer. (n.d.). Retrieved from http://bio-mirror.im.ac.cn/mirrors/bioscience/news/scientis/biolcloc.htm

TheraPhi Plasma device. (n.d.). Retrieved from http://theraphi.net/

Three Initiates, T. (1912). Chapter II. The seven Hermetic principles. In W. Walker Atikinson (Ed.), . [The Kybalion by Three Initiates]. Retrieved from http://www.sacred-texts.com/eso/kyb/index.htm

Tsarion, M. (2015, April 16,). *MICHAEL TSARION - SHIVA* [PDF]. DocSlide: uprvimredovima. "The Irish Origins of Civilization", http://docslide.us/documents/michael-tsarion-shiva.html.

Tveter, D. (2001). The transactional interpretation of quantum mechanics . Retrieved from http://www.dontveter.com/qi/online.html#cramer1

Tzu, L. (2008). *Lao-Tzu: The Tao Te Ching.* . New York, NY: Penguin Putnam.

Veda-Pulse. (n.d.). Retrieved from http://vedapulse.com/

VedaPulse. (n.d.). Retrieved from http://vedapulse.com/

Verner, M. (2013). Temple of the World: Sanctuaries, Cults, and Mysteries of Ancient Egypt. Retrieved from http://cairo.universitypressscholarship.com/view/10.5743/cairo/9789774165634.001.0001/upso-9789774165634-chapter-4

Vincent Bridges, Angels in our DNA. (n.d.). Retrieved from http://academysacredgeometry.com/faculty-profile/vincent-bridges

Ward, D. (n.d.). Zero point energy. Retrieved from http://www.zamandayolculuk.com/html-3/zero_point_energy.htm

Wicherink, J. (2008). *Souls of Distortion Awakening*. Ontheemde Zielen Ontwaken: Ontheemde Zielen Ontwaken.

Winter, D. (2012). Compressions, The Hydrogen Atom*, and Phase Conjugation. Retrieved from http://www.fractalfield.com/mathematicsoffusion/

Winter, D. (2015). 2015. Retrieved from http://www.fractalfield.com/fractalphotosynthesis

Winter, D. (2015). 7 Arrows. Retrieved from http://www.sevenarrows.net/7ArrowsShamanEmbeddingCourse.pdf

Winter, D. (2015). Phase conjugate wave mechanics as the cause of consciousness/ perception: . Retrieved from http://www.fractalfield.com/conjugateperception/

Winter, D. (n.d.). *Alphabet of the Eartheart* [PDF]. Prague,Czech Republic: Aethyrea. (),, .

Winter, D. (n.d.). Heart coherence. Retrieved from http://theraphi.net/

Winter, D. (n.d.). History & Physics of fire in the blood Origin of bioelectric - negentropy. Retrieved from http://www.fractalfield.com/negentropicfields/

Winter, D. (n.d.). Implosion physics, The real grail is in your DNA. Retrieved from http://www.soulsofdistortion.nl/Dan%20Winter.html

Winter, D. (n.d.). Peak Experience activates Phi harmonics of the brain and heart . Retrieved from http://www.fractalfield.com/conjugateperception/

XRay Tsunami rolls through galaxy. (2017). Retrieved from http://www.space.com/36698-x-ray-tsunami-perseus-galaxy-cluster-video.html?utm_source=sp-newsletter&utm_medium=email&utm_campaign=20170503-sdc

About the Author

D r. Shelley Evans has been a trainer and educator of esoteric philosophies for well over 35 years. As a Marriage Commissioner, TheraPhi and DNM Wellness Practitioner in Alberta, Canada she shares insights of quantum nature throughout diverse genres and domains.

Printed in the United States
By Bookmasters